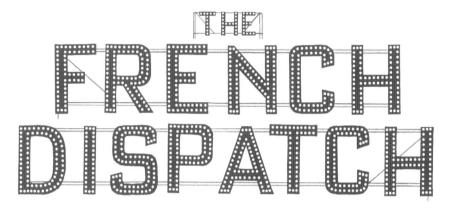

## OF THE LIBERTY, KANSAS EVENING SUN

by
**MATT ZOLLER
SEITZ**

with an
introduction by
**NICOLAS SAADA**

**ABRAMS, NEW YORK**

Introduction by NICOLAS SAADA ... 11

## The Making of Wes Anderson's *The French Dispatch* ... 17

PART I: An American in Paris ... 18

PART II: In the Forest ... 29

PART III: The Masthead ... 39

PART IV: Embracing Angoulême ... 56

PART V: Stretching the Canvas ... 89

PART VI: To the Barricades ... 118

PART VII: Death Comes for Everyone ... 142

PART VIII: On Rails ... 160

## The Covers of *The French Dispatch*

Illustrations by JAVI AZNAREZ ... 179

## The Rosenthaler Plates ... 193

## Music for *The French Dispatch* ... 201

Composer Alexandre Desplat on *The French Dispatch* ... 203

Interview with Jean-Yves Thibaudet ... 207

## Fondu Enchaîné

**DISPATCHES ON *THE FRENCH DISPATCH* ... 219**

"Wes Anderson's 'Framerica': A New Antiterra" by MARC CERISUELO ... 220

"The Real and Imagined Worlds of Wes Anderson" by SIDDHANT ADLAKHA ... 223

"The Concrete Masterpiece" by PADDY JOHNSON ... 229

"The Purposeful Period Fashion of *The French Dispatch*" by ABBEY BENDER ... 231

"No Crying: How to Overcome Blasé Ennui" by DAVID BORDWELL ... 236

"The First Cut Is the Deepest" by AARON ARADILLAS ... 242

Acknowledgments ... 252

*Introduction*

Dear Matt,

First of all, thank you for asking me to write this piece about Wes.

I am not sure that my contribution to your series will be helpful, but I will try to write something.

I met Wes for the first time in 2005, at a party organized at the celebrated French nightclub Castel. The host was a man called Pierre Edelman, a French producer known for his work with David Lynch and Pedro Almodovar. The whole thing looked more like a wedding, with several tables set up and guests' names on each. The big event that evening was a small concert by legendary singer-composer Christophe, who showed up unexpectedly to perform some of his finest songs.

As dinner went on, and I sat en pleine reverie, Pierre showed up at my table asking me to meet the American director Wes Anderson, who was attending the dinner and was curious to meet an ex Cahiers du Cinema jounalist freshly turned filmmaker (I had just directed my first short movie). By an extraordinary series of coincidences, I had just seen a few days before The Life Aquatic and had been immensely moved by the film.

After a brief introduction to Wes, I felt the need to ask a question in the form of a confession: "Did your parents divorce when you were a kid?" Wes was surprised by the abrupt question, but to me, his answer would set up the logic of what I wanted to tell him about his film.

Wes replied with a laconic "yes," and yet, although he could have been taken aback by the bluntness of my demand, he may have felt that I was trying to make a point. And I was. The Life Aquatic seemed to me a wonderful chaotic tale about a group of people who prefer to invent family rather than suffer the hazards of real family life. I had the impression when I watched it for the first time that for Wes, the whole world was just a huge dysfunctional family.

Did this monologue strike a chord with Wes? Or was he just happy to talk about movies? Maybe both. I had to let him know how I felt a sort of bond to his film, a secret connection, as if The Life Aquatic was strangely in key with my sadness as a child, only comforted by the friendly presence of movies within the turmoil of my parents' separation.

I met Wes again at the wrap party of Marie Antoinette. We exchanged phone numbers and a few days later made plans to go to a movie. I had the difficult task of choosing the theater and the film. I went for an obscure noir directed by Anthony Mann, Side Street, which was showing in one of the most celebrated repertory theaters in Paris, Le Christine. Side Street is a pure New York movie, a dangerous thriller starring Farley Granger and Cathy O'Donnell, filmed on location in Manhattan in 1949. Wes enjoyed every minute of it and realized that one scene was shot right near his apartment building.

I have since regularly shared with Wes my enthusiasm for under-the-radar films, noir or others: Richard Lester's Juggernaut, Basil Dearden's Pool of London. . . . I sometimes send him clips from movies that, isolated from their narrative logic, seem to have a life of their own. For instance, the attack of the casino in Ouistreham in The Longest Day has become one of our favorite long takes in the history of cinema. Who else but Wes would appreciate a hidden gem in a big sixties production like The Longest Day?

But another important stage of our friendship was in late 2005, when Wes decided to direct a short feature that would be the set-up of his forthcoming film, The Darjeeling Limited. Wes always wanted to direct a film in Paris, and he asked me to help him during the production; I was very happy to contribute to this wonderful gem of a film, Hotel Chevalier.

I think that when friendship and work mix well, friendship gets stronger. But the other way round can trigger disasters. I was happy to be part of the joyful experience of Hotel Chevalier.

Wes proved also a close advisor on my feature films as a director, and I have always sought to ask him practical questions on my projects. For Taj Mahal, my second feature, partly shot on location in Mumbai, Wes gave me vital information on the best way to adjust to the realities of filming there. I always ask him for advice when it comes to making, writing, or even dreaming up a film.

Wes has often been taken aback by my old-fashioned English, which I borrow from film dialogues of the past: super-duper, deft, fine and dandy . . .

Wes also introduced me to restaurants that I never imagined could exist: His taste for classic French food, at a time when people are obsessed with organic and healthy cuisine, was quite a revelation. There is a place he loves called Auberge Bressane; every time I meet him there for dinner, I have the feeling that the whole locale is straight from a Paramount picture from the thirties, a set built on some soundstage, just for Wes.

As Wes began to stay in Paris on a regular basis, I made sure to introduce him to some of my close friends. This is how I made the connection between Fred Wiseman and Wes. Wes had told me of his admiration for Fred's work and explained how he had borrowed a phone scene from High School in Rushmore. So, I arranged a dinner with him and French director Arnaud Desplechin; we have been trying to have these dinners going since. I feel like the fourth Beatle every time we have dinner together! (Mind you, Ringo was a great drummer.) We had a reunion a year ago, at Georges, near the Palais-Royal.

Wes also introduced me to his family: his magnificent wife, Juman, and their daughter, Freya.

And I was lucky enough to meet more of his friends: Jake Paltrow, Bob Balaban, Owen Wilson, Bill Murray, Jason Schwartzman, and the wonderful, poetic Michael Lindsay-Hogg. Not to mention Roman Coppola, Jeremy Dawson, Octavia Peissel, and Bob Yeoman, close associates of his filmmaking universe.

Last but not least I finally got to meet the great Matt Seitz, and now, I really feel part of the "family." But the Wes Anderson family is unlike any other: It's a juxtaposition of brilliant minds, creative people, explorers. A gallery of colorful individuals that add glow to the sometimes dull palette of life.

In November 2018, the Kunsthistorisches Museum in Vienna hosted an exhibition curated by Wes and his wife, Juman: Spitzmaus Mummy in a Coffin and Other Treasures. He was just a few weeks away from the beginning of the production of The French Dispatch. Many of his friends attended the opening and it was a glorious weekend, punctuated with museum visits including an unforgettable tour of Sigmund Freud's office, with Jake Paltrow and his wife, Taryn Simon.

I tried to document these few days in Vienna and edited a strange 10mm film, just with music, which I showed to Wes a few months later: It was a Jonasmekasesque exercise in which I was aiming to capture the feel of unity, extravaganza, and warmth we all experienced during these few days. I don't know if I succeeded, but this "Vienna weekend" remains a personal landmark to which I often return since we entered these horrid and depressing days.

If I were asked to define Wes's film style, I would actually have a very hard time doing so.

I was no longer writing about film when I became acquainted with his films, so I watched them both as a filmmaker (or aspiring one) and as an audience.

What I admire most about Wes is that his films are built like traps: They seem to display a richness of style, visuals, and sound that are actual delusions to the audience. I would not say that these films are not designed to please an audience, but, as I have realized lately, they are deceptively glamorous. It's all about not taking what you see for granted: There is always something lurking in Wes's films --- violence, sorrow, melancholy.

I understand that he has built a passion for Proust, and his movies look like recollections, often using a narrator's voice to make us think that what we are watching actually happened in some unreal parallel universe. His films explore the Twilight Zone of our sentiments: They tackle hidden, common traumas, past, personal injuries.

If I compared Wes to a musician, I'd choose Brazilian singer Caetano Veloso. Veloso's albums are both immediate and complex; they epitomize "sense and sensibility" --- experience of pop music and bossa nova, a constant adjustment between heart and reason. Wes's films manage to reach that fine line between depth and spectacle.

I am all the more honored to have been physically part of Wes's film world.

I was invited to dub in French one of the dogs in Isle of Dogs, a terrific experience which I then repeated live during the production of French Dispatch. I was cameoed as a lawyer with little experience, supposedly defending the cause of an incredible, bigger than life character: artist Moses Rosenthaler. The filming in Angoulême proved a wonderful experience; watching Wes work with Bob Yeoman and the whole French/US crew was inspiring. Even in such a small scene, I managed to understand the somehow paradoxical position of a film performer.

As part of a Wes Anderson film, I had to trade my personality for something else, as if I had to paint myself, reinvent it into some sort of cipher: l'avocat francais avec la moustache.

I knew the scene was shot in black and white, and I wonder if it had any impact on my non-performance. I still don't know if this was satisfactory for Wes, but I am very proud to have been part of what he calls his "French film."

French Dispatch is a miracle of a movie, a portmanteau film, which I saw as a celebration of creativity and its importance over death, affliction, and gloom. It's a film for our times, even though Wes directed it before the pandemic. It's comforting and funny, yet you leave it with an uncanny sense of gravitas. It's pure Wes Anderson.

In French Dispatch, one character, the young orphan, Gigi, was a reference to my father.

During the production, Wes finally decided to call the character by that unusual name.

I often talked about my dad with Wes, and my greatest regret is that they never had the chance to meet in person, because I am sure they would have clicked.

There's a story I told Wes about my father that he has always loved: In the mid-eighties, while I was still a very dreamy and unsettled French alumni and was just beginning to write for Cahiers du Cinema, I remember going to see Au Revoir les Enfants by Louis Malle at the local cinema. That very same evening I had dinner with my father and told him how much I loved this new Louis Malle film.

He told me, "It figures; wasn't Louis Malle Robert Bresson's first AD?"

"Dad, Louis Malle was never Bresson's first AD."

"He was."

"He wasn't!"

A pause.

"You know what? Let's call Robert Bresson."

My father was able to find Bresson's name in the phone book and actually called him. I remember sitting beside him, in awe. It was Bresson's wife who picked up the phone.

"Yes?"

"Could I speak with Robert Bresson?"

"Hold on a minute. ROOOOBBBERT!"

A deep, powerful, yet controlled voice took over.  Bresson.

My father introduced himself and added, "Nicolas Saada, my son, asserted that Louis Malle was never your AD, although I am certain that it is true."

Bresson replied:  "You are both wrong . . . and both right. I worked with Malle on A Man Escaped.  He was my first AD, and we didn't get along at all.  He left after a week." I believe that no one but us got such information.  Wes loved the story because it shed a special light on my father's extravagant personality.

My father passed away in 2014 while I was prepping Taj Mahal. A few weeks after the funeral, Wes took me for dinner at Auberge Bressane, ordering a glass of red wine for each of us. "What was your father's first name again?"

"Gilbert.  But we all called him Gigi."

Wes raised his glass, looked at me, and said, "To Gigi."

I was moved to tears, as I think these moments measure the deepness of a friendship.

The character of Gigi embodies a sense of isolation and solitude that any outsider can relate to:  He is adopted and has to adjust to all sorts of challenging circumstances. He is a true wanderer.

I would end by saying that whenever I am in the company of Wes, my feeling of disconnection with the world vanishes, as I realize that we all belong to the same country: cinema. Film.  Movies.  Everything makes sense, and I cherish his friendship --- that lifts my spirits up.  Wes has enabled his friends to reinvent the sometimes restrictive concept of family.

So, I raise my glass and will end with a toast.

TO WES!


    Nicolas Saada

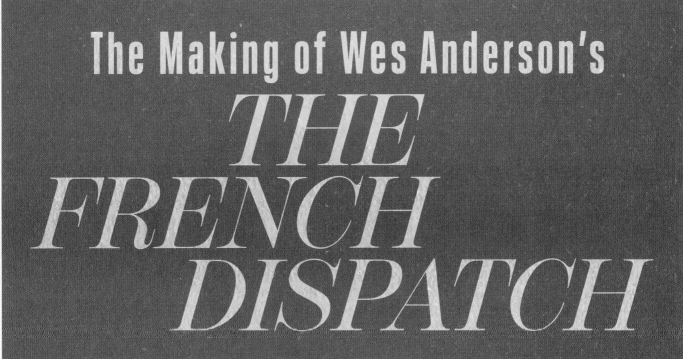

# AN AMERICAN IN PARIS

The seed of Wes Anderson's tenth feature film, *The French Dispatch,* was planted in 1987, in Houston, Texas, when Anderson started reading *The New Yorker* in his high school library. Sometime after that, he saw a TV commercial selling *New Yorker* subscriptions and convinced his parents to get him one. He has subscribed ever since.

"I read it, even though I had no idea what they were talking about most of the time," he told me. "One of the first pieces I remember reading in it was about Oxford dons, and I had absolutely no idea what I was reading about. But I was interested because I knew that it wasn't anything you were going to come across anywhere else. Also, I was interested in jazz music, and there was a whole section of the arts listings about jazz. All the great famous clubs were still there, and some of the famous names were still playing in them—the Blue Note records musicians. And I liked this Pauline Kael[1] who wrote the movie reviews. And all the short stories—fiction came first in *The New Yorker*. I mean it literally came first, right after the 'Talk of the Town' section. But it also seemed like it came first in the sense that it was the focus of the magazine, and writing fiction was what I always wanted to do."

Despite his affinities, Anderson did not begin delving into the history and lore of *The New Yorker* until a decade later, in the fall of 1997, when he visited New York City and had tea with me a few years after I'd moved there from my hometown of Dallas, where, at the local alternative weekly, I was the first person to review a Wes Anderson movie: the short film version of *Bottle Rocket*. Shot on location in Dallas with his University of Texas at Austin classmate Owen Wilson and his brothers, Luke and Andrew, it later became a Columbia Pictures feature.

"Do you remember, Matt, telling me about Joseph Mitchell back around 1996?" he asked me, during a phone conversation soon after production wrapped on *The French Dispatch*. "Because in a way, that's one of the beginnings of this movie: me having in mind certain pieces, little short things that had been in *The New Yorker* that I thought might eventually add up to some kind of movie. I had never heard of Joseph Mitchell until that conversation, which would've been twenty-five years ago. We were walking somewhere between the East and West Village, and you described for me his piece 'The Rats on the Waterfront.'"[2]

"A classic," I said. Mitchell didn't write a word after 1964 but remained on staff at *The New Yorker* until his death.[3] The two of us (like many fellow Gen Xers) first learned about Mitchell in the years following the publication of *Up in the Old Hotel,* a 1992 anthology of his work. He'd been on National Public Radio a

[1] Film critic of *The New Yorker* from 1968 to 1991. Kael's irreverent, conversational, sometimes bawdy style revolutionized and popularized writing about cinema, influencing multiple generations of journalists and filmmakers. Anderson's fascination with Kael was so intense that, seven years after her retirement, he arranged to visit her at her home in Great Barrington, New York, and show her *Rushmore*. He then wrote an article about the experience that served as the introduction to the publication of the *Rushmore* screenplay.

[2] Published in 1944, the piece was a taxonomic study of waterfront rats and the exterminators tasked with rooting them out. Mitchell's interest was sparked by a report that rats carrying bubonic plague had been intercepted on a cargo ship and prevented from infecting the city. "In New York City, as in all great seaports, rats abound," Mitchell wrote. "In the whole city relatively few blocks are entirely free of them . . . some authorities believe that in the five boroughs there is a rat for every human being."

[3] It was subsequently revealed that sometime around the 1964 publication of *Joe Gould's Secret*, Mitchell's alcoholism worsened to the point where he couldn't write anymore.

# "I started to think I might like to do a movie about The New Yorker, or a magazine like The New Yorker."

—WES ANDERSON

couple times, telling stories of the old days and reading excerpts from his greatest hits in a lilting North Carolina accent.

"Mitchell died right around the time of that conversation," I said, "but they hadn't memorialized him in *The New Yorker* yet. I was in the process of writing his obituary for the *Star-Ledger,* so I was full of stories about his work methods—how he didn't believe in so-called news hooks, and he just sort of wandered around the city doing what's called 'pure reporting' about daily life, where you just meet people and talk to them and tell their stories. What I remember most about that day, Wes, was commenting that the hem of your sports coat and your slacks seemed a bit short to me. You told me that this was a deliberate aesthetic choice."

"I would not have said that," Anderson said. "I would have said, 'I did it on purpose.'"

"But yeah, you were fascinated by all these Joseph Mitchell facts. And I remember that you wrote down the title of the anthology—I think on a napkin?"

"Yes—and somewhere around that point in time, I started really reading about the magazine, and that's when I discovered that there was such a thing as *New Yorker* lore—all of these stories about the founder and original editor, Harold Ross, and his successor, William Shawn, and about putting the magazine together, and all the other memorable characters who were involved in it, that sort of thing."

Anderson read Brendan Gill's book *Here at the New Yorker.* He read *Remembering Mr. Shawn's New Yorker: The Invisible Art of Editing* by Ved Mehta. He read Ben Yagoda's *About Town: The New Yorker and the World it Made,* and James Thurber's *The Years with Ross.* Around 2008, Anderson started delving even more deeply into *New Yorker* lore with his friend David Brendel, a writer who would end up editing the anthology *An Editor's Burial: Journals and Journalism from* The New Yorker *and Other Magazines: Inspirations for* The French Dispatch. It was an ongoing process of self-education.

In 2001, Lillian Ross—like Mitchell, a pioneering New Journalist who never would have described herself in those terms—told Anderson a few of her own *New Yorker* anecdotes while interviewing him for a "Talk of the Town" piece about the filming of *The Royal Tenenbaums.* The piece was titled "Wes Anderson in Hamilton Heights." By that point, Ross had published her own memoir, *Here But Not Here: My Life with William Shawn and the New Yorker,* which detailed her fifty-year affair with William Shawn, Harold Ross's successor. Shawn navigated among the magazine's offices; his wife, Cecille, and their three children; and Ross and her adopted son, Erik. Cecille Shawn was still alive when Ross's book was published, as were their children, one of whom is actor and playwright Wallace Shawn, of *The Designated Mourner, My Dinner with Andre,* and *The Princess Bride.*

Ross's "Talk of the Town" item briefly turned Anderson into a *New Yorker* character. This seemed inevitable, given that Anderson and cowriter Owen Wilson's screenplay was influenced by J. D. Salinger short stories that had originally been published in *The New Yorker,* and the film's chapter/title inserts suggested horizontal *New Yorker* covers. Ross's piece described Anderson as ". . . the most waifish-looking film director since François Truffaut. He has, from the top, nondescript brown hair, sharp features, clear-frame glasses, shoulders permanently hunched in behind-the-camera position, and no noticeable hips. On the set, he was elegantly clothed in mauve corduroy pants, a maroon corduroy sports jacket, and red sneakers."

I was and still am obsessed with Ross. My ten-thousand-word *Dallas Observer* cover story "Slouching Towards Hollywood,"[4] about the making of *Bottle Rocket,* blatantly cribbed its style from Ross's making-of book *Picture,* about John Huston's *The Red Badge of Courage.* I was delighted by the Ross piece on *Tenenbaums,* though disappointed that she didn't mention Anderson's hems.

"Somewhere during that period," Anderson said, "which I guess was maybe four years, I started to think I might like to do a movie about *The New Yorker,* or a magazine like *The New Yorker.* And around the same time, I had this other idea, which was to do a movie that was a collection of short stories—a straight-up anthology-type of movie that doesn't disguise that it's split into different stories. And, also, I had always wanted to do a movie set in France, or a movie that's partly in French. And somehow all of these three things got mixed together."

[4] September 7, 1995.

Wes Anderson standing in front of the Angoulême Cathedral on Place Saint-Pierre for the shooting of the façade of the magazine's headquarters

ABOVE: Somehow the director finds time to moonlight as a magazine delivery truck driver.

OPPOSITE: Anderson checks focus on a shot of Owen Wilson being chased on his bike by kids in front of a river. (See pages 82–85 for more production details about the scene.)

## "THE FAMILY OF FILM"

"Wes was destined to make a movie in France," said *The French Dispatch* producer Jeremy Dawson, a former visual-effects designer and supervisor who began working with Anderson on 2004's *The Life Aquatic with Steve Zissou*, assisting animator Henry Selick on the film's stop-motion sea creatures. "Wes has been a fan of French cinema forever, and has lived in France and spent a lot of time there. It's a country that has always been close to him, and there are a lot of French filmmakers who he's friends with now, or has been historically influenced by. So this wasn't an accident."

From the short film and feature versions of *Bottle Rocket,* which stole shots and cuts from Jean-Luc Godard and François Truffaut and made 1990s Dallas look like a spiritual sister of 1950s Paris; through *Rushmore*'s beret-and-blazer-clad hero; the *Darjeeling Limited* prologue *Hotel Chevalier*; the array of French music and fashion and Antoine Doinel–type sensitive-and-melancholy youth who appear throughout Anderson's projects; and the thread of Jacques Cousteau shoutouts in his early features (culminating in *The Life Aquatic with Steve Zissou,* about an American version of Cousteau), Anderson is a Francophile to the marrow.

But he's an amateur compared to one of his other main producers, Octavia Peissel, who holds dual American and French citizenship and speaks French and English with equal fluency. "I'm half American and half French, so this film is sort of perfect for me, right?" said Peissel, who started working with Anderson on 2009's *Fantastic Mr. Fox.* "Most of the cinematographic influences here are very French, but then, the whole world of the literary magazine in the film is very American—all the stuff that concerns the journalists. So it feels very much as if the script and screenwriting draws from the American experience, and the filmmaking from the French.

"As for the point of view on France, it's not France through French eyes, but it's not France through the eyes of a tourist, either," Peissel continued. "It's France through the eyes of the sorts of people who actually have *lived* here. When I was speaking to Franco-French people whom we made the film with, after they had gotten to see it, it resonated with them. The kind of writing shown in the movie comes from a period in France that was hugely influenced by the presence of

Americans after World War II and by American culture. That means there's something very American about that period of French history, inherently."

Peissel describes *The French Dispatch* as a film that's about being an American expatriate and a Francophile, but that also understands and correctly identifies aspects of the French national character. "It's a film about expats and the stories and experiences of being an expat, but at the same time, it's very French," she said. "There are things about the film that are intrinsically French and things that are intrinsically Western and things that are about the expat experience."

"Wes is probably the most European of all the major American directors," says French actress Léa Seydoux, who has worked with Anderson four times as of this writing, most recently on *The French Dispatch*. "He's very influenced by European cinema, and by French cinema especially. I can feel that in his movies. Even though Wes is not French, he loves French culture. I grew up on French cinema and I carry French cultural baggage with me everywhere, so it's delightful seeing him recognize that part of me from carrying it around himself. I spent time in the United States as a child, at a summer camp with a cousin where my family thought I could learn English, and I have spent a lot of time in America and watched American films, so I know what it's like to feel as if a culture other than yours is a part of you. I feel like Wes wanted to make a movie about that phenomenon—that feeling that you can hold a culture within yourself even though you weren't originally born into it."

Parisian writer-director Nicolas Saada, who befriended Anderson during the wrap party for *Marie Antoinette*, calls the director an "international filmmaker," in the sense of not seeming intrinsically tied to any specific country.

"I think when we talk about Wes being international, we need to talk about family," said Saada. Beyond *The Royal Tenenbaums*, there's Anderson's next feature, *The Life Aquatic*, which struck Saada as being about the creation of an invitation-only family that supplements or replaces biological ones. "We're a pack of strays," Steve Zissou declares. The strays form their own pack with Zissou as alpha, guiding them in hunts, play sessions, and burials, and presiding over the admission of new members.[5]

"All of Wes's movies are about family," Saada said, "whether it's the one you were born with or the one you make. His characters want to leave families that they were born in. Or they run away from them. Or they go somewhere else in order to come to terms with problems in their family. In France, *The Royal Tenenbaums* was released as *The Tenenbaum Family*, so that's how I've always referred to it. In *The French Dispatch*, too, you have a man who left his homeland and his biological family to start a publication in another country where another language is spoken. The dynamics of the staff makes it seem very much as if he has created a new family in another country. The patriarch, who is the founder of this new family, invites additional people to join, enlarging the size and richness of the new family."

Saada said that when he spends time with Anderson, he is no longer a "French director," but part of "a common family group" that shares "a love of film. Filmmaking is our common home. I believe this is why Wes loves to have friends in different countries and live in different countries and discuss movies with people from all over the world. Wes's connection to family is, I believe, an explanation of his aesthetics. That is, his aesthetics are not isolated or closed, you know? He can find a connection with Satyajit Ray and Akira Kurosawa and Jean-Luc Godard as well as Stanley Kubrick. They're all in the family: the family of film."♠

5   Zissou's statement unknowingly anticipates *Isle of Dogs*, which is literally about a pack of strays.

# FRENCH CINEMA STARTER PACK

### RIFIFI
### (1955)
### JULES DASSIN

Not many quintessential French films were made by Americans, but the caper picture *Rififi* is a conspicuous exception: Jules Dassin, an actor-director who was equally successful on Broadway and in Hollywood, was shut out of the American entertainment business after being blacklisted, and reinvented himself with this timeless piece of entertainment, which invented or perfected many of the elements so strongly associated with heist pictures that viewers feel disappointed when they're not included (such as sawing a hole in a ceiling to retrieve something in a guarded room beneath). *The French Dispatch* tips its chapeau to *Rififi* not just in its reproduction of particular images and incidents, but also in its jocular presentation of the enmity between gangsters and police as a never-ending game of one-upmanship.

### MON ONCLE
### (1958)
### JACQUES TATI

Actor-filmmaker Jacques Tati's filmography was built around his self-created character Monsieur Hulot, an affable, befuddled, but adaptable innocent, in the vein of Chaplin's Little Tramp, who meandered through an increasingly urbanized and mechanized postwar France. *Mon Oncle* is a perfect starting point for newcomers to his filmography, which is modeled on silent film comedies, burying dialogue deep in the mix and using music and sound effects to drive and shape the action. Anderson's approaches to choreography, scene-building, and set design owe a lot to Tati, an auteur who conceived projects in terms of sets and shots that were built not just to advance a story, but to create an alternate world. Many moments in opening sections of *The French Dispatch* have a Tati flavor, in particular the neighborhood stirring at dawn and the waiter glimpsed through windows while he climbs a series of stairwells.

### THE 400 BLOWS
### (1959)
### FRANÇOIS TRUFFAUT

Critic-turned-filmmaker François Truffaut's autobiographical debut was loosely based on his childhood in Paris; the movie's empathetic eye and Nouvelle Vague visual grammar influenced every coming-of-age story made afterward. Gritty, precise, and intimate, yet somehow also grand and overflowing with feeling, it's one of the best first films ever made; its international success inspired Truffaut to make four more features charting the maturation and evolution of his avatar, Antoine Doinel (Jean-Pierre Léaud): *Antoine and Collette*, *Stolen Kisses*, *Bed and Board*, and *Love on the Run*. The influence of *The 400 Blows* is plain to see in both the black-and-white short and feature-length color versions of *Bottle Rocket*.

### LA RÈGLE DE JEU
(1939)
**JEAN RENOIR**

Talk about prescience: In 1938, filmmaker Jean Renoir became convinced that a second world war was inevitable and announced that his next film would be "a precise description of the bourgeois of our age" who were oblivious to the turmoil, and capture his belief that France was "dancing on the edge of a volcano." The result was shot in February of 1939 and released in July of that same year, two months before Hitler invaded Poland and war officially broke out in Europe. *La Règle de Jeu* is an account of an aristocratic estate party right before the outbreak of World War II, by turns a satire on class, a knock-down farce, and a rueful comedy of manners strongly influenced by *A Midsummer Night's Dream*. It is also noteworthy for its immaculate blocking of actors and its use of the camera to set up and pay off jokes.

### LE PLAISIR
(1952)
**MAX OPHÜLS**

Like *The French Dispatch*, this Ophüls anthology film offers three stories linked by themes and motifs, and switches between satire, romance, and intrigue in the course of a single tale. There are episodes about a mysterious man who attends dance halls wearing a mask; a madam of a small-town brothel bringing some of her working girls to her niece's first communion; and a painter who falls for his model without anticipating how tempestuous the relationship will be. Scene for scene, this might be Ophüls's most fully realized movie. Every joke and plot twist lands just right, and the director's trademark marathon tracking shots don't register as virtuoso displays because the viewer is too focused on the characters to wonder how they were achieved.

### LOLA MONTÈS
(1955)
**MAX OPHÜLS**

Max Ophüls, who was born in Germany but made many classic features in France, died of a heart attack two years after the release of this epic chronicling the life of Irish circus performer, dancer, and courtesan Lola Montez (Martine Carol) and her affairs with Franz Liszt (Will Quadflieg) and Ludwig I of Bavaria (Anton Walbrook). Ophüls was known for his sinuous tracking shots, elegant mise-en-scène, and wry observation of social protocols and class differences; all of those gifts are on display here, along with spectacular crowd scenes that immerse viewers in the funeral of Ludwig I and a circus that provides the story's organizing metaphor (with Peter Ustinov serving as ringmaster). Shot in English, German, and French simultaneously, the movie's flashback-driven story was recut chronologically in the aftermath of disappointing reviews and box-office returns, then partially restored in the decade following Ophüls's death.

### BREATHLESS
(1960)
**JEAN-LUC GODARD**

Jean-Luc Godard's first feature was both a sensational lovers-on-the-run drama made in the style of US crime pictures he adored, and a wry account of American culture colonizing France's imagination (Jean-Paul Belmondo's Humphrey Bogart–styled antihero worships Bogart, and even owns a poster of him). Its jagged editing, disregard for continuity and the 180-degree rule, and down-and-dirty showmanship (including the use of a wheelchair as a dolly) continue to inspire independent filmmakers.

### CONTEMPT
(1963)
**JEAN-LUC GODARD**

Godard's opulent, corrosively satirical CinemaScope melodrama follows a screenwriter (Michel Piccoli) hired to script-doctor an adaptation of *The Odyssey*, who must contend with the demands of an intransigent, legendary director played by Fritz Lang, an obnoxious American producer played by Jack Palance, and his own disaffected wife (Brigitte Bardot).

### THE UMBRELLAS OF CHERBOURG
(1964)
**JACQUES DEMY**

Legendary for its production design, costumes, vivid use of color, Michel Legrand score, and cast full of up-and-coming future French cinema stars that includes Catherine Deneuve and her sister Françoise Dorléac, Jacques Demy's film and its follow-up, *The Young Girls of Rochefort*, are key influences on the students-in-revolt episode of *The French Dispatch*. The acclaimed, multiple Oscar-nominated *Cherbourg* chronicles the love lives of young men and women in a small town affected by compulsory military service in French-occupied Algeria. Like many mid-century French films, it is knowingly naive, rapturously embracing some Hollywood manipulations even as it subverts others. It is a "sung-through" musical, meaning there is no spoken dialogue, only lyrics set to music. Songs include "I Will Wait for You," which won an Oscar for Best Original Song.

### CLÉO FROM 5 TO 7
(1961)
**AGNÈS VARDA**

Agnès Varda's most acclaimed dramatic feature covers two hours in the life of singer Cléo Victoire (Corinne Marchand) as she attends a fortune-telling session that predicts a negative change in her life just ninety minutes before she's to receive the results of a cancer test. Unfolding in not-quite-real time, *Cléo* is an essential work of Nouvelle Vague cinema, in part because of the writer-director's empathy for her heroine, who has to deal with blithe sexism from her boyfriend and two male artistic collaborators on top of everything else; where many of the famous male directors in the movement treated women as alluring but opaque, Cléo treats its main character as a person with ordinary problems of a sort rarely shown in films.

### THE BATTLE OF ALGIERS
(1966)
**GILLO PONTECORVO**

Italian filmmaker Gillo Pontecorvo's drama charts the fight for Algerian independence from the occupying French army. It's notable for both its uncompromising depiction of colonial violence and resistance, and its kinetic neorealist approach to the subject: The production employed nonprofessional actors, most of whom were veterans of the occupation, and the entire story is shot in a flowing, loose-limbed style more characteristic of documentaries than commercial features (a technique that allowed the editor to interpolate actual newsreel footage into the fiction). Its success cemented a subgenre of historical drama that interweaves documentary and invented images, and inspired filmmakers (including Anderson, in the student protest segment of *The French Dispatch*) to embrace instability and chaos when depicting scenes of large-scale public violence.

### LA CHINOISE
(1967)
**JEAN-LUC GODARD**

Jean-Luc Godard's comedy-drama about French students protesting imperialism was released a full year before the protests of 1968 but seems to anticipate them. Inspired by Fyodor Doestoevsky's *The Possessed*, the movie follows five members of a radical Maoist group known as the "Aden Arabie Cell" through a world of capitalist excess and shallow people. Godard is known for his "dialectical" filmmaking approach, in which competing or opposite ideas are allowed to coexist; this Godard film is packed with scenes where characters literally argue with each other about everything from whether assassination is morally acceptable in certain circumstances to whether Nicolas Ray's 1954 Western melodrama *Johnny Guitar* is misunderstood.

### LE SOUFFLE AU CŒUR
(1971)
**LOUIS MALLE**

Louis Malle's coming-of-age drama is one of the consummate examples of a film that's about childhood but most assuredly is not for children. *Le Souffle au cœur* follows jazz-loving teen Laurent (Benoît Ferreux) as he learns about adult hypocrisy, disillusionment, and disappointment, losing his virginity in a brothel and accumulating unwanted knowledge of his mother's extramarital affair. Controversial in its day for its frank depiction of sexuality, and for its ending, which breaks one of the ultimate taboos.

### DAY FOR NIGHT
(1973)
**FRANÇOIS TRUFFAUT**

Truffaut's 1973 meta-film about a director trying to shoot a movie was his answer to Fellini's *8½*, but it had its own beguiling, hermetic energy, and an unusual insistence on the collaborative nature of the art form. Anderson used it as inspiration for a 2004 American Express ad that he directed and acted in (opposite regular collaborators Jason Schwartzman and Waris Ahluwalia), and he generally seems to have an intense affinity for it, perhaps in part because, like so many of his own movies, it focuses on obsessive, self-involved, often oblivious characters whose yearnings and agonies are taken seriously even when the audience is being wryly reminded that they're watching a fictional construct devised by craftspeople and performed by actors.

### JEAN DE FLORETTE/ MANON DES SOURCES
(BOTH 1986)
**CLAUDE BERRI**
**MARC CARO**

In one of the most ambitious French cinema productions of the 1980s, cowriter-director Claude Berri adapted a two-volume novel by early twentieth century novelist-filmmaker Marcel Pagnol into *Jean de Florette* and *Manon des Sources*, a pair of films totaling four hours that were shot back-to-back and released sequentially. Set in a small rural town in the nineteenth century and revolving around a sought-after but water-deprived property with a spring that has secretly been blocked with concrete, it's an intimate epic about how it takes a village to enable long-term civic corruption. It builds to a wrenching yet dramatically satisfying finale in which everything happens as it should.

### LE SAMOURAÏ
### (1967)
#### JEAN-PIERRE MELVILLE

Alain Delon stars as a hitman who is known for his clean getaways and airtight alibis; his luck fails him after a contract killing in a nightclub, and he is identified and investigated by police and betrayed by his unknown employers, who would rather erase him than risk exposure. Jean-Pierre Melville's moody, cool, testosterone-soaked crime and war dramas anticipated the careers of directors like Walter Hill, John Woo, and Michael Mann. This one finds the writer-director embracing a mythic-poetic story-telling model, presenting both conversations and violence in a way that feels more figurative than literal. Hill's *The Driver*, Mann's *Thief* and *Heat*, Woo's *The Killer*, Johnnie To's *Vengeance*, and Nicolas Winding Refn's *Drive* are but a few of the subsequent films that feel like extended riffs on Melville's classic.

### THE YOUNG GIRLS OF ROCHEFORT
### (1967)
#### JACQUES DEMY

A more jumbled, entropic companion to *The Umbrellas of Cherbourg*, with another Legrand score and a star-packed cast that includes Catherine Deneuve, George Chakiris, Michel Piccoli, and Gene Kelly, *Rochefort* continues Demy's fascination with the interaction of civilian and military spheres (but substitutes the navy for *Cherbourg*'s infantry) and intertwines it with multiple showbiz subplots (characters include fraternal twins, one a dancer and the other a musician, who move to Paris to pursue their art; a couple of carnival workers involved in the creation of a fair; a sailor who considers himself a painter and poet; and an American composer).

### LA PISCINE
### (1969)
#### JACQUES DERAY

Part of cinema's appeal is rooted in the opportunity to stare at beautiful people in beautiful places wearing beautiful clothes (or few clothes, or none) for long stretches without any fear that they'll notice the gawking and call the cops. Jacques Deray's slow, quiet, opulent psychological thriller *La Piscine* understands this better than almost any film of its era, and that's why its appeal has persisted despite the fact that, story-wise, not a lot happens in it. The principal cast includes Alain Delon, Romy Schneider, and Jane Birkin, all of whom look smashing in their bathing suits, sunglasses, shorts, and partially buttoned shirts and blouses, and drive sporty cars that look like hard candies on wheels.

### ROUND MIDNIGHT
### (1986)
#### BERTRAND TAVERNIER

Bertrand Tavernier's 1980s period piece *Round Midnight* stars legendary saxophonist Dexter Gordon as Dale Turner, a stylized version of himself (by way of Lester Young and Bud Powell), who attempts a late-life reinvention by moving from New York to Paris, where he hopes his art will be more appreciated. Much of the movie focuses on the relationship between Turner and Francis Borler (François Cluzet), a film poster designer and divorced single parent who gives Dale shelter and support as he struggles with addiction and tries to rebuild in hopes of returning to New York. Circuitously plotted and alternately warm and sorrowful, *Round Midnight* (named for a Thelonious Monk tune) is a French filmmaker's love letter to jazz, or at least a romanticized version of what he perceives to be the jazz life. Gordon was nominated for an Oscar for Best Actor for his first and only film performance in a leading role, and Herbie Hancock's original score (featuring Gordon on sax) won both an Oscar and a Grammy.

### LA HAINE
### (1995)
#### MATHIEU KASSOVITZ

Actor-filmmaker Mathieu Kassovitz's debut feature covers roughly a day in the lives of three marginalized young immigrant men whose lives are turned upside down by a riot that resulted in a friend being brutalized in police custody and ending up in intensive care. There's an Afro French boxer and drug dealer named Hubert (Hubert Koundé) whose gym burned down in the riots; a volatile young Jewish man named Vinz (Vincent Cassel) who is obsessed with vengeance and idolizes Travis Bickle from *Taxi Driver*; and a thoughtful North African Muslim named Saïd (Saïd Taghmaoui) whose inclination is to defuse violence. A small gem of social criticism with an arresting style that draws on such prior urban classics as *The Battle of Algiers*, *Dog Day Afternoon*, and *Do the Right Thing*.

### THE TRIPLETS OF BELLEVILLE
### (2003)
#### SYLVAIN CHOMET

Sylvain Chomet's animated comedy follows Madame Souza, her loyal dog Bruno, and the eponymous sisters (former vaudevillians) as they try to free Souza's grandson from kidnappers who abducted him during the Tour de France. It's a mobile riot of marginalia, each frame stuffed with more details than one viewing can absorb. In a modern era of shaded 3D computer animation defined by Pixar and DreamWorks, it's a treat to watch one that uses high-tech assistance sparingly, and is intoxicated by the scratchy, wooly, wiggly texture of lines drawn with pens held by human hands. *The French Dispatch* has a strong Belleville feeling, not just in the final episode, which climaxes in an animated car chase, but in its casting, which prized faces so distinctive that they seem to have been created on a drafting table.

Illustration by
Javi Aznarez

# IN THE FOREST

**PART II**

**A**NDERSON hashed out the plot of *The French Dispatch* with some of his regular collaborators, including Roman Coppola, Jason Schwartzman, and Hugo Guinness. The publication that gives the film its name was envisioned not as a native French publication but a Sunday magazine supplement of the Liberty, Kansas *Evening Sun,* staffed by transplanted Americans. The city would be Paris, essentially, but renamed Ennui-sur-Blasé, a fusion of two words that Americans often associate with French characters.[1]

In honor of his original affinity for *The New Yorker,* "at least one of the stories in the magazine would need to be a work of fiction," Anderson said. It was decided that the "fiction" component would be a short story by a Japanese writer. "That one eventually turned into *Isle of Dogs,*" Anderson explained, referring to his ninth feature. "Once that idea expanded itself and became a movie of its own, it got pulled out of our magazine movie."

With the "fiction" removed from the publication, only "journalism" remained.

Now all that *The French Dispatch* needed were journalists and stories.

After extensive collaboration with writing partners who helped him work out the plots, Anderson settled on three long "feature stories," about a mentally disturbed artist who goes to prison for double murder, falls in love with a prison guard, and becomes an influential painter; a *French Dispatch* writer who has an affair with a teenage activist while covering student uprisings modeled on the 1968 Paris demonstrations; and a profile of the private chef to a police commissioner that turns into a crime story when the commissioner's only son is kidnapped by gangsters. These longer stories would be preceded by a short, whimsical journal entry, modeled on the "Talk of the Town" items at the front of *The New Yorker,* establishing the city and its residents and planting bits of geographical information and foreshadowing that would come into play later.

As the "Talk of the Town"—later the Sazerac—segment took shape, it was decided that each piece would be "presented by" the character who wrote it. This would allow each *French Dispatch* writer spotlighted in a segment to serve as the de facto narrator of events depicted therein.

Additionally, said Anderson, this device would please viewers "who saw my other movies and came away thinking that what they really needed [were] more framing devices."

Anderson did not originally intend *The French Dispatch* to have a master framing device about the death of Arthur Howitzer Jr., founder and publisher of *The French Dispatch*. Anderson had originally pictured the movie as "a pure anthology"—a bunch of short movies loosely tied together by a shared setting, like *New York Stories* or *Paris, je t'aime*. Anderson also knew he wanted Bill Murray, a presence in all his projects since *Rushmore,* to play a role. He settled on casting Murray as Howitzer. At some point, it was decided that the film would start with Howitzer's death and the reading of his will, which specified that the magazine be shut down,

---

[1] There are no blasé characters in the film, and nobody suffers from ennui. All of the characters, French and American alike, are deeply invested in whatever they happen to be preoccupied with.

# "What happens next?"

LEFT TO RIGHT: Jeffrey Wright, Wes Anderson, Owen Wilson, and Tilda Swinton on set during the filming of the memorial for *French Dispatch* editor-publisher Arthur Howitzer (Bill Murray, horizontal)

the staff bought out, and the presses dismantled, melted, and sold for scrap.

"I guess I feel like he didn't trust anybody to carry it on, so he decided 'That's the end of it,'" Anderson told me. This touch, too, was inspired by *New Yorker* lore. "I don't know if Harold Ross gave a lot of thought to naming a successor to *The New Yorker* at first. In the years before Ross died, the other people at *The New Yorker* always had this anxiety that the thing couldn't last after he was gone. I think it was only when Ross got himself this sort of genius, William Shawn, into his orbit that it became clear that there was a way to keep it going."

There was early talk of Howitzer appearing only at the beginning and end of the movie, but he ended up making cameos in every segment. We see him enthusiastically footing the bill for reporting, publishing longer-than-anticipated manuscripts, giving notes on structure and word choice, and (in the Roebuck Wright segment) changing the trajectory of a writer's life in the course of a conversation.

"We didn't know going into this Howitzer was going to be woven into all the other stories in some way," Anderson said. "It just happened."

After the prologue, a *Citizen Kane*–like account of Howitzer's death and the reading of his will, Herbsaint Sazerac (Owen Wilson) takes viewers on a cycling tour of the city, narrating into the camera à la *Our Town* or a Spike Lee movie while suffering slapstick indignities.

This is followed by three longish, bittersweet feature stories (the painter, the students, the kidnapping) and a concluding montage that returns the anthology to its starting place: the staff contemplating a hazy future.

The closing line, spoken by Roebuck Wright (Jeffrey Wright): "What happens next?"

When Anderson started thinking about putting the entire story together, that was the question he kept asking himself. It is always the question.

Anderson's chronologically organized collection of *The New Yorker* magazines, dating back to the 1940s

## THE PROCESS

The screenplay for *The French Dispatch* was devised through a collaborative process Anderson has been honing since his days at the University of Texas at Austin, where he and his first writing partner, actor Owen Wilson, came up with stories for what eventually became Anderson's first four movies. The process consists of Anderson and various configurations of friends getting together in pairs or groups and hashing out plots, characters, and situations, within a rigorous daily work structure that's meant to drive the writing forward.

"There's this perception of Wes as having everything all figured out and then everybody's just executing the plan," said Jason Schwartzman, cowriter (with Anderson and Roman Coppola) of the script for *The Darjeeling Limited* and a contributor to the stories of *Isle of Dogs* and *The French Dispatch*. "And that's definitely true with the directing part—he plans everything out so that he knows each shot and how long it is. But what people maybe don't realize is that Wes is finding the story in the writing just like anyone else would. I think that maybe one of the more surprising things for people to find out about Wes is that he's as free in the writing as he is meticulous on the set."

Schwartzman, of course, first met Anderson on *Rushmore,* in which he starred as Orson Welles wannabe Max Fischer.

Coppola was an early fan of *Bottle Rocket,* first the short and then the feature. After Schwartzman, Coppola's cousin, played Max in *Rushmore,* Anderson became a familiar presence in the Coppolas' lives, an Eli Cash to their Tenenbaums. The Schwartzman-Anderson-Coppola collaboration began in Paris in 2006, where Coppola worked as a second unit director on his sister Sofia's historical drama *Marie Antoinette,* which costarred Schwartzman. On Anderson's productions, Coppola is a utility player who goes wherever the project most needs him, whether it's helping to revise a shooting plan on the fly, going off set to direct second unit footage, or solving a sudden logistical problem.

"Roman is involved in everything whenever he's with us," Anderson said.

Anderson was in Paris in 2006 at the same time Coppola and Schwartzman were there shooting *Marie Antoinette. The Darjeeling Limited* and its short-film prelude, *Hotel Chevalier,* originated in conversations among the three. "We had the John Cassavetes movie *Husbands* in mind," said Anderson, laughing at the memory. "Somehow we thought to combine India and *Husbands*!" The trio wrote a draft of the script in Paris and refined it months later while staying together in Anderson's apartment in New York. Then they decided to finish writing the movie in India. "We did a lot of traveling by train," Anderson said. "We finished writing it in the foothills of the Himalayas."

"We were just kind of gathering these experiences and living our parts," Coppola said. "There were three brothers in the story. Jason was his character in the movie. Wes was the elder brother, the Owen [Wilson] character. I was the middle brother, the one played by Adrien [Brody]. We would get in character and sort of play out scenes, improvise a bit, have our observations. It's hard to describe all this stuff to other people, but we basically had a sense of what we were doing. Wes was guiding the process. He had a sense of the destination."

Schwartzman explained that when Anderson works out stories with others—for instance, with Schwartzman and Roman Coppola on *The Darjeeling Limited,* or with Hugo Guinness on *The Grand Budapest Hotel,* and with Schwartzman, Coppola, and Guinness on *The French Dispatch*—he might have a general idea of the story when the process begins, but the plot and scenes tend to get worked out in more or less linear order, through a mediated process of discovery that Schwartzman said is ". . . no kidding, kind of like playing detective. That's what it feels like to me."

Anderson is the detective. He throws out ideas and asks follow-up questions of whoever's in the room, insisting that all participants concur on a scene's events and details before moving on. At the end of a session, Anderson will type up the session's notes on his laptop in screenplay format.

Hugo Guinness, who cowrote the Oscar-nominated script for *The Grand Budapest Hotel* with Anderson, describes the process as rigorously linear: "You have to try to at least somewhat finish whatever you're currently working on before Anderson will agree to move on to something new."

Guinness is the only member of Anderson's trusted inner circle of writers whose career doesn't revolve around the entertainment business. A British writer, artist, and designer, he moved to New York in the late 1990s after spending his twenties and thirties in London, working as an advertising copywriter and investment banker. Now he's a painter. He and Anderson met in New York through Anderson's then-girlfriend, Jennifer Wachtell, and Guinness's wife, painter Elliott Puckette.

"I first met Wes in about '99, I think," Guinness said. "He was thirty and I was forty, and what I really remember from those times was how curious he was about everything. He really was like a sponge, just soaking up everything culturally: books, films, theater. A little bit shy, very forceful, and very sensitive. Wes used to spend a lot of time at our house. I think at one point he wanted to shoot *The Royal Tenenbaums* in our house, but decided it was too narrow."

Guinness contributed artwork to *The Royal Tenenbaums* and *The Life Aquatic with Steve Zissou* and played the voice of Farmer Bunce in *Fantastic Mr. Fox* but didn't begin working on scripts with Anderson until years later. Anderson's official invitation was sparked at a lunch with himself, Guinness, and their mutual friend Roboin Hurlston (partial inspiration for M. Gustave in *Grand Budapest*).

"Robin is this sort of extraordinary character, really, who's lived a wonderful life and done amazing things on a limited budget, and is much admired by both men and women—just sort of an eccentric English character," Guinness explained. "He doesn't really do anything. He's never had a job. He's very good at reciting these great chunks of poetry. He's very good at one-liners. He's a very well-mannered, beautifully dressed, old-fashioned English gentleman bachelor. In a way, he himself is a made-up character. He's picked up bits from everywhere, from the books he's read and the films he's seen. That's what people do. They invent themselves.

"Anyway, I made up a eulogy for Robin over lunch, and Wes and Robin thought it was very funny, and in retrospect I think that was the beginning of the two of us writing together. Wes made the offer to have both of us collaborate with him, but Robin declined—I don't know why. Wes is very much the boss when we're writing together, and that's fine with me, as I have no desire to be in charge of anything. Much of the time, when Wes and I are writing, I find myself just sitting with him. I help with the dialogue, mainly. Wes might set up a scene and then say, 'So and so comes in, and

TOP: Wes Anderson and coproducer and creative collaborator Roman Coppola

BOTTOM (LEFT TO RIGHT): Bill Murray; production designer Adam Stockhausen; Jason Schwartzman, who plays *French Dispatch* illustrator Hermès Jones; first assistant director Ben Howard; and Javi Aznarez, the actual illustrator of the cover images used in the film

Wes Anderson and Bill Murray on set

such and such happens—What should they say next?' Wes will sit in a chair, I will sit in a chair, and he might have a tiny little notebook that he would jot things in. Later that night or perhaps the next day he might type up the bits in his notebook that he thought were good. The main goal for me is to get into that notebook."

Schwartzman says Anderson is a taskmaster in writing sessions, insisting he and his collaborators flesh out whatever they're working on to the maximum extent possible before looking ahead to the next thing. "A lot of times you'll necessarily get ahead of yourself when you're talking stuff out in this way. You might say something like, 'Oh, yeah—and maybe after he's done talking to this guy, he can go over to this other place and talk to this other character about this other thing that's gonna be important later!' And then Wes will stop you and make you back up and finish the scene that you were supposed to be working on. He'll sort of politely wave you away when you're getting too far ahead. He's like, 'We'll get to that.'"

The relentless linearity of Anderson's process, says Guinness, channels everyone's energy and keeps them fixed on the goal of finishing the scene, the sequence, the act, and ultimately the first draft. A standard writing day might find Anderson and one or more collaborators meeting virtually or in person in the morning, perhaps for a shared breakfast, then working through to lunch, then picking up again afterward and working through to dinner, which typically happens at six. On *The French Dispatch,* Guinness worked with Anderson on the entire script separately in New York and Paris, then Anderson did multiple separate sessions with Coppola and Schwartzman in various physical locations and online.

"The whole thing is always pretty regimented," Schwartzman said, "and when you get done for the day, you're kind of exhausted. I think Wes likes to do it this way because it makes him and everybody stay focused on what's in front of them."

For Schwartzman, Anderson's openness during the writing phase cuts against the perception that he goes into every project with a fully formed vision and is mainly about the execution after that. "I think Wes honestly doesn't know what happens next when he's working on a story," he said. "I mean, he sort of does. How to explain this? It's not like he knows everything that needs to happen and then it's just a matter of getting other people to help him write it all down. It's more like Wes wants things to happen in a way that makes sense."

"We have a little private quote between us, where we'd ask whether it was 'in the forest,'" said Coppola. "We had this analogy that it was as if Wes had already been to this destination in a dream. He was aware of the destination, but we were trying to retrace the path to get there, and Wes remembered kind of going through a forest, which was our metaphor, in order to get to this destination. So whenever we were discussing an idea, Wes was really the only one that had the sensitivity to know whether it was 'in the forest'—meaning, on the path to our destination. So we might throw out an idea like, 'Oh, maybe they do this thing,' and Wes would say, 'No, that doesn't feel right,' and then another thing would make him go, 'Ah, that feels right,' and we would know that now we were in the forest."

When a conference gets deep and tangled or somebody gets on a roll, talking too fast for Anderson to transcribe, Coppola might record the discussion with his phone. "Roman does a lot of recordings," Anderson said. "He's a dictation guy." If there's any disagreement about what was said, or if the writers worry that they might've failed to write down a usable idea, they'll check the audio.

Owen Wilson, who began working with Anderson at the University of Texas in the nineties and cowrote the screenplays to *Bottle Rocket, Rushmore,* and *The Royal Tenenbaums,* was surprised to hear how rigorous the writing process had become since the last time he and Anderson wrote together. Their system wasn't really much of a system.

"I was never any good at typing," Wilson said, "so I preferred writing it out, and Wes would write stuff out, too, and then Wes would type up some pages, and then maybe I would have some feedback on the pages, or he'd have feedback on more stuff I'd written in longhand," Wilson said. "I vividly remember this one part of the notes that Wes made for *The Life Aquatic,* because that was all worked out on yellow legal pads. He had a whole paragraph saying that the name of the ship was the *Belafonte* and the captain's name was Steve Cocteau and the crew was in pursuit of the jaguar shark, 'so rare as to quite possibly constitute a one-off mutant fluke.' When we were working on the screenplay for *Bottle Rocket,* the feature, at Gracie Films,[2] Wes had an office next to mine. He'd always be at his desk so that he could be the one doing the typing, and sometimes I'd be in the room, talking or lying on the couch. There was a lot of talking."

Hearing a description of the most recent iteration of Anderson's writing process, Wilson chuckles at "how much more evolved it is. . . . It probably is a reaction to how long it would take the two of us to get anything done, and probably to how much wasted time there was, and going down different sorts of roads that didn't necessarily lead anywhere but that could be funny to talk about for a couple of weeks!"

The final stage for any feature script is Anderson doing multiple drafts solo. Just him and the keyboard.

"Wes is really the only one who puts pen to paper, so to speak, as far as the actual writing of the screenplay," Coppola said. "He's sort of the filter, and he'll often just decide to move on his own."

In the case of *The French Dispatch,* Coppola said, the first full story in the anthology (the love affair between the inmate painter and the prison guard) was plotted mainly by Anderson, while the prologue, the other two stories, and the framing device were collective efforts. Guinness contributed bits to all of the segments, in separate sessions spread out over a period of six weeks, mainly in Kent, England. ♠

---

2  Los Angeles–based production company of James L. Brooks (*Broadcast News, The Simpsons, The Mary Tyler Moore Show*), who brought *Bottle Rocket* to Columbia Pictures and oversaw its expansion from a short film into a feature.

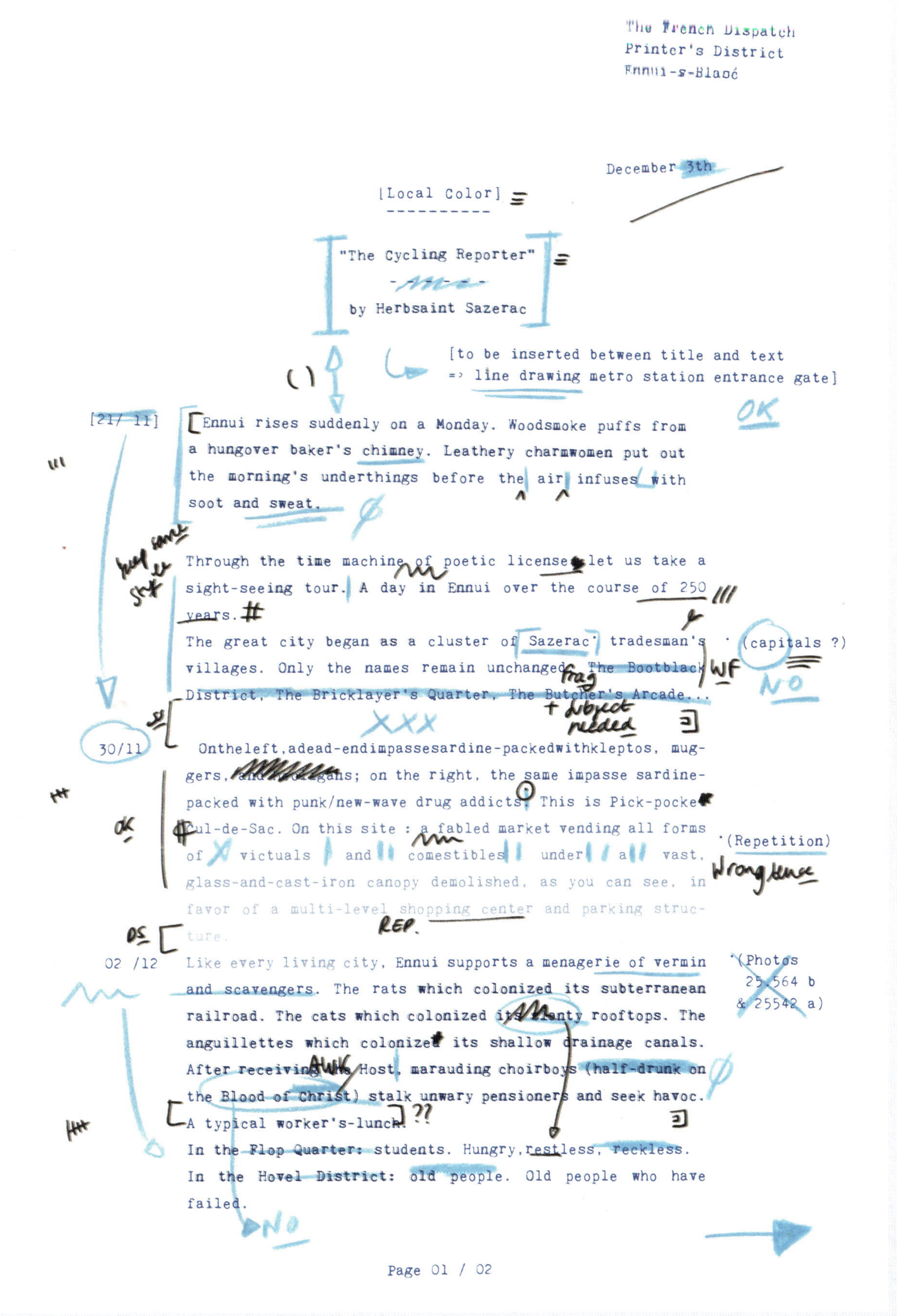

```
                                            The French Dispatch
                                            Printer's District
                                            Ennui-s-Blasé

                                                       December 3th
            [Local Color]
            ----------

            "The Cycling Reporter"

              by Herbsaint Sazerac

                            [to be inserted between title and text
                            => line drawing metro station entrance gate]

  [21/11]  Ennui rises suddenly on a Monday. Woodsmoke puffs from
           a hungover baker's chimney. Leathery charwomen put out
           the morning's underthings before the air infuses with
           soot and sweat.

           Through the time machine of poetic licenses, let us take a
           sight-seeing tour. A day in Ennui over the course of 250
           years.
           The great city began as a cluster of Sazerac tradesman's        (capitals ?)
           villages. Only the names remain unchanged. The Bootblack
           District, The Bricklayer's Quarter, The Butcher's Arcade...      NO

  30/11    Ontheleft,adead-endimpassesardine-packedwithkleptos, mug-
           gers, and hooligans; on the right, the same impasse sardine-
           packed with punk/new-wave drug addicts. This is Pick-pocket
           Cul-de-Sac. On this site : a fabled market vending all forms    (Repetition)
           of  victuals  and  comestibles  under  a  vast,              Wrong tense
           glass-and-cast-iron canopy demolished, as you can see, in
           favor of a multi-level shopping center and parking struc-
           ture.                     REP.
  02/12    Like every living city, Ennui supports a menagerie of vermin    (Photos
           and scavengers. The rats which colonized its subterranean        25 564 b
           railroad. The cats which colonized its slanty rooftops. The      & 25542 a)
           anguillettes which colonize its shallow drainage canals.
           After receiving the Host, marauding choirboys (half-drunk on
           the Blood of Christ) stalk unwary pensioners and seek havoc.
           A typical worker's-lunch.
           In the Flop Quarter: students. Hungry, restless, reckless.
           In the Hovel District: old people. Old people who have
           failed.

                                    Page 01 / 02
```

Prop used for the "Local Color" segment, showing Howitzer Jr.'s markup to Sazerac's original typed draft.

Wes Anderson and Owen Wilson on the set of Sazerac's office

# THE MAST-HEAD

THE first *French Dispatch* writer invented for the film was Herbsaint Sazerac, to be played by Owen Wilson, a sardonic chronicler of city life who travels the city on his bicycle, writing observations and quotes in a notebook. "You could say that the character is Joseph Mitchell with bits of other people mixed in," Anderson said.

Although Mitchell's literary voice was the seed for Sazerac—Wilson's North Texas accent standing in for Mitchell's North Carolina drawl—the character's affection for French bourgeoisie and working-class life draws heavily on Agnès Varda's *Daguerréotypes*, her 1975 documentary about life on Rue Daguerre, where Varda was living at the time with her two-year-old son.

"We saw Sazerac as a chronicler-of-his-city character, like Varda in *Daguerréotypes,* and a guy who's wandering around like a street photographer, but with a notepad, the way Mitchell wrote about pockets of New York, capturing characters and little microcosms," Anderson said. "As far as other influences, there was Luc Sante, who wrote about New York and was an advisor on Scorsese's *Gangs of New York,* and who also wrote a book about Paris called *The Other Paris,* which is all underbelly, and very interesting. Sante always finds the kind of unforgettable detail or bit of information that sticks in your mind. And we thought a bit about Bill Cunningham, who used to take pictures of people's clothes for the Thursday fashion section of the *New York Times* and rode around the city on his bicycle."[1]

Another inspiration was Belgian writer Georges Simenon, publisher of hundreds of books and the creator of a beloved detective hero, Commissaire Maigret. Anderson recalls how he and Nicolas Saada were talking

[1] 1929–2016, a *New York Times* photographer known for candids and street photography. His career took off in 1978 when he published a collection of impromptu photographs in the *Times*, of famous people captured during seemingly unguarded moments. The paper's then-editor, Arthur Gelb, called it "a turning point for the *Times*, because it was the first time the paper had run pictures of well-known people without getting their permission." The series led to a regular feature titled "On the Street." Although Sazerac is not a photographer, his written descriptions of citizens have a touch of Cunningham's spontaneity.

about Simenon one day when "Nicolas got out a book of Simenon and began translating some of his favorite Simenon writing from French into English on the spot, and that became part of the character, too. Simenon describes a neighborhood of, he literally said, 'old people who have failed,' and 'the occasional, very old person who jumps out the window of the dilapidated building,' and we decided to work those bits into the prologue."

Sazerac was the first of many *French Dispatch* characters who could be described as "Yanks abroad." This felt intuitively correct to Anderson, as he was one such person, and the hall of fame of *New Yorker* contributors contained surprisingly few writers born and raised in the city.

In the name of due diligence, I put together a spreadsheet of past and then-current *New Yorker* writers. The theory held up. "E. B. White was from Mt. Vernon, New York. Lillian Ross was from Fresno originally. William Shawn was born in Chicago and raised in Las Vegas. And then you have our guy Joseph Mitchell from North Carolina, and Truman Capote from Alabama, Pauline Kael from the San Francisco Bay Area, William Saroyan, Fresno. James Thurber, author of *The Secret Life of Walter Mitty*, Columbus, Ohio. Brendan Gill, from Hartford, Connecticut, attended the Kingswood Oxford school, graduated Yale, and was in the Skull and Bones Society with John Hersey, another *New Yorker* guy—of course, Hersey was the author of *Hiroshima,* which took up a whole issue of the magazine when it was published. It said here that Hersey was born in China and didn't come back to the US until he was ten."

"There you go," said Anderson.

"Seems like the transplant thing holds true today. David Remnick, the current *New Yorker* editor, is from Hackensack, New Jersey. Emily Nussbaum, the lead television critic, was born in Scarsdale and grew up in Rhode Island and Atlanta. Kelefa Sanneh is from Birmingham, England. Jia Tolentino is from Toronto. It's unusual to have a *New Yorker* contributor like A. J. Liebling, who was born on the Upper West Side, or James Baldwin, who was born in Harlem, both born-in-New-York New Yorkers. Although you do have a Baldwin-like character in your movie—"

"A combination of Baldwin and Liebling! So I guess he's two New Yorkers rolled into one."

THIS PAGE: **Still-frame images from the Sazerac section of *The French Dispatch***

### NATIVE, RESIDENT, TRANSPLANT

E.B. White, the author of *Charlotte's Web* and *Stuart Little* and the coauthor of *The Elements of Style,* somewhat self-servingly argued for the supremacy of the transplanted writer in 1949's *Here Is New York,* defining the three types of New Yorkers thusly:

> There is, first, the New York of the man or woman who was born here, who takes the city for granted and accepts its size and turbulence as natural and inevitable.
>
> Second, there is the New York of the commuter—the city that is devoured by locusts each day and spat out each night.
>
> Third, there is the New York of the person who was born somewhere else and came to New York in quest of something. Of these three trembling cities the greatest is the last—the city of final destination, the city that is a goal. It is this third city that accounts for New York's high-strung disposition, its *poetical deportment, its dedication to the arts, and its incomparable achievements. Commuters give the city its tidal restlessness; natives give it solidity and continuity; but the settlers give it passion. And whether it is a farmer arriving from Italy to set up a small grocery store in a slum, or a young girl arriving from a small town in Mississippi to escape the indignity of being observed by her neighbors, or a boy arriving from the Corn Belt with a manuscript in his suitcase and a pain in his heart, it makes no difference: Each embraces New York with the intense excitement of first love, each absorbs New York with the fresh eyes of an adventurer, each generates heat and light to dwarf the Consolidated Edison Company."*

"Hugo Guinness calls it 'reverse immigration,'" Anderson said. (Guinness is specifically referring to the reversal of his own journey, that of a European who came to America.) "Immigration, to an American, is when people from other countries come to America. Reverse immigrants are basically expatriates. They're

Still-frame image of Sazerac on the Ennui Métro, describing the rats that inhabit the tunnels. Those are real rodents behind him, enclosed within a set element.

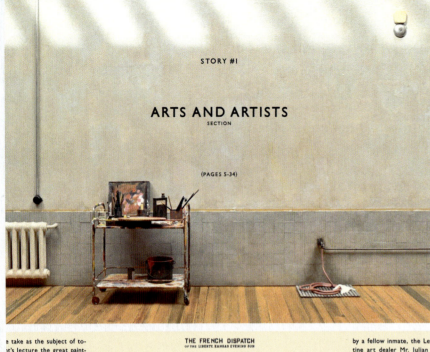

THIS PAGE: Still-frame images from the "Arts and Artists" segment of *The French Dispatch*

OPPOSITE AND PAGE 44: Tilda Swinton rehearsing the "Berensen Lecture," which were shot on location at the Théâtre d'Angoulême

leaving America because they want to experience someplace else."

"So you're sort of saying up front, 'This film is not a culturally authoritative view of France'?" I asked (admittedly a leading question).

"Well, I'm not sure what that means. These writers are Americans. They write for an American magazine in France. Whatever the 'there' is that we're trying to get to, we're not doing it through factual reporting. We're doing a fiction of journalism."

The conversation turns to a discussion the two of us had in *The Wes Anderson Collection: The Grand Budapest Hotel*, about the difference between being a tourist and a resident in a city with customs and a language different from the ones that the visitor grew up with. A resident is not on par with a native citizen in terms of bragging rights, but the word does imply a comfort level that goes beyond "tourist." Residents retain the humility of the newcomer and would never represent themselves as an authority on their adopted surroundings, but they can go into a local hardware store and ask for a certain kind of lightbulb in a language other than the one that they grew up speaking without needing anyone else to translate.

"Maybe I'm at that point with France now," Anderson said. "I don't feel like a tourist. I feel like a resident visitor."

It was a long, strange trip. Anderson didn't leave the United States until he was in his early twenties, for a brief trip to England and France. In his early thirties, while touring to promote *The Royal Tenenbaums*, he spent quality time in England, France, Spain, and Italy, and fell in love with international travel. His fourth feature, *The Life Aquatic with Steve Zissou*, was originally set on the Atlantic coast of the United States, but once he visited Rome, he became smitten with the atmosphere and cultural history of the region, and impulsively decided to film interiors at Rome's Cinecittà Studios, and exteriors on the Mediterranean and Aegean Seas. He set his fifth feature, 2007's *The Darjeeling Limited*, in India after watching Jean Renoir's 1950 film *The River* (a French director's vision of India) in Martin Scorsese's screening room.

After that, Anderson began roaming with intent. He spent weeks or months in countries other than the US—solo, with friends, or in the company of Juman Malouf, his partner and the future mother of their daughter. He also became more purposeful in his travels across the US. Where most Americans treat travel as a dull but unavoidable means of getting where you want to go, Anderson treats it as an activity with its own experiential value.

"Wes is a person who very much appreciates living your life in an artful way, or a way that allows you to have good experiences," said Roman Coppola. "When we travel together, we'll often do a lot of preparation as far as how we're going to get somewhere, and what manner of transportation we're going to take. Wes loves traveling by rail or by bus. He'll travel throughout the US and Europe by train, often stopping to get food at local restaurants he's heard of, and so

on. There's a lot of detail with Wes when it comes to travel, food, and accommodations."

Anderson and Malouf are based mainly in England and France now, "but that allows you to just get on a train and go visit a lot of other countries," Anderson said. "So we take advantage of that. You just go to the train station, and the next thing you know, you're in Switzerland."

Anderson draws inspiration from many collaborators and sources, and layers them so that when you look at a finished movie, it's difficult to identify a character or story as having been inspired by just one thing. For example, during *The French Dispatch*'s story germination phase, Anderson decided he wanted at least one of the feature stories to be about a painter. That's all he had at first: the idea to do a story about a sort of abstract expressionist painter and an art dealer inspired by Joseph Duveen.

Anderson's friend David Brendel, future author of *An Editor's Burial,* described the origin of Anderson's interest in "the grande dame of art lecturers, Rosamond Bernier." A 2011 *Vogue* profile, published on the occasion of Bernier's ninety-fifth birthday, called her "the world's most glamorous art lecturer turned memoirist," a woman who has "tamed wild animals, flown her own plane, and befriended the likes of Henri Matisse, Leonard Bernstein, and Frida Kahlo. As an expatriate American in Mexico during the 1940s, she presided over a menagerie that included an ocelot, an anteater, spider monkeys, various tropical birds, and (most incongruously) a small penguin, which she took swimming off the coast of Acapulco. As the first-ever European Features Editor for *Vogue* in postwar Paris, she lived at the Hôtel de Crillon—where, in a city still recovering from wartime deprivations, she had the benefit of hot water—and charmed Picasso with her Mexican-accented Spanish."

"It started a dozen years ago over a yearly dinner with our friends Hampton Fancher[2] and Annie Ohayon,"[3] Brendel said. "Annie knew Rosamond through her own French-American cultural work. I'd just met Rosamond, and she seemed like, well . . . a character in a Wes Anderson film. Rosamond's story zigzags from Mexico, Diego Rivera, and Frida Kahlo, to France and Jean Cocteau, to Barcelona and Brassaï. After she was the Paris Editor of *Vogue,* she started the art journal *L'Oeil.* There she published original work by icons who to her were friends: Joan Miró, Henri Matisse, and Pablo Picasso."

Bernier's life captured Anderson's imagination, so he tracked down videos of her lectures, which inspired the framing scenes of J.K.L. Berensen (Tilda Swinton) talking about Moses Rosenthaler (Benicio Del Toro) before a rapt audience. Brendel contrived to connect Anderson and Bernier, expecting "a perfect match." But attempts at an introduction never worked out, and Anderson, like the writers of *The French Dispatch,* soon moved to France. Bernier died in 2016 at one hundred years old, having just written her second memoir. She would live on in disguised form through Berensen, staff writer for *The French Dispatch,* art historian, clotheshorse, and lecturer extraordinaire, played by Swinton, a presence in all of Anderson's projects since *Moonrise Kingdom.*

"Bernier was a very real and shameless model," said Swinton. "Art fangirl and critic; friend—and, possibly, 'friend'—to the Surrealists/Post-Impressionists; self-professed 'professional talker.' Her flamboyantly prestigious and highly subjective lectures on the history of art—presented at the Met in the highest of Parisian couture and the most impeccable diction imaginable—were our template."

"Even though Tilda's character is based mainly on Bernier, and modeled physically in the way she speaks and the way she's written," Anderson said, "the person whose role she's filling in this story is another *New Yorker* writer, S. N. Behrman, because the first inspiration for that story was Behrman's famous piece about Joseph Duveen, the art dealer.[4] Our story ended up being something completely different from the Duveen profile—it started out as a story about an art dealer, but it became about an artist and an art dealer. And we steal a little bit from the Emile de Antonio film *Painter's Painting.*[5] But the germ still comes from that Duveen story. And the character that Adrien [Brody] plays in our movie, Julian Cadazio, is kind of our version of Duveen."

Berensen's *French Dispatch* article, "The Concrete Masterpiece," focuses on the life and art of Rosenthaler (Del Toro), described by Berensen as being "at the Vanguard of the French Splatter-School Action Group." He's a mentally disturbed painter sentenced to life in prison for killing two people in a bar. Moses takes up painting again after falling for a prison guard, Léa Seydoux's Simone. One of Moses's portraits of Simone attracts the notice of Cadazio (Brody), who is serving a brief prison sentence for financial crimes. Cadazio admires Moses's gifts but sees him mainly as a future income source for himself and his art dealer uncles. He pressures Moses to create a monumental work that will be unveiled in the presence of assembled press and potential buyers. With Simone serving as his muse and life coach, Moses reaches his fullest potential via the eponymous masterpiece: a multipaneled abstract fresco, painted on a concrete wall.

The dominant tone is gently satirical. But when the segment contemplates the redemptive purity of Moses's love for Simone—who, even though she cares for the inmate, is revealed to have had self-interested reasons for driving him onward—it is poker-faced, much like the central love stories in *Bottle Rocket, The Royal Tenenbaums, Moonrise Kingdom,* and *The Grand Budapest Hotel.* Berensen's narration, delivered in a lecture hall and in voice-over, puts a bit of space between the characters and the viewers by regularly reminding us that this is not what happened, merely one writer's account of events—a storytelling choice that unites every section of the movie.

---

2   Filmmaker and screenwriter who adapted *Blade Runner* for Ridley Scott, and wrote and directed *The Minus Man,* starring Owen Wilson.

3   Once a publicist for notable musicians, including Annie Lennox, Lou Reed, Laurie Anderson, and Bebel Gilberto, Annie Ohayon curates and produces an acoustic concert series at The Standard in Manhattan.

4   "The Days of Duveen," published in *The New Yorker*, Sept. 22, 1951, is an account of the life and work of Joseph Duveen, aka 1st Baron Duveen, a British national whose wheeling and dealing and almost personal-assistant-level spoiling of wealthy clients created a new cultural stereotype of the art dealer-as-rock-star—somebody who knew the value of art mainly because he understood the value of money. "Probably never before had a merchant brought to such exquisite perfection the large-minded art of casting bread upon the waters," the piece observed. "There was almost nothing Duveen wouldn't do for his important clients. Immensely rich Americans, shy and suspicious of casual contacts because of their wealth, often didn't know where to go or what to do with themselves when they were abroad. Duveen provided entrée to the great country homes of the nobility; the coincidence that their noble owners often had ancestral portraits to sell did not deter Duveen."

5   1972; documentary feature by Emile de Antonio charting the New York visual art scene from 1940–1970, featuring Philip Leider, Leo Castelli, Willem de Kooning, Helen Frankenthaler, and other luminaries. Considered by many to be the definitive documentary on the New York School.

THIS PAGE: **Still-frame image of Lucinda Krementz (Frances McDormand) hard at work on a manifesto about the manifesto**

OPPOSITE: **Still-frame images from the "Politics/Poetry" segment of *The French Dispatch***

6   *Les Parapluies de Cherbourg* (1964) is a musical with a score and songs by Michel Legrand following a few years in the lives of a young man and woman. Their relationship is defined by the young man getting drafted into the Algerian War and the woman giving birth to a child resulting from a tryst the night before he joined the army. Songs include "I Will Wait for You" (the main theme, also known as "Devant le Garage," was a huge international success) and "Watch What Happens" (originally "Récit de Cassard" or "Cassard's Story"). *Les Demoiselles de Rochefort* (1967), another collaboration between Demy and Legrand, is about the summertime attraction between two women in a seaside town and a couple of carnies who are passing through while working on the local fair. As in the *French Dispatch* segment, a lot of the significant action revolves around an adorable café. The most famous songs are "A Pair of Twins" ("Chanson des Jumelles" in French) and "You Must Believe in Spring" ("Chanson de Maxence").

7   A film-and-literature inside joke, once removed: The star-crossed couple are essentially Romeo and Juliet at the Revolution, and the most famous screen version of Shakespeare's tragedy, at least until Baz Luhrmann got hold of it, was directed by Zeffirelli, as luck would have it, in 1968.

8   "The Events in May: A Paris Notebook," published in the "Reflections" section of *The New Yorker* on September 21, 1968.

## ICONIC PORTRAITS

THE second long article, "Revisions to a Manifesto," concerns a student uprising in 1960s Ennui-sur-Blasé, inspired by the 1968 Paris demonstrations. Cinematically, this segment draws on midcentury French cinema riffs on pre–World War II American genre films that were popular at that time, including *The Umbrellas of Cherbourg* (a musical)[6] and *The Battle of Algiers* (a counterinsurgency war picture).

Timothée Chalamet and Lyna Khoudri star as Zeffirelli and Juliette,[7] leaders of rival student factions that oppose the government. One is male-dominated and accommodationist in character, and seems primarily interested in gaining access to girls' dormitories. The other faction is more radical, agitating against imperialism and the conscription of soldiers. Frances McDormand, an Anderson regular since *Moonrise Kingdom,* plays Lucinda Krementz, a *French Dispatch* correspondent who, while profiling different types of student revolutionaries for the magazine, has a secret fling with Zeffirelli and helps him sharpen his manifesto. ("This isn't the first manifesto I've edited," she assures him.) Lucinda is loosely based on Mavis Gallant (1922–2014), an American in Paris who wrote

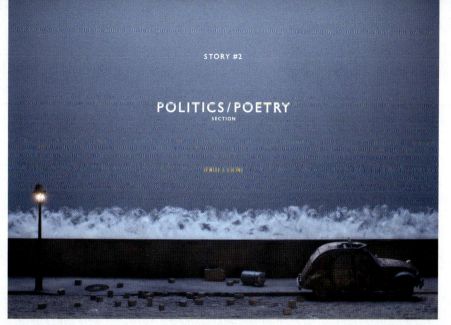

> "One of their issues was, literally, access to the girls' dormitory."
>
> —WES ANDERSON

a two-part memoir/analysis of the 1968 student uprisings for *The New Yorker*.[8]

Chalamet's Zeffirelli and Khoudri's Juliette are drawn to each other, despite Juliette's disapproval of Zeffirelli's self-exculpating centrism and his age-inappropriate relationship with Lucinda, which even Zeffirelli finds confusing. On the day the students confront police and government officials, ritualistically battling each other via chess, Lucinda admits her affair with the teenager and gives Zeffirelli and Juliette an unusually eloquent "get a room" speech, and they do, fleeing the scene on Juliette's scooter. Their affair radicalizes Zeffirelli. Sometime later, while restoring power to a downed transformer atop a pirate radio station that broadcasts antigovernment sentiments, Zeffirelli is electrocuted to death. He becomes a commodified martyr whose image appears on flyers, posters, and T-shirts: a vaguely inspirational emblem, shorn of personal and political context, like the iconic portraits that his friends argued about in the café.

As is always the case in Anderson's films, and as is the case in every *French Dispatch* episode, the tale of the student uprising happens in a parallel universe that's not the same as our own. Recognizable timelines and events are alluded to, combined, or reimagined, but never mirrored exactly. The story in the student protest episode is "pretty clearly supposed to be our version of the events of May 1968," Anderson said, "but ours, I think, happens more like in 1965. Maybe that's because of Godard." The male students are worried about being forced to serve in "the Mustard Region." The area (though it sounds like Dijon) isn't identified as being a part of France or a colony beyond; it's just a (potentially) lethal place where young men go to fulfill mandatory service. "I guess it could be in the south somewhere, or maybe it could be a colonial outpost in North Africa," Anderson said, "where they grow condiments, I suppose."

The protest of gender segregation in dormitories, however, is an exact reference to something real. "Daniel Cohn-Bendit, as you know, was an important voice during May '68. Two months earlier, in Nanterre, where he was a student, he was a principal leader of the March 22 protest," Anderson said. "And one of their issues was, literally, access to the girls' dormitory for all male students, which we put in our story because, I guess, I thought it had a sort of innocence and charm to it."

Anderson directs McDormand and Chalamet on the set of the barricades sequence as Roman Coppola listens.

THIS PAGE: Still-frames of the title card and opening page of the "Tastes & Smells" segment of *The French Dispatch*

OPPOSITE AND FOLLOWING SPREAD: Photos from the filming of Roebuck Wright's interview, which used period-accurate TV cameras and monitors

9   Anderson said that although Roebuck Wright was written with Jeffrey Wright in mind, he didn't intentionally give him the actor's last name. "Oddly," he adds.

10   Judging from the set's Braniff-goes-to-the Actors Studio production design.

11   Roebuck Wright's uncanny memory is reminiscent of a claim made by *New Yorker* contributor Truman Capote (*In Cold Blood*) that he never took notes during interviews because he could recall every word his subjects uttered.

## A NEW FLAVOR

THE final segment, "The Private Dining Room of the Police Commissioner," is a combination caper picture/crime thriller wrapped in an origin story about the piece's author, Roebuck Wright (Jeffrey Wright).[9] Like the prologue, this segment has moments of direct address (not as frequent as in Sazerac's) as well as interactions between the writer and his editor (although here we get to see what Roebuck was like before he became a professional writer, a privilege not afforded any other character). We're told that Wright was originally assigned to profile M. Nescaffier (Steve Park), personal chef to Ennui-sur-Blasé's Commissaire de la Police Municipale (Mathieu Amalric). The assignment morphed into a cops-and-robbers farce when Gigi (Winsen Ait Hellal), only child of the widowed Commissaire, was kidnapped by a local crime boss known as the Chauffeur (Edward Norton), who refused to release Gigi until police handed over a jailed accountant (Willem Dafoe) with knowledge of the gangster's finances.

The entire contraption is nestled within an even wider frame: Wright being interviewed sometime in the 1970s[10] by a talk-show host (*Ray Donovan* star Liev Schreiber, Jeffrey Wright's college buddy from Amherst). It's a *Grand Budapest*–y multilayered metafiction: Wright is recounting the creation of his signature piece, and the interview includes a summary of the kidnapping and police action, plus a digression recounting how he became a magazine writer to begin with (he was jailed by homophobic police officers; Howitzer paid Wright's bail and assigned him to review a poetry book). There are also ruminations on the craft of writing, Wright's supposedly "typographic memory,"[11] and the blend of estrangement and independence Wright felt as an expatriate reinventing himself in France (an experience that bonds him to Nescaffier, and that he has in common with the film's writer-director). The intricate arrangement of the film's storytelling techniques becomes a spectacle in itself as the segment tries to conjure the cinematic equivalent of Nescaffier's dream: a new flavor.

But even as the anthology tries to stretch Anderson's imagination, familiar Andersonian themes persist. The most significant, said Anderson, echoing his friend Nicolas Saada, is the invention and embrace of a new family. "As much as these writers decided to go somewhere else to live, and to put themselves in the position of being outsiders, that doesn't mean that you don't also seek out family," he said. "This magazine is probably something like that for them. Even though it may not be a close-knit family, it's their little anchor that they share in a city abroad. So yeah, Bill Murray's character is the father, looking after all of them a little bit."♠

**Behind-the-scenes photo of the "Issue in Progress" board**

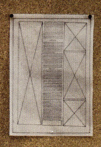

**ROEBUCK WRIGHT**

22-23   24-25   26-27   28-29   30-31   32-33   34-35   36

**KREMENTZ**

48-49   50-51   52-53   54-55   56-57   58-59   60-

# ROGRESS

### le N. 47

## E OF ENTS

| 8-9 | 10-11 | 12-13 | 14-15 | 16-17 | 18-19 | 20-21 |

**BERENSEN**

| 38-39 | 40-41 | 42-43 | 44-45 | 46-47 |

## LEVEL OF COMPLETION

    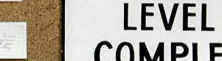

**RAC**

| 62-63 | 64-65 | 66-67 | 68-69 | 72 |

|  | MILESTONE | \multicolumn{8}{c}{WRITERS} |
| | | RW | HS | LK | JvB | CW | BW | FQ |
|---|---|---|---|---|---|---|---|---|
| 1 | BRIEFING | X | ✓ | ✓ | ✓ | ✓ | ✓ | ✓ |
| 2 | FIRST DRAFT | OK | ✓ | X | X | X | ✓ | N/A |
| 3 | SECOND DRAFT | ✓ | X | X | X | X | OK | |
| 4 | PHOTOGRAPHY APPROVED | AM | ✓ | AM | ✓ | | FM | X |
| 5 | ILLUSTRATION APPROVED | | | OK | N/A | ✓ | ✓ | |
| 6 | COPY CHECKED BY COPY EDITOR | ✓ | ✓ | X | ✓ | X | | |
| 7 | COPY CHECKED BY EDITOR-IN-CHIEF | AM | AM | | AM | AM | AM | AM |
| 8 | HEADLINE WRITTEN | | | X | X | ✓ | ✓ | |
| 9 | HEADLINE SIGNED OFF | | | AM | AM | | | |
| 10 | GALLEY PROOF READING 1 | | | | X | | | |
| 11 | GALLEY PROOF READING 2 | | | ✓ | X | | X | ✓ |
| 12 | GALLEY PROOF SIGNED OFF | AM | AM | | | | | AM |
| 13 | LAYOUT APPROVED | | | | | | | ✓ |
| 14 | HEADLINE TYPECAST | | | | | | | ✓ |
| 15 | STEREOTYPING | | | | | | | |
| 16 | SENT TO PRESS | | | | | | | |

**EDITOR'S NOTES**

ISSUE NO.

## PART IV

# EMBRACING ANGOULÊME

Once the script was worked out to Anderson's satisfaction, the next step was storyboarding and planning the shoot. Step one was finding a city that could stand in for Ennui-sur-Blasé, the film's main location.

As outlined in the screenplay, Ennui-sur-Blasé is a large French city that's like Paris, but is not exactly Paris. It's more of a movie buff's fantasy of urban France, mediated by classic films set there—an exhaustive list that includes such features as *La Ronde, Rififi, The 400 Blows, The Murderer Lives at Number 21, Quai des Orfèvres, Mon Oncle,* and countless others.

Anderson considered several different cities as shooting locations, but in the end, he chose Angoulême. Like so many aspects of film's production, this was a decision that just *happened*.

Nicknamed "the balcony of the southwest," Angoulême is a walled city, or "keep," roughly fifteen kilometers wide, located in the Charente region of France. Angoulême was built on a plateau at the intersection of multiple bodies of water and important trade routes, which of course made it a target of sieges throughout its history. The city was occupied by the Visigoths and sacked by Vikings, and its Jewish population was targeted many times over the centuries, from a massacre by Crusaders in 1236 through the Nazi occupation of the 1940s. The population of the outlying region of Angoulême is about 110,000, the city center (known as Old Angoulême) roughly 42,000. Angoulême is known as one of France's most important artistic centers outside of Paris. Jean-Louis Guez de Balzac, best known for his epistolary essays, was born in Angoulême, and became one of the founding members of Académie française.

At the time of *The French Dispatch*'s production, the city was most widely celebrated as a center of publishing, literature and illustration, comics art, and animation. All these industries proceeded inexorably from the city thriving after the invention of the printing press. It became a hub for paper manufacturing and publishing, and soon after that—

Ah. But why let a dry recitation of data set the scene for us? Instead let's consult Florent Gaillard, a historian of Angoulême, born and raised in the city.

It is impossible to convey the effect of Gaillard's honeyed Gallic rumble of a voice in the pages of this book. Imagine him seated at a corner table in an ancient pub, wreathed in cigarette smoke, swirling a snifter of port, a three-legged dog snoozing at his feet:

OPPOSITE: **Overhead view of filming of a scene in the student protest episode. The trees were provided by the art department, along with the auto-junk ramparts and piles of stones. In the background: Église Notre-Dame d'Obézine, which is behind Rue du Sauvage, where the film's barricades scenes were shot.**

"Angoulême has become the capital of comic books in France. It was declared a UNESCO site for creativity."

—FLORENT GAILLARD, ANGOULÊME HISTORIAN

*It's like something out of a dream, this city. It's kind of like a mountain on a rock, a place that's surrounded by rocks. It has been compared, to some extent, to the Acropolis. It is perched. Its glance is towards the sky.*

*Let me tell you about the first time when a person could say "Angoulême" and have another person immediately say, "Yes—I know what that name means." It dates back to the sixteenth century, to the Renaissance. There was a count called François d'Angoulême, who would eventually become king: François I.[1] At that particular moment, François's ascension really shone a light on Angoulême—it really put it on the map. Angoulême became the territory of François's sister, Marguerite, and during that period, Angoulême became especially associated with arts and literature.*

*At the time that the count became king, his family had an incredibly extensive library full of manuscripts. These are still preserved in the National Collection today. François's ascension to king also sparked the construction of several castles in the area, including one very famous castle, [Château] La Rochefoucauld. This all spurred a burst of artistic creativity in and around Angoulême.*

*The fact that Angoulême was built by a river is important to note. People call it "Le Fleuve du," which is kind of an adjective—a nickname for the river. It has to do with feeding, with food. The reason they call it that is because that river was crucially important to feeding economic development in the area. Anything that was produced in the Charente region would use the river to transport the goods to other markets. The river was a very important trade route. Because there were few alternate routes at the time—no trains, paved roads, things like that—the river was crucial to the economic development of Angoulême.*

*One of the most important of all products in this heavily forested region was paper—a major export that was transported elsewhere by river. The area became known for producing artisanal paper, and this tradition continued on through the industrial revolution. During the industrial revolution there was a real boom. The production of paper became more industrialized. Productivity increased exponentially. Angoulême had, during the nineteenth century, approximately ten thousand workers in various paper factories. The paper factories remained a center of Angoulême's economy until about the 1960s. Deindustrialization continued through the 1970s.*

*With the death of mechanized industry, Angoulême needed a new direction, and in 1974, they got one, with the founding of a comic-book festival:[2] Festival international de la bande dessinée d'Angoulême, aka The Angoulême International Comics Festival. What people outside of France may not know is that comic books are huge in France. The appearance at the 1977 festival of Hergé, creator of Tintin, brought the festival to international attention. The Angoulême International Comics Festival would go on to become the second largest such festival in Europe, and the third largest in the world, drawing two hundred thousand visitors a year, with events occurring simultaneously all over the city.*

*Angoulême has since become the capital of comic books in France. It was declared a UNESCO site for creativity, on account of having become a capital of comic books. Many important comic-book publishing houses have since established themselves in Angoulême, and several prominent authors as well. It's definitely an area where comic books are exported, and where deals over comic books are made.*

Then Gaillard adds some details that make *The French Dispatch* seem destined to shoot in Angoulême. One is Angoulême's evolution into an international center for animation—an outgrowth of its centrality to comics. Angoulême is now home to RECA, 2d3D Animations, and Superprod Animation, among other production houses, and hosts many training programs and schools, notably École de la CCI Charente.

This would all prove convenient for Anderson, who is fond of comics art and animation and has previsualized every shot of his features as animatics (i.e., moving storyboards) ever since directing his first animated feature, 2009's *Fantastic Mr. Fox*. "You can really see what the film is going to look like when you watch Wes's animatics," says Léa Seydoux. "He's very visual, with a specific aesthetic. He wants to know the structure of the film and all the shots before he goes on set. They're like little, rough versions of the finished movie. He does all the voices himself."

Anderson wanted *The French Dispatch* to contain animated sequences long before finding out that Angoulême was uniquely equipped to help realize them.

## COMICS AND CARTOONS

**P**REVIOUS live-action Anderson films have had animated elements (notably *The Life Aquatic*, which showcased stop-motion sea creatures by animator Henry Selick[3]), and many of Anderson's later features rely heavily on digital compositing to fill out the shots (most outrageously, the ski chase in *The Grand Budapest Hotel*, of which Octavia Peissel says, "We were thinking about shooting out of helicopters and we were thinking about the Alps, and all of a sudden we end up, like, in a parking lot shooting a miniature skier on a miniature mountain slope.") But *The French Dispatch* marks the first time that Anderson has switched between animation and live action within the course of a single, continuous story—and,

**1** Francis I (1494–1547, King of France 1515–1547); the son of Charles of Orléans.

**2** Founded by French writers and editors Francis Groux and Jean Mardikian and comics writer and scholar Claude Moliterni.

**3** Director of *The Nightmare Before Christmas* and *James and the Giant Peach*.

in one instance, without explanation. The kidnapping of little Gigi by local criminals via hot air balloon was written into the screenplay from the start, and plays like a parenthetical interlude or joke (and is framed by the narrator, Roebuck Wright, as a graphic from the magazine).

Peissel said she was relieved when Anderson confirmed that the chase sequence would not, in fact, involve actual persons leaping from moving cars and crashing into things. The decision to do the entire thing as an animated cartoon, she said, ties the film into a local tradition that became a center of Angoulême's commercial life.

"*Bande dessinée* is the traditional Franco-Belgian style of comic books, and Angoulême is the *bande desinée* and animation capital of France," said Peissel. "Wes was writing that third story while we were already prepping the other stories that had been finished. Angoulême's importance in the history of *bande desinée* definitely had something to do with the decision to do the chase as two-dimensional animation in *bande desinée* style."

"Well, that's all accurate," Anderson said. "But there are other things going on here. One is, let's face it, I'm never going to do a car chase as well as somebody like John Frankenheimer. And suddenly switching over to animation is something I think maybe I can get away with doing. Also, at this point, people accept that a thing like that can happen in my movies. Whereas if you were watching a Christopher Nolan film, and the big chase scene was about to start and all of a sudden the movie switched to hand-drawn animation without any explanation, the audience would revolt. To be honest, I think I might have issues with it myself."

## NEW YORK, NEW ANGOULÊME

THERE'S another historical detail about Angoulême that makes its selection feel preordained: Before New York City was named after a city in England, and before it was claimed by the Dutch—and before one of its rivers was named after Henry Hudson, an English explorer employed by the Dutch East India

PREVIOUS SPREAD AND OPPOSITE: Still-frames from the animated chase sequence in the final episode

BELOW: Wes Anderson with Willem Dafoe (the Abacus) and Mathieu Almaric (the Commissioner) at Rue du Minage, where both the Abacus's capture and the shoot-out between cops and gangsters were filmed

Company—Manhattan was known as Angoulême. Gaillard is an expert on this aspect of the city's history, having appeared in (hosted, really) a documentary called *Et si New York s'appelait Angoulême,* by filmmaker Marie-France Brière.

The city we now know as New York was christened Angoulême by explorer Giovanni da Verrazzano[4] on January 17, 1524, during a voyage sponsored by none other than King Francis I, the once and future favorite son of Angoulême. Verrazano dubbed the harbor "Angoulême" to flatter His Majesty. The ship's mapmaker was Verrazano's brother, Girolamo. In 1529, Girolamo drew a world map incorporating information from all Verrazano's voyages, identifying what we now call New York Harbor as "Angoulême." Subsequent maps by Italian and French cartographers would variously identify the harbor, the inlet, and an area upstate as "Angoulême." Centuries later, Angoulême would be renamed New York.

And so—like a pinball appearing to careen at random, only to land in the right spot time and again—Anderson's suburban Texas origin story brings him into contact with issues of *The New Yorker,* which pushes him toward New York, which inspires him to make *The Royal Tenenbaums,* which is visually and literarily influenced by *The New Yorker,* which leads to Anderson embarking on a European promotional tour for *The Royal Tenenbaums,* which inspires Anderson to shoot his next three features plus assorted short films and TV commercials outside of the United States and transforms him into a dedicated traveler whose nesting places include New York and Paris.

Flash forward to 2019: Anderson finally shoots a feature in France, concerning a magazine inspired by *The New Yorker,* but published in English, and founded by an American who, like Anderson, grew up in a flyover state.[5]

The shooting location: Angoulême. New York before New York was New York. It's as if the cosmos itself sent Wes Anderson to Angoulême.

Then again, it might've been the beef.

## THE BEEF

**W**ES Anderson loves food as much as he loves movies. As Roman Coppola has noted, the director's travels are shaped by what type of food a city or region is known for and what restaurants he wants to try. If he likes the place, he'll return, bringing friends and coworkers. If he adores it, he'll go back so many times that the place will become a second home.

The production of Anderson's feature films revolves around communal dining as well. This was always the case. I remember the food available during the shooting of Anderson's first feature, *Bottle Rocket,* to be of suspect quality, but there were large quantities of it. The energy among cast and crew as they ate, however, was more like that of a boardinghouse scene in an Old Hollywood movie than a commissary or "mess tent" on a typical film set.

The commitment to communal dining became more pronounced on *Moonrise Kingdom, The Grand Budapest Hotel,* and *The French Dispatch.* Anderson started planning his shoots so that as many scenes as possible, interior as well as exterior, could be done in the same city, preferably in the same neighborhood, and ideally within walking distance of the hotels.

"I don't think people understand how important it is to Wes to keep things as intimate as possible," Jason Schwartzman said. "You might be watching *The Grand Budapest Hotel* and there'll be a shot of the exterior of a location that's supposed to be on the other side of the country from the Grand Budapest Hotel, and if you ask Wes where they filmed it, he'll tell you, 'Oh, that was the building across the street.' I think that if Wes could shoot an entire movie without having to walk more than five minutes in any direction, he'd do it. He's definitely tried."

Although there were artistic and architectural reasons for choosing Angoulême, and perhaps certain historical-cosmic forces involved as well, one might speculate that the quality of the food might've been what kept Angoulême in the "yes" column.

Of particular note is a restaurant named Le Bruleau Charentais, owned by a chef named Frédéric Guidoni.

Guidoni was born to French dentists who lived in Algiers when it was still a colony. They fell in love while serving on the faculty at a university in Bordeaux. The family moved to Angoulême when Guidoni was still an infant. His father died when he was six. His mother eventually remarried. Guidoni "didn't get along" with his stepfather, but says he will always be grateful to the man for teaching him to fly single-engine planes.

---

[4] 1485–1528. The Verrazzano Narrows Bridge, which connects South Brooklyn to New Jersey, is named for him.

[5] No, seriously. Think about it.

TOP: Art department rendering of the Ennui-sur-Blasé skyline

MIDDLE: Rue de l'Échêvé in Angoulême as it normally appears

BOTTOM: Still-frame of the same location in the finished film, after being painted, set-dressed, lit, and built out with digitally composited miniatures (see upper-right corner of frame)

The postcard of the original city market that Herbsaint Sazerac holds in his hand while he tells readers/viewers about the remaking of the place by the forces of modernity

As a teenager, Guidoni enlisted in the French navy and studied for two years to fly fighter jets, but never completed his training. Later, while studying math at university, Guidoni decided he was tired of eating takeout food and premade meals, so he bought cookbooks and taught himself the basics. He enjoyed cooking and had good instincts, and although he never formally studied the culinary arts, he became so skilled that his friends began angling for invitations to dine with him.

Over the decades, Guidoni studied many different subjects, including accounting and business management, and pondered setting down roots in various regions of France. But he always returned to cooking and Angoulême, and in 2005, Guidoni cemented his destiny by purchasing Le Bruleau Charentais, an Angoulême restaurant built with stones gathered from Charente. Guidoni describes Le Bruleau Charentais as "a space with fifteen tables and a big-ass chimney made of big-ass quarry stones, not little bricks stacked on top of each other." The chimney proved ideal for smoking meats with chestnut and beech firewood gathered from nearby forests. Thus smoked meats—especially beef—became the food the restaurant was known for. Guidoni now lives full-time in Angoulême with his wife and sixteen-year-old son, and his existence revolves around the restaurant. "I am content," he said. "I'm really happy with my life. What I want most is for my son to be as happy as me in his life."

Anderson would make Le Bruleau Charentais his default Angoulême dining spot and cast Guidoni as the owner of the Sans Blague Café. But as it turned out, Guidoni already knew somebody was shooting a film in his hometown long before the director walked into his restaurant and took a liking to him. A few weeks earlier, a casting agent had stopped Guidoni on the street and asked him if he wanted to be in a film. He said "no" because they wouldn't tell him what the film was about, or who was making it.

Hundreds of Angoulême residents could tell their own version of this story. In the months leading up to principal photography in 2018, Anderson's people were out on the streets with clipboards and cameras, trying to fill in the backgrounds of *The French Dispatch*.

### EXTRAS, EXTRAS!
### READ ALL ABOUT THEM!

**G**UIDONI was surprised that anyone would have considered him as an extra. No one had ever asked him to do that kind of thing before. At the time, the casting agent didn't tell him the name of the movie or director. She was just trawling the city for interesting faces.

This came out of Anderson's affinity for nonfiction writing and cinema. He's a fan of French documentaries as well as dramas and comedies, in particular Agnès Varda's nonfiction films about Paris,[6] and he has a history of casting nonprofessional or unknown actors, dating back to 1996's *Bottle Rocket*. He decided to cast as many supporting and background roles as possible with citizens of Angoulême. No acting experience required. The person would just need to be comfortable on camera, have an interesting face, and be willing to stay on set as long as they were needed.

The extras casting was overseen by Amélie Covillard and Martin Scali. Scali, the second unit director of *The French Dispatch*, and an associate of Anderson's since *Fantastic Mr. Fox*, started the search

---

[6] 1928–2019. A pioneering filmmaker of the French New Wave, Varda switched between fiction and nonfiction, always hewing close to street-level experience. Her documentaries include *The Beaches of Agnès* (2008), *The Gleaners & I* (2000), *Documenteur* and *Mur Murs* (both 1981), and *Daguerréotypes* (1975).

A gallery of some of the extras and prospective extras photographed, often on the streets of Angoulême, by *The French Dispatch*'s casting department

**Wes Anderson poses with Ennui-sur-Blasé law enforcement officers on the police headquarters set, created at the abandoned felt factory where many key locations were built.**

when he arrived in Angoulême in August 2018. "Wes told me, 'We want the most Fellini-an faces that have ever been on-screen. Every time you see someone who has the most character, the most distinctive look, whatever draws your attention that is uncommon, a bit extraordinary, go for it.' I knew the city, so I devised a plan. I went to coffee shops, I went to gyms, I went to the prison and hung around in the prison."

Amélie Covillard—who worked with Anderson for the first time on *The French Dispatch*—took over extras casting in September, and managed everything having to do with extras through the following year.

"I went to drugstores, I went to flea markets, I went everywhere I could go, you know?" she said. "I went to boxing classes, art classes. I went to so many places I can't even remember. When we were looking for people that are climbers, I went to climbing clubs to find the real people who do that. I went to fields where you have workers that work outside to pick the vegetables and stuff, and as they are always outside, their skin is really tanned and burned, and you can see the life in their faces. I went outside the lower courts, you know, waiting for the guys that had problems with the police, who were waiting to go before a judge, you know, and I'd look at their faces and be like, 'Oh, he's interesting, I have to talk to him.' And then I would take a picture of them—two pictures: one close-up, another from head to toe. And I would write down the name, the phone number, how old they are, how tall they are, what they do for a living, and if they have brothers and sisters or dogs or cats. The dogs and cats question was important because Wes needed a lot of dogs and cats for the movie, too. So sometimes he wasn't just casting a person, he was also casting their dog or cat."

Three extras ended up being cast in recurring roles as members of the Ennui police force. Anderson dubbed them "The Hero Group," and threaded them through the entire movie. One is Jean-Pierre Chabernaud, a retired bank employee who had just recovered from a long illness when a casting agent interviewed him outside the local rugby stadium. Anderson chose Chabernaud to play Ennui's chief of police based on his picture. When Charbernaud heard he had been selected, he said, "I will accept on one condition: that you assure [me] that this is not a porno, because at my age there's no way that I would make it through to the end."

The only member of the Hero Group with actual police experience was Noël Wojcik, an Angoulême police officer, twice married and the father of an eight-year-old daughter named Eloise, after the heroine of the children's books. Wojcik was approached by a casting agent while on duty in his patrol car. Breaking protocol, the casting agent asked Wojcik if he would agree to be photographed for possible casting in a Wes Anderson film that was supposed to begin filming soon.

"I suppose that I was trusted with this closely guarded bit of information because I was a police officer," said Wojcik.

# "Now my Starsky & Hutch car has Owen Wilson's signature on it!"

—NOËL WOJCIK, ANGOULÊME POLICE OFFICER

At first he said he did not want to appear in the movie because he didn't know if Wes Anderson "was the name of the director, the actor, or what," plus, "I was very involved in my duties at the time because of the threat of terrorist attacks across France, and I didn't want to be distracted."

He relented and let himself be photographed in a "discreet location" after learning that Owen Wilson would be in the movie. Wilson had costarred with Ben Stiller in a film version of Wojcik's favorite imported American TV program, the 1970s cops-and-robbers potboiler *Starsky and Hutch*. As a child, Wojcik was "crazily, madly obsessed" with the original series. Today he owns a replica of Starsky and Hutch's car, a red Ford Gran Torino with white vector stripes on both sides, which he bought from a collector in Los Angeles and shipped to Angoulême.

"I went and asked my superiors for a special dispensation to appear in this film because Owen Wilson was in it," he said. "Fortunately, they said 'yes.'"

At the end of production, Wilson met privately with Wojcik and his family and signed toy Starsky and Hutch cars and set photos as gifts. "I also brought Owen one of the drawers from my Gran Torino, which I was able to detach, and asked him to sign that as well. So now my Starsky and Hutch car has Owen Wilson's signature on it!"

The Hero Group's third member is Thibault Descamps, an animator who has worked on comics projects for thirty years and now lives in Angoulême with his partner and two sons. Descamps is an Angoulême native who lived for ten years in Paris and then moved back home for quality-of-life reasons. "It's a little paradise," he says. He was scouted for *The French Dispatch* while shopping at a market next to his house. "I had heard of the possibility of a Wes Anderson movie shooting in Angoulême, so I instantly knew when I was approached that that's what this was about." At the time, he had long hair and a beard because he'd been confined to his house for a long time while working on storyboards; he asked if his scruffy look meant he would be playing part of a criminal gang. "The casting person replied, 'I can't tell you who you might be playing, I can't tell you about the plot of the film, I can't tell you anything or even the title, because it's top secret,'" he said. "I started doing the costume fittings to play a prison guard, and the adventure began." By the time production began, he had been shifted over to playing a street cop.

Months later, Thibault found himself in the unique position of animating himself in a sequence of a movie that was shot in his hometown.

"The last shot in the film before it goes into the animated chase sequence is a close-up of me, Noël, and Jean-Pierre," he said, "and then immediately after that is a shot I did of the three of us, and it's animated."

Among the film's most striking nonprofessional cast members is Mauricette Couvidat, a home care worker for terminally ill senior citizens. She ended up being cast as the mother of the police commissioner (a role ultimately played by Mathieu Amalric). Couvidat was discovered at a drugstore, a bit of serendipity reminiscent of Lana Turner being discovered by director Mervyn LeRoy at the soda counter of Schwab's Pharmacy in Los Angeles. But where the Turner story was fabricated,[7] this one is true.

"The pharmacy is where I met Covillard, the casting person who was prospecting for Wes Anderson's movie," says Couvidat, a delightful woman who looks as if she could've been drawn by Hergé, and whose voice is a soulful croak. "I had a cold and was there looking for meds. She had a cold and was there for meds, too. She heard my voice, which she later told me was distinctive, and which was greatly exaggerated at that moment because I had a cold, and then she looked at me, and once she saw the kind of person I am, she asked the pharmacist to ask me if I would agree to be in a movie. And I said 'yes' right away! The entire casting process took place in the pharmacy—just like that! She took a photo of me, which she showed Wes Anderson, and he immediately said, 'She'll play the role of Maman.'"

All told, the production interviewed and photographed over fifteen-hundred citizens, entering their names and contact details on a form that was stored in a Dropbox folder on the production website along with their photos. About nine hundred ended up appearing as extras.

Covillard says the production would have happily interviewed ten times that number, but the ratio of yeses to nos is always slim when you're throwing a net over a city. "I tried to make them understand that it would be a great experience, because they would get to see how we make a film, how we fabricate it," says Covillard. "I tried to make them feel special, you know? I'd tell them, 'I went to you—not this other person, but you!' Sometimes they would be happy

---

[7] Turner was actually discovered at Top Hat Cafe, 6750 Sunset Boulevard, near her school, Hollywood High, by Billy Wilkerson, then-publisher of *The Hollywood Reporter*, a trade publication based one block east of Top Hat.

that I talked to them, but not all the time. Sometimes it could get really annoying because ten people in a row would tell me, 'No, I'm not interested.' I wanted to chase after them and say, 'Where are you going? Don't you know this is a Wes Anderson movie?' But I couldn't tell them that, you know? Most of them don't even know Wes Anderson, anyway!"

But those who said "yes" got more emotional investment from their director than they could have reasonably expected. Covillard, Scali, and Peissel say that Anderson was involved in the extras casting process to an extent that is unusual on Hollywood-level productions. Poring over hundreds of photos and dossiers to find the right faces gave him a baseline familiarity with each candidate that he carried on set when it was time to roll the picture.

"It seems crazy enough to me that Wes personally chose every extra in this movie," says Covillard, "but what's even crazier is that he memorized the first names of everybody he chose, and when they arrived on set, he was like, 'Oh, hello, Annette!'"

## HOME BASE

**W**HEN Liev Schreiber was cast in a small role as a TV talk-show host in the third segment of *The French Dispatch*, his only prior experience working with Wes Anderson was as a voice actor in the English-language cast of *Isle of Dogs* (as Spots). Now Schreiber was about to get a taste of what it was like to work for Anderson on a live-action movie.

"The first night I got to Angoulême," he said, "Wes invited me to what was called, I think, the 'company dinner.' And I was instructed to go to my room at this tiny little quaint French bed-and-breakfast and get my slippers first. So I went to my room and there were these nice, plush, sort of tartan, plaid slippers. I put them on, even though I felt it was a risk for me, because what if the other guests didn't have them on? But sure enough, I get to the dining area and every person down there is wearing plaid slippers."[8]

Some cast members only stayed at the hotel for a brief time span that included their shooting days. Others arrived before their time in front of the camera and stayed as long as they could afterward, the better to enjoy the communal atmosphere that has become a signature on Anderson productions since *Moonrise Kingdom*. The latter, a modestly budgeted fable about a romance between two young teenagers, was shot mostly on location on Prudence Island in Narragansett Bay, Rhode Island.

*Moonrise* also offered an opportunity to refine specific production techniques that had been honed over the course of previous live-action features, including Anderson's preference to have the hotels and the sets close together, which avoids so-called "company moves" where the entire production has to travel somewhere else.

"We had a hotel that we were renting from Monday through Friday every week, where two storyboard artists and an editor would come from London every Monday," said Scali of his time working on *Fantastic Mr. Fox*. "They were setting up the editing room in the suite of the hotel. We were editing the animatics there. The storyboarders were drawing. I was xeroxing or scanning their drawings, and the editor was putting them all together, and Wes was directing them."

Scali and others believe *Mr. Fox* was the laboratory in which Anderson learned production techniques that would define the second act of his career. In his next live-action feature, *Moonrise Kingdom*, he got to test approaches he'd been thinking about during production of the animated film. A shuttered felt factory served as a makeshift studio where key *French Dispatch* interiors were built quickly and cheaply. The number one rule was, "Never build anything the camera won't see." Film students learn this in school, but the lesson is sometimes forgotten on big-budget productions, particularly by directors who don't have a strong visual style, or who want to shoot a scene in a lot of different ways and keep their options open during editing.

The "don't build what you can't see" rule led to quite a few cinematic sleights of hand. For instance, all of the train scenes in *The Grand Budapest Hotel* where characters are looking through windows by having the actors sit at a table next to a chunk of "train wall" on a rail-mounted dolly platform that was being pushed through the snow by grips. Most of the money spent on those shots went into building what people saw through the moving windows of the "train car." The most important material on all of Anderson's post–*Mr. Fox* productions is plywood.

"I remember visiting Wes in Paris when he was going over [*Mr. Fox*]," said Owen Wilson. "He was doing it by remote at that point. So I'm there in Paris, and the production is going on in London, and he's looking at it all. It all just seemed to be so tedious and demanding. I told him I was worried it was going to end up like that scene in the movie *Shine*: 'I'm gonna come back here and you're gonna be slumped over, like the kid that collapsed on the piano when he tried to play Rachmaninoff—and then we're going to cut to the older version of you!' That's what I felt was happening, because it all seemed to be so unbelievable, the level of exacting attention that was required of him. I'm still not sure how they finished the thing! But I guess the flip side of the experience is, being able to control everything helped him discover new ways to exercise control."

"Wes's process now has definitely been influenced by, and evolved from, doing the animated films," says Jeremy Dawson. "There are things from animation we bring into live-action filmmaking, and things from live action that we bring into animation. Wes kind of breaks the rules in both directions, and ultimately it's a very bespoke way of making movies that works for him."

Kevin Timon Hill, who art-directed on the film, said "Throughout the process of working on a film like *Isle of Dogs*, you get to design every single thing. It's all miniature so he could pick every pattern and shape. It wasn't a huge shock to me that when I came onto *The French Dispatch* that he was working that way."

---

8 The slippers were made by Rondinaud, a local shoemaker that went under during the 2020 pandemic. At the time of this volume's publication, they were exploring plans to reopen.

The art department of *The French Dispatch* assembled in a group photo. Those who had already gone home by that point, or who were continuing to work remotely, are represented by 8 by 10-inch headshots.

ABOVE, LEFT: **May Ziadé, producers' assistant (on the left); Andréa Hachuel, 3rd AD (on the right)**

ABOVE, RIGHT: **Vincent Audion, sign painter**

## A WELL-CURATED FAMILY

As on previous Anderson productions, *The French Dispatch*'s headquarters had the feel of an artist's colony wherein every participant was laser-focused on a common project.[9] The base of operations was the Hôtel Saint Gelais, which is located in a part of town that *The French Dispatch*'s associate producer Ben Adler describes as "kind of its own little area, a world within a world. It certainly was when we were making the film, and Wes and the actors and everybody were living there."

Yannick Lamuraille, the proprietor of the Hôtel Saint Gelais, says the hotel was built in 1853 at the same time as a church that is directly opposite (and that was also used as a background in the film). The hotel was originally a rectory where chapel employees lived.

When France instituted a separation of church and state in 1905, the chapel became the only one in Angoulême still owned by the Catholic Church (the rest being owned by the state). In 1946, the structure became a retirement home for priests. In 2006, it was bought and renovated as a house; the residents sold it to Lamuraille in 2015. There was pressure to turn it into apartments, but the partners who bought the place argued that due to its intimate layout (there are only twelve rooms, and a restaurant with a separate entrance) and proximity to a park, it made more sense as a hotel.

The Hôtel Saint Gelais opened to the public in 2017, just in time for Wes Anderson and his film crew to move in. Lamuraille found Anderson to be "almost like someone from another time. The day we met, his look was very sixties or seventies. He was wearing brown corduroy trousers. He was very diligently looking for more places in the city where he could shoot the film. Later that same day, I happened to see Wes scouting locations in the town square. He recognized me and approached me, and we got to talking about the film, and I told him I was renovating another building, La Residence Sainte, and I showed it to him. This later became Place du Minage, where there is an enormous shootout in the final episode of the film. The courtyard of that building was also used for a scene where the police capture The Abacus, the accountant played by Willem Dafoe."

All the key members of the production team who were closest to Anderson and were in town for the duration of the shoot lived at the hotel. A certain number of rooms were set aside to host lead actors who came in for a limited period and then left. Spillover cast were housed in a separate hotel, but all were invited to attend dinners at the restaurant, which had been turned into the cast's dining area for the duration of the shoot. Anderson chose the meals and wines with input from Lamuraille and the restaurant's kitchen staff. "Wes was the boss during that time, and for a while, it was as if Wes had become the maître d' of the hotel," Lamuraille said. "From the moment that the production began, we stopped being a hotel and restaurant and simply became Wes's house."

"All the production people would be always at the hotel," said Stephen Park, who played Nescaffier, the master chef profiled in the "Private Dining Room of the Police Commissioner" segment. "It was like the hotel staff was kind of gone, and it was just the production left. Wardrobe and hair people were set up behind the hotel's front desk. We were in Wes's world now."

Cast and crew were invited to watch rough cuts of scenes while meals were being prepared—an unusual practice, according to pretty much everyone on the shoot with prior industry experience. It's more typical for film editing to be done off-site, and it's a rare director who encourages cast and crew to watch the rough assemblage of a day's footage, for fear that an unpolished glimpse might shake their confidence in the production or make them self-conscious about their own contributions.

9   Or, alternatively, like the *Belafonte* in *The Life Aquatic with Steve Zissou*, a decommissioned frigate rebuilt as a floating research lab, movie studio, barracks, and spa.

ABOVE, LEFT: **Aurélien Cheval, set dresser**

ABOVE, RIGHT: **Vincent Gazier, sculptor**

Anderson wasn't bothered by any of that. According to some of his longtime collaborators, he started showing rough assemblages to select cast and crew on *Moonrise Kingdom* and ramped up the practice with each new live-action shoot. By the time he set up shop in Angoulême, the viewing of rough-cut scenes had become an everyday occurrence, like picking up the day's call sheets and sides.

"If dinner wasn't quite ready yet," said Wilson, "and everybody was kind of lingering around waiting, you might have a drink or something, or wander back into where they're editing and maybe look at something. There might be days where I would wake up at the hotel, and since I was going [on set] later in the day, I might wander around and kinda see what I could see. Wes would usually be there, if it was before the day's shoot, or after dinner at night. He might be looking at a scene he's working on with other people, and if you popped in and said 'hi,' he'd show it to you. I don't like seeing stuff that I'm involved in, but I like seeing stuff with other people in it. I remember seeing something with Benicio and Léa from the one about the painter, a scene that had just been cut together, and thinking it was cool."

Working this way is so relaxing that it has spoiled Wilson for other productions. "I don't understand why more people don't make movies the way Wes does, where everyone stays together and works together," he said. "There are no trailers when you get to the set. Everybody's just there, together."

"Wes makes a point of having dinner every night with whoever is there, because obviously people come and go," says Martin Scali, "and Bill [Murray] comes and then Jason arrives and then Jason leaves and Owen arrives. But every night, with whoever is there, Wes is doing a dinner. Obviously, cast members and heads of departments are always welcome. You see Wes on set doing certain things—you know, being Wes—and he's exactly like that at dinner. He really keeps on with the vibe."

"Wes likes to work with the same people, always," said Seydoux, who met Anderson when he directed her in a Prada commercial. She took small roles in *The Grand Budapest Hotel* and voiced Nutmeg in the French dub of *Isle of Dogs,* a role played by Scarlett Johansson in the original. "I was delighted to be able to enter into his orbit. It's very intimate and relaxed, the way Wes runs a production. It almost doesn't feel like—how do you pronounce the word? A hierarchy? Levels? You feel as if you're all on the same level."

"I hesitate to say this," Wilson said, "because I know it sounds a little bit corny, but it feels like a family. A very well-curated family."

There was even a lending library of French films, curated by the director, to get everybody in the right headspace—and just to encourage them to watch older movies, which is something Anderson does anyway.

"The films in the library were open for anybody on cast and crew to borrow and watch and return," cinematographer Robert Yeoman said. "I watched all the films in it, and a lot of them I'd never seen before. There was *Vivre Sa Vie, Les Diaboliques, The Fire Within.* A lot of Jean-Luc Godard, François Truffaut, Agnès Varda, Louis Malle."

Said Tilda Swinton, "*Moonrise Kingdom* was my introduction to this rhythm, and this world. There is, at the heart of that film, a community play, *Noah's Flood,* which drives into the curve pretty exactly how the gaggle feels. On *The French Dispatch,* we lived off and on in Angoulême for several months. I was lucky enough to come and go several times over the course of the winter and into the spring. Wes and I were actually invited to switch on the Christmas lights, which was a major thrill for us both. We all became very fond of the city: By the time we wrapped, I reckon a good part of the population had either appeared in or played some part in the making of the film. The attitude of the people to our shoot can maybe best be described as insouciant. We became neighbors. We made the film together. And it's impossible to imagine making it anywhere else."

The alleyway where the crew shot one of the close-ups of Herbsaint Sazerac riding his bike, before (TOP) being painted and redecorated with signage and after (BOTTOM)

## THE RIGHT PLACES

NEXT, the crew had to figure out where each scene would be filmed. The process kicked off with key production personnel—including Anderson, Dawson, Peissel, Scali, Yeoman, and production designer Adam Stockhausen—scouting locations in and around the central city. Anderson prefers to scout by golf cart rather than automobile because the pace is slower and he feels connected to the environment that he's traveling through.

"This process is a huge amount of fun," said Stockhausen. "Wes's determination to have an entire production happen in close proximity gives it this kind of incredible, multiuse backlot quality, where you're really exploring every single nook and cranny, and it's like a puzzle to figure it out. You know: Here is the story, and within the space you've decided to restrict shooting to, how can you rearrange all of the available pieces? How can you see it differently, configure it differently, and try to use every last scrap of what the place has to offer to fill in the blanks of the story?"

It's this cost-and-labor-saving mindset that led to Anderson using the exterior of the Hôtel de Bardines as the exterior of the university where J.K.L. Berensen lectures; as a source of furniture and decorations for Zeffirelli's apartment; as a background structure in one of the shots of the young Moses painting; and in the background of a still photo at the end of the segment that tells how Simone eventually became "a woman of considerable property." (The woman in the photo, Odile Fougère, is actually the owner of the hotel.)

The process begins, says Stockhausen, with "sort of a full dossier. You're like, 'Okay, let's look at every street and let's start to knock on doors and get in every building.' And by the end of it, in a town the size of Angoulême, you've seen quite a bit." But despite the aggressive use and reuse of locations, the vast majority of *French Dispatch* scenes would end up being shot indoors, on the premises of two facilities converted into temporary soundstages. One of them, listed on call sheets as "Navy Yards," was a dormant factory that once manufactured equipment for the French navy. It was at the Navy Yards that most of "The Concrete Masterpiece" would be shot (including the scenes on the "bridge" leading into the prison, actually a set grafted onto an existing overpass). The other production hub was Les Feutriers, or "the felters," a factory that once made felt-tipped pens. Located just outside the city limits, the "Felt Factory," as it became known, was the production's headquarters for a year. The space housed production offices and equipment storage as well as soundstages. The latter were ideal for creating one-off "gag" shots built around theatrical/unreal sets, such as an image of Herbsaint Sazerac and other subway passengers on a stalled train car, a colony of tunnel rats looming behind them[10] in what feels like an exterminator's reimagining of one of Anderson's patented dollhouse

**10** "That's a little tribute to one of the Joseph Mitchell pieces that kind of started me down this road," Anderson said, alluding to Mitchell's 1944 *New Yorker* article "Thirty-two Rats from Casablanca."

The home of the Zeffirelli family, actually shot in the Banque de France building

Collage of 35mm black-and-white and color photos shot in Angoulême by *The Grand Budapest Hotel* costar Tony Revolori, who played the young Rosenthaler. CLOCKWISE FROM TOP LEFT: Église Notre-Dame d'Obézine; an alley overlooking the corner where the Sans Blague Café exterior would be built; high-angled shot overlooking the city; two images of Revolori in makeup; denuded trees at sunset; Benicio Del Toro, reporting for work.
COURTESY OF TONY REVOLORI

# "Everything was vintage and had a special look to make you think it was exceptional." —STÉPHANE CRESSEND, SUPERVISING ART DIRECTOR

shots. "They had a bunch of different factory bays in there," says Stockhausen, "and we sort of took them over and made them into our stages. We had all of our workshops there, all of our storage there, and it became our studio, totally from scratch, without even electricity when we walked in the door."

"At points on the film, we had everyone working on different sets," said Kevin Timon Hill, who art-directed on the film. 'We had such a huge workload and so many locations to work across. Everyone in that art department had very different approaches to how we work individually but they all seemed to complement each other as the sets were all so different, too. You also have to really try to understand Wes's feedback and what he's trying to achieve to hit the nail on the creative head."

Any furniture and accessorizing objects featured in the film that were not already present in a room were added by the art directors, who sent buyers to vintage and antique stores throughout Paris and Western France to stock up on items with Andersonian vibes. Their purchases were kept in storage in a room of the Felt Factory until they were required on set.

"We were in a good part of France to find perfect stuff in," said supervising art director Stéphane Cressend. "Everything was vintage and had a special look to make you think it was exceptional. In the end, we had a real antique shop in the factory."

With rare exceptions—such as scenes of Berensen lecturing on Rosenthaler, which were shot inside a local college auditorium, with costumes and lighting complementing the decor that was already on-site—the crew never used locations as-is. The crew temporarily altered many building facades and indoor spaces to bring them in line with the movie's aesthetic. Sometimes they built extra elements or details onto the structure. Other times they just added splashes of paint here or there and hung the appropriate signage.

"There's always a certain amount of work that's done, even on real locations," said Yeoman. "There's always a modification that's made for shooting."

"One thing we talked about a lot," said Stockhausen, "was the question, 'What is Angoulême? What is the town that we're in, and what is the overall, overarching sense of the place?' And I think that the combination of this gritty, dirty, crumbly, murky, musty architecture with the flashes of bright Citroëns and things like that kind of gave an umbrella palette to the whole thing. And there were individual pushes and pulls here with vivid colors, like the strong orange colors in the "Berensen Lecture" and the other [colors] all throughout that episode."

The first close-up in *The French Dispatch* sums up Anderson's presentational aesthetic: a choreographed list of details, each presented with a dancer's grace. A narrator (Anjelica Huston) continues a voice-over that began two scenes earlier as a lazy Susan spins left and right and objects are placed upon it. Per Anderson's screenplay: "A demi-tasse, coffee in a tiny pitcher, and hot milk in a creamer; a crimson-colored cocktail one finger deep; a short-stemmed glass of amber aperitif, a jigger of off-black digestif (which gets an egg cracked into it, two jolts of spicy sauce, and a raw oyster carefully slid from its half-shell); a small chocolate sundae; a Coke in a bottle; a box of cigarettes with a book of matches; and a little glass of water with an effervescent tablet dropped in, fizzing." Then the camera follows a waiter as he lifts the tray above his head and carries it down a narrow hallway and up several flights of stairs to the office of publisher Arthur Howitzer.

This brief series of shots required the construction of three sets in three different parts of the Felt Factory. There was Howitzer's office, packed with details and built to accommodate multiple angles and a large ensemble cast; the hallway down which the waiter carries the drink tray, which is basically plywood; and the back wall of the *French Dispatch* building, viewed full frame, the waiter disappearing from one window and reappearing in another as he climbs to the top. The back of the newspaper office passes muster as an old building in an ancient French city, but it's a relatively cheap theatrical fabrication, just like the plywood hallway: pieces and more pieces, snapped together jigsaw-style across the back wall of the factory where so much of the film would be made.

"The shot with the waiter going up the stairs was one of our more ambitious builds," said Yeoman. "But building it as a set was the only way Wes could really control everything about the shot: the way it looked; where and how we shot it. That little bit tells you everything about how Wes shoots a movie. He's very much in control of all the visuals of the film. By building to the shot, he can make it exactly what he imagined, in terms of the rhythms and look of the shot."

The Sazerac prologue provides a grand summation of the production team's methods. In the screenplay, Sazerac calls it a "sightseeing tour" that uses "the time machine of poetic license." Cutting quickly from one locale to the next, often with Sazerac in the frame, it is the only segment of *The French Dispatch* that could be described as more of a sketch than a story.

Coproducer Peissel loves the Sazerac prologue because of how it confesses to the audience that they're watching a film about France made by an American from Texas: "Owen has a Texas accent, he's totally American, but he's wearing a beret and explaining the city and the history of it and everything. France, seen through the prism of these Americans, is a specific France. It's a specific Paris, but it's one that French people also love. The French writers that

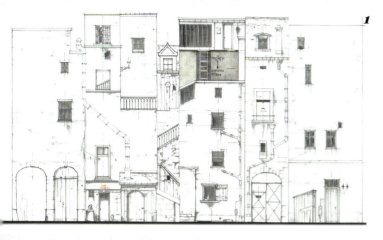

Series of images that convey the planning necessary to create the rear exterior of the French Dispatch offices where the waiter climbs a series of stairs while bearing a tray full of drinks—a set that cinematographer Bob Yeoman called "one of our more ambitious builds."

(1) Production design sketch; (2) blueprint/schematic; (3 & 4) three-dimensional maquettes built from thin cardboard, with details inked on their surfaces; (5) the full-scale set actively under construction, with scaffolding; (6) the finished product.

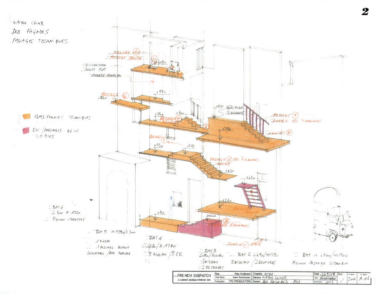

TOP: **Still-frame from the finished movie, showing the waiter's hands putting together the drinks tray with help from a lazy Susan**

BOTTOM: **Still-frame of the finished rear exterior of the magazine, with the waiter seen bringing the drinks up flights of stairs**

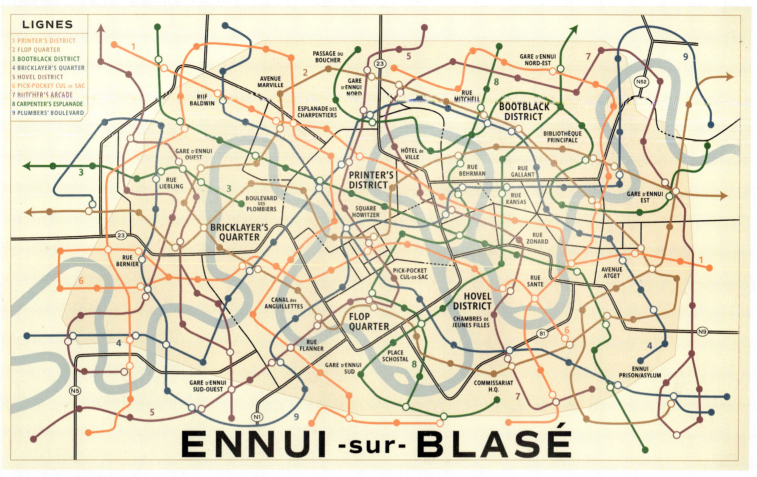

**The Ennui-sur-Blasé Métro map**

Wes nods to in this film are that type of writer and that type of expatriate American. Every French person knows these kinds of people. They are not French, but they have French friends and are very much involved in the local literary or artistic or filmmaking circles that they are a part of. The French love that. They love seeing themselves through the eyes of such people."

The segment begins with a wide shot of a "Public Square" early in the morning. No one is on the street yet. Then Sazerac declares, "Ennui rises suddenly on a Monday," and the frame fills with life. People and animals emerge from indoors and start their routines. Filmed in one take in a wide shot, the scene is composed and lit to make the alley feel like a stage set—perhaps a French-language answer to Thornton Wilder's *Our Town*.[11] Sazerac's narration seems to cue action in the manner of a movie director.

The alley set was created behind the Felt Factory. Existing facades and street elements were spruced up with overlays, props, and paint. The framing—which makes space for people and animals to scurry and bustle—evokes scene-setting wide shots in classic urban films with a voyeuristic bent: the rear exterior of the apartment building in Jacques Tati's *Mon Oncle;* the complex with the garden courtyard in Alfred Hitchcock's *Rear Window;* the self-contained city blocks where the events of *Do the Right Thing* and *Dog Day Afternoon* unfold.[12]

"Wes likes to place things all in one shot, if he can," said Yeoman, "and he wants you to feel the atmosphere and location. He wants you to feel like you're there. And I think when you shoot wide shots, viewers go away feeling like they actually experienced living in that place."

"A big part of Owen's part of the film is about how the architecture of the city relates to the people, and just trying to express something visual and French that has some detail and some history to it," said Anderson.

A montage depicts the ebb and flow of life in the city, for the buildings as well as the citizens. Sazerac stands before a construction site where a beloved old market is being bulldozed to make way for a "multilevel shopping center and parking structure." The foreground elements were built at the Felt Factory, while the background (including the crane) consisted of stop-motion miniatures and digitally composited elements. Then comes the bit about the city's "menagerie of vermin and scavengers." The previously mentioned rats appear in a cross section of lair, embedded in the subway wall like a hellish art installation. The shot of the anguillettes that "colonized [the city's] shallow drainage canals" is a second-unit shot overseen by second-unit director Martin Scali. It was taken at a real canal, with real eels; those are Scali's hands holding the net. A shot of a snow-covered plaza required that biodegradable material be trucked in from a prop house in Germany. There was snow foam fired from a cannon and "snow candles" that released white flakes into the air when burned. "The snow effects

[11] Wilder's meta-dramatic play about the denizens of Grover's Corners is a lodestar for stage, film, and TV storytellers. The tale is narrated in third person by a character known only as The Stage Manager, who breaks the fourth wall to address the audience. Anderson has used third-person narration in many projects, including *The Royal Tenenbaums* (narrated by Alec Baldwin in the spirit of Orson Welles's narration of *The Magnificent Ambersons*) and *Moonrise Kingdom* (where Bob Balaban's narrator character regales viewers with facts about New Penzance Island, then joins the action and is revealed to have been a member of the community the whole time).

[12] Both films observe Aristotle's unities of time and place: All action occurs in one day, in a single locale.

Collage of images of bike-related scenes in the Herbsaint Sazerac segment.

(1) Grip and camera team modifying a golf cart with a platform rig that can safely carry Owen Wilson on a bike at high speed while getting closeups with a 35mm film camera; (2) Wilson trying out the rig as Anderson checks the framing in the camera's viewfinder and monitor, with Benicio Del Toro seated behind him; (3) City taxicab created by the art department, with roof rack to carry multiple bikes to city locations; (4) Wilson and Anderson on the set at the Felt Factory, testing the elevated rig that will dip the actor safely down for the stunt shot where Herbsaint inadvertently rides down into an open Métro entrance; (5) Wilson tests out a possible "Oh no!" expression.

**Still-frame of Owen Wilson riding through the finished, decorated Angoulême side streets**

were handled by the same people who did it for *The Grand Budapest Hotel*," said Robert Yeoman. "They're very good at snow."

The shot of hundreds of cats mewling on rooftops necessitated the wrangling of several dozen felines, all belonging to humans cast as extras elsewhere in the picture. Anderson insisted that all the cats in the shot be pets belonging to the extras, not from animal wranglers. There appear to be more than two hundred fifty cats in the shot, but it's really the same forty or so cats placed atop three fabricated "rooftop" elements, all shot separately with the intent of being digitally merged in postproduction, like puzzle pieces snapping into place. The felines had to be arranged in a certain way to lead the eye through the shot and minimize the chance that a hypervigilant viewer would realize the filmmakers had endlessly repurposed the same animals.

Unfortunately, said Scali, it wasn't always easy to get a cat to stay in one spot, and once the crew had succeeded, they had to repeat the miracle thirty-nine more times. "As you might have heard, cats don't take direction well," said Scali. "Even though we never had more than forty cats on set at once, that's still an enormous amount of cats. We had to have food and water and litter for all of them. There was a lot of psychology involved because we didn't have a handler, which would have at least centralized any problems. Instead it was kind of like we had forty parents and forty babies on set. We had a greenroom for the owners where they could relax and eat and so forth, but a big part of the job was still making sure that the owners were happy, you know? It took two weeks to figure out and three or four days of shooting for this three-and-a-half-second shot," Scali said.

The shot of Herbsaint Sazerac being ambushed by marauding schoolboys and knocked off his bike ended up being one of Yeoman's favorite images. It required the camera rig to be pushed on a wheeled dolly platform at a rate of speed that matched the velocity of the bike as it zipped into the shot with Sazerac on it, then disappeared behind a bookseller's stall and exited sans rider ("surprisingly balanced," per the script).

Two identical bikes were used in the shot: one with Wilson on the seat, the other riderless. The riderless bike had to be pushed out from behind the bookseller's stall by a props person, at the right moment and the correct velocity to continue the motion arc established when Sazerac entered the frame. A string tied to the front of the riderless bike helped keep it upright.

Nevertheless, certain physical challenges needed to be solved. One was how to make sure that the camera and both bikes were always traveling at more or less the same rate of speed. The camera team figured out they had to start the dolly shot at full power, like sprinters pouring it on the instant they heard the starter's pistol. Key grip Sanjay Sami—problem-solving superhero of Anderson's camera department—found a way to cheat a bit: The crew attached a thick bungee cord to the front of the dolly that could yank it up to full speed, slingshot-style, after Anderson called "action" and the brakes were released. This let Sami push the dolly at a consistent trot for the rest of the scene without requiring a Herculean wind sprint at the start of each take.

But the day was still exhausting. "Wes's films are the Grip Olympics," said Sami. "I feel like you need to physically train to work on his movies. But the reward, I think, is comparable to winning a medal at the Olympics. You have the pride of knowing that you're one of the people that Wes Anderson chose to show up on his set every day and help solve the challenges that he comes up with. The shot where you see the handlebars of the bike, that's the front of a bike mounted on the back of a golf cart with a [35mm motion picture] camera fixed behind it. To get two hands on the handlebars, we had to have two people reaching into the shot. We couldn't get one person's arms around the camera. So it was like one of those Muppets where you need two people to do both the hands."

Anderson said that his goal was to "take each of these little vignettes and try to do some bit of movie-type magic with each one, to have some sort of a trick or a Jacques Tati–like moment. Which is how you end up with Owen hanging off of a garbage truck."

The shot in question finds Sazerac coasting through traffic on his bike while hanging on to a garbage truck and inveighing against the sins of the automobile, then dropping out of frame and tumbling downstairs into a Métro station. This gag was filmed indoors in the Felt Factory, with Wilson on a stationary platform in front of a green screen, gimbals jostling the truck and other vehicles to sell the illusion that they were all on a road. Sazerac's bike was mounted on a contraption that Sami describes as a "banister" with a seesaw midpoint. Wilson was perched on the high end of the seesaw. When the timing was right, the crew dropped Wilson below the frame line. Background plates of the city whizzing by were filmed after Wilson left France and would be added to the scene in postproduction. The actor and all the vehicles had to be raised several feet above the studio floor to give Wilson enough room to drop out of sight.

One prologue moment in Anderson's screenplay didn't make it into the finished segment: Sazerac in a cemetery eating "a simple worker's lunch" among the tombstones. One of the stones bears the inscription, "Lucette Sazerac, 1920–1955."

Anderson says the audience was supposed to intuit that Lucette was Herbsaint's wife. But the moment ended up getting cut for flow. "The thing just got too long, I suppose," said Anderson. "I consider it part of his character, though. Just one that the audience doesn't get to know, unfortunately."

Had it stayed, it would've given a different feel to the moment when Sazerac tells Howitzer, "I hate flowers."♠

Wes Anderson and Owen Wilson between takes at the cemetery set where Herbsaint Sazerac takes his simple worker's lunch

Still-frame images showing the "pasts" and "futures" of various Ennui neighborhoods

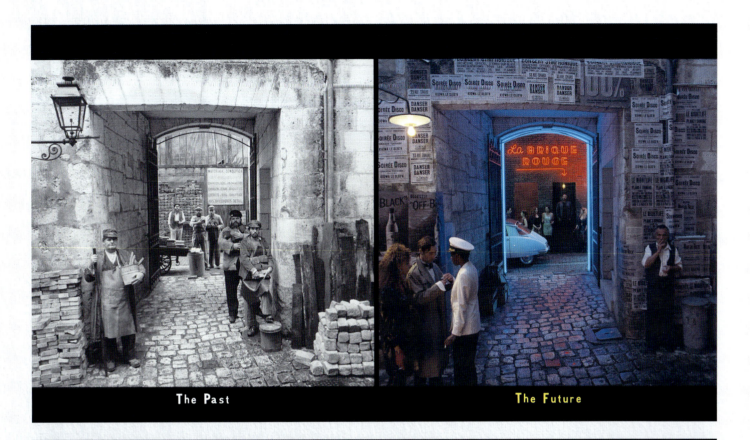

The Past | The Future

The Past | The Future

# STRETCHING THE CANVAS

**E**ven though Wes Anderson animates his movies before he shoots them, he can't draw. Not really. When a pair of visiting journalists described his drawings as "cartoons" and "comics," he politely corrected them, because he didn't want to "devalue" the work of "real artists." Asked if he could paint, he laughed a little. "I don't even think I really know how to move paint around on a canvas," he said. Perhaps for this reason, Anderson has always been fascinated by painters, representational and abstract, of every school and era. When he was in sixth grade, he fixated on Renaissance painters, particularly Michelangelo, Raphael, and Da Vinci. In seventh grade, he moved on to Picasso. "I was more likely to look at paintings in books than paintings in museums," he said, though he fondly recalls taking in an exhibition of Bonnard paintings with his mother at New York's Metropolitan Museum of Art as an adult, and being enamored enough with the painter's still lives to "try to look at more pictures from that point in time on," including work by the Abstract Expressionists.

It was the latter school that inspired the first full-length story in *The French Dispatch,* "The Concrete Masterpiece," in which imprisoned painter and double-murderer Moses Rosenthaler (Del Toro) creates an enormous, multipaneled, abstract fresco in tribute to his lover, model, and muse, the prison guard Simone (Seydoux). A framing device finds art historian and *French Dispatch* writer J.K.L. Berensen (Swinton) giving a lecture on Moses and the artistic movement that he was a part of, the "French Splatter-School Action Group," a fictionalized Gallic answer to the New York–based "action painting" movement that became so popular in the 1950s.

As in so many Anderson productions, it's hard to tell exactly when the story takes place; the production design mixes elements from the 1930s, forties, and fifties, and the violence, sexuality, and nudity are of a sort that wouldn't become permissible on-screen until the 1960s. The story is mainly about an artist losing his urge to create, thanks to mental illness and a hard-knock life, then finding it again thanks to the love of a woman who believes in his as-yet-untapped creative potential. But there are also echoes of art-world satires, true-crime stories about guards falling in love with prisoners, and film noir. In the end, Simone comes across as the constructive and good-hearted version of a femme fatale (a *femme donner la vie?*), identifying Moses as the key to escaping her tedious, depressing job, and a means of financing her reunion with her daughter. But there's no cynicism in this aspect of the story because it's clear that Simone and Moses genuinely love and respect each other.

OPPOSITE: **Moses Rosenthaler (Benicio Del Toro) contemplates a work-in-progress.**

Anderson said that when preparing to shoot this segment, job one was figuring out what Moses Rosenthaler's work would look like, and how to convince viewers that it was "original and interesting, convincingly good." He decided to make him a nonrepresentational painter because ". . . if it's abstract art up there on the screen, how is the audience going to say what's good and bad, what's interesting or not interesting? Especially if it's in the form of paintings that are going to be sharing the frame with a lot of other, real things, and if you're not going to see the painting for too long at any given moment?"

Even with those built-in safeguards, though, the assignment would not be easy for the person hired to create Moses's work. Brilliance is in short supply in the real world, and it's hard to fake when you're working in the art department on a film set, inventing work by a fictional character who is supposed to be as good as anybody who ever picked up a brush.

"That's a tricky thing because paintings in movies are often really terrible, and almost invariably, even in Old Hollywood movies that were shot under the studio system, back when there was an entrenched system in place for making everything, they rarely were able to produce good paintings, because on a film, you just never have enough time to do anything," Anderson said. "However good your film production assembly line is at making costumes and building sets and all of that kind of stuff, a painting is something that you have to sit there and really *paint*. You can't make it *seem* like a good painting. It just has to actually *be* a good painting. Fortunately, we decided to spend a lot of time on Moses's paintings, and it was a very long, long process, and the person doing them was a wonderful painter named Sandro Kopp."

Sandro Kopp was born and raised in Heidelberg, Germany, finished his education in Wellington, New Zealand, and now lives in the Scottish Highlands. He broke through to international attention in 2008 after painting portraits via Skype. His work has been compared to that of Alice Neel and Lucian Freud. A 2012 *Autre* interview described Kopp as "part of a new wave of post-modern figurative artists." Kopp names David Hockney, Marlene McCarthy, John Currin, and Vincent van Gogh among his influences. He's been part of Anderson's extended circle of friends and collaborators for over a decade. One of his best-known subjects is designer Waris Ahluwalia, who acted in four Anderson pictures, beginning with *The Life Aquatic*.

Kopp is also a multimedia artist who has worked in the film industry in various

For the shot where Young Rosenthaler is shown in the same frame with his right hand as it applies paint to a still life, painter Sandro Kopp, who created Rosenthaler's work, was nestled behind him, doing the brushstrokes through an opening in the back of the actor's smock.

A gallery of Sandro Kopp portraits, painted over the last two decades

of Simone were rendered in that spirit. The style is nearly identical, the main difference being that the big paintings favor orange while the nude favors black. All are based on nudes that were painted from a body double who assumed poses based on the animatic.

Kopp and Anderson thought of Francis Bacon, Willem de Kooning, Jackson Pollock, Frank Auerbach, Anselm Kiefer, and other painters "to find sources that we could take a little bit of energy from," but agreed that Moses's work "should not look 'like' any specific painter. It had to be believable as the work of someone completely new. It wasn't supposed to be me, either. It had to be its own thing." And there had to be two identifiable phases or "periods" for Moses: the early one, which is figurative and has recognizable faces, and the later period, when things get abstract.

The paintings were "a team effort," said Kopp, that involved himself, two assistants, Anderson, and members of the design and art departments who answered any questions Kopp had about the shots that the paintings would be part of. Kopp sketched the early Rosenthalers based on conversations with Anderson, then had his assistant Sian Smith "build the frameworks" of pieces for him to finish. Another assistant, Edith Baudrand, helped with "the technical side, mixing up a unique formula to make it look more like the shackle grease, pigeon blood, and other substances described in the film."

The self-portrait of Moses was entirely Kopp's. When you see young Moses, played by Tony Revolori of *The Grand Budapest Hotel*, painting it on camera, Kopp's hand is holding the brush. "They shaved my arm and put makeup on me to match Tony's skin tone, then splattered me with paint," Kopp said, "and then I crouched behind Tony and put my painting arm up through his sleeve while the camera filmed us from the back. Movie magic—the simplest kind."

Kopp said he was comfortable making Moses's earlier paintings, as it's "somewhat close to my normal mode of working—I mainly do portraits and nudes, although I have worked entirely abstract for two decades." The abstracts required more of an imaginative leap. He was a bit anxious about working so far outside his usual mode due to the short window of preparation and production time, and his trepidation increased when he lost a month of prep time while completing another project. "I had two and a half months to make paintings that needed to look like a genius had worked on them for three years," he said.

Kopp arrived on set and went to his studio, a high-ceilinged room in the Felt Factory. He wanted to start on the large abstracts immediately. Anderson said they weren't ready for that yet.

"Wes said, 'First I want you to do a test of how you would paint flesh. Show me the way that you're going to represent flesh, using the entire canvas, end to end, just flesh. Whatever you want,' Kopp said. "So I did that, and then in the evening he looked at it, and he said, 'That's very good. Now I want you to do another one that's more faceted, with elements sort of pushing into each other.' And I did that. And then

capacities, including producer and photographer, and he's done work in other media, including sculpture. "But painting has been the only real thing I've ever done as a career, since my teens," said Kopp, during an interview in his Scotland studio. "Wes has always been encouraging of my painting. He's attended many gallery openings in support of my work and owns a number of paintings that I've done. I think he chose me because we've known each other such a long time, because he knew I'd be comfortable with a sort of long-haul approach to the paintings that would be seen in the film, and because he knew I wouldn't have an issue with moving between the figurative work that represents the paintings of the young Moses and the stuff he starts doing in prison."

The early Moses works were inspired by a variety of artists, including Pierre Bonnard, Albrecht Dürer, Ferdinand Hodler, and Gustave Courbet. Although the art Moses creates in prison could be described as Abstract Expressionist, Anderson cautioned that ". . . it's not *really* French." It's somewhat in the vein of abstract painters that were part of the New York School in the 1950s, but *en français*.[1]

Kopp said both the large-format fresco panels that give the segment its title and the small nude

[1] The New York School was a loose amalgamation of dancers, poets, improvisational theater performers, novelists, composers, artists, and filmmakers who were inspired by nonrepresentational and avant-garde art movements. Major painters from this period included Jackson Pollock, Willem de Kooning, Robert Goodnough, Rosemarie Beck, and Philip Guston. Lionel Dobie, the middle-aged expressionist "action painter" played by Nick Nolte in Martin Scorsese's segment of *New York Stories*—an influence on both Anderson's writing of Moses and Del Toro's performance—appears to have been part of that movement as well.

Kopp's assistant painters Edith Baudrand and Sian Smith working on the *Boxcar* painting. TOP: Self-portrait of young Moses Rosenthaler (Tony Revolori). BOTTOM: Poster announcing Cadazio Uncles and Nephew Galerie's exhibition of Rosenthaler's painting of Simone.

he said, 'Now do another one, and when you're done, I want you to take a pallet knife and attack it with two or three slashes through the entire structure.' We were blowtorching sometimes. Sometimes we were mixing up enormous amounts of color and hurling it. We were doing all kinds of funky stuff to come up with something that was unusual, something that had a visual language of its own." He and his assistants were working on the early Rosenthalers at the same time, Kopp says, "but the main order of business was getting the [late Rosenthaler] style up to the point of maximum energy. When we got to that point, Wes said, 'All right! Now it's time for you to do a full-sized one, about five by ten feet.'"

Kopp went to work on the first canvas. He put the canvas horizontal and applied paint by hand and with brushes. Then, during the forty-five-minute window when the paint was still pliable, Kopp placed the canvas flat on the floor and "messed around" with the gobs and splatters. "We didn't move the panels until the paint was dry, but there were elements later that were done vertically," Kopp said. Then he let the work dry overnight and returned the next day to repeat the process. It took about four days to create the first panel. "Then Wes came into the studio and said, 'Okay, that looks good—now you need to do nine more.'"

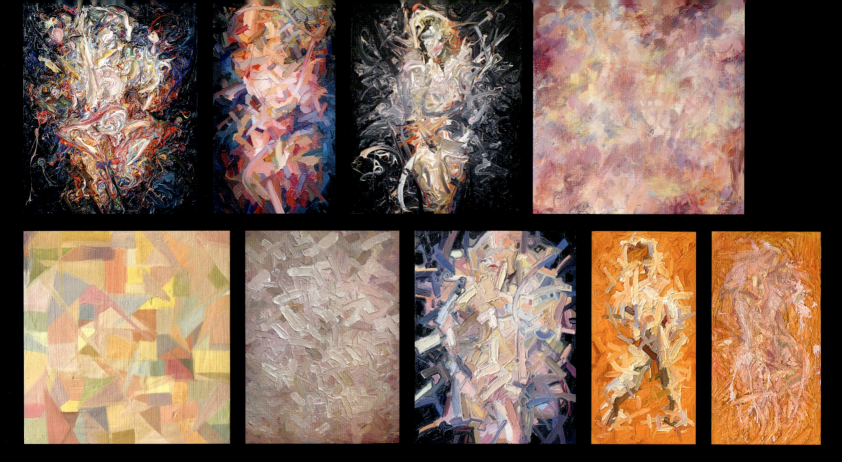

TOP: Seven abstracts created by Sandro Kopp in the development of Rosenthaler's Splatter-School style.

BOTTOM: Kopp does detail work on one of the Concrete Masterpiece panels.

A delighted Sandro Kopp pauses during work on the Concrete Masterpiece in preparation to film the sequences that recount its unveiling.

## THE METICULOUSNESS BONANZA

**J**.K.L. Berensen, the painter's biographer and the segment's narrator, was another panel in a gallery of oddballs that Tilda Swinton had been painting with Anderson since *Moonrise Kingdom*. Swinton had been a fan of the director for sixteen years before she began working with him. "I have seen every Wes Anderson film as they have appeared in order over the years, starting with *Bottle Rocket* and onward," she said. "Like all masters, he creates a unique world with its own landscape, rhythms, and textures and that world was something I recognized immediately as one I wanted to be in, as a spectator and fellow traveler. It never occurred to me in those early days that I would ever be invited to step into that frame."

Eventually, Swinton realized that would never happen if she didn't take the initiative, so she wrote him a fan letter. "A formal fan letter," she clarified. "A declaration of willingness to serve. Rather like someone seeking engagement as a stowaway: kinda honestly admitting nefarious designs."

The collaboration developed via email and phone long before the two got together in the same room. "I have no memory of ever meeting him for the first time," she said. "Crazy. Where were we? Possibly Rhode Island? To shoot *Moonrise Kingdom*? Which means he would've been in some sort of springwear: seersucker or a lighter corduroy. Almost certainly his ginger suede crepe-sole Clarks Wallabees. And a silk knitted tie? Or am I thinking of George Brent in *Dark Victory*?"

Swinton felt synced up with Anderson after her first reading of the *Moonrise* script. Her character reminded her of one of her favorite supporting characters from one of her favorite films. "I was immediately and irrevocably struck by the memory of Nurse Irma in Powell and Pressberger's *Life and Death of Colonel Blimp*: she with the brisk and breezy bedside manner and 'really excellent English,'" she recalled. "There is something about that portrait that I have always loved and found terribly funny, and for some reason, she became the familiar of Social Services, with her irrepressible cheeriness and energy, her spick and spanness, her emphatic diction and bombproof silhouette. The detail I remember best about putting that figure together was positioning her unsecured wig at a slight angle and coloring my own hairline silver to peek out underneath it at the front."

Her next film with Anderson, *The Grand Budapest Hotel*, cast her as Madame D., a wealthy but doddering older lady whom

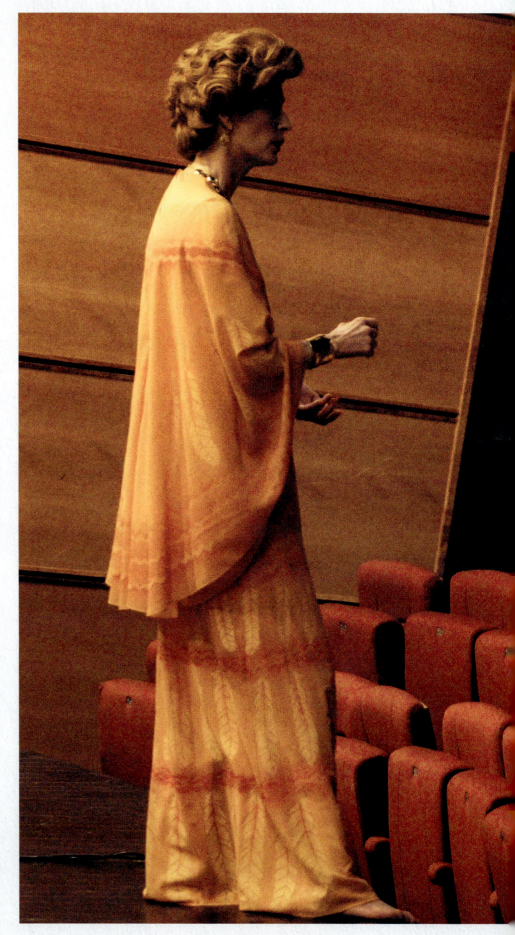

Tilda Swinton and Wes Anderson on site at the "Berensen Lecture"

M. Gustave keeps satisfied. She spent eight hours a day in a makeup chair, which didn't leave much time to act. Even more so than on a typical shoot, she had to make every second count.

"Robert Mitchum—allegedly—ran on the benzine of the dictum: least possible effort for the greatest possible return. Madame D., for me, was a matter of two days' work; five hours, early morning, in a chair, chatting to my friends as they created a miracle on my face; three hours at the end of the day taking it all off, culminating in delicious hot towels like in the fanciest restaurant. Apart from that, my funny bone was so thoroughly tickled by that character, her ancient sprightly besottedness and innate glamour. I downloaded some details I especially love from grand old girls I have known and baked them in. My grandmother provided possibly my favorite detail. I was always enchanted by her practice of bringing out an enameled powder compact at the end of luncheon in public, snapping it open, bashing the powder puff five times into her face—cheek, cheek, forehead, nose and chin—then uncapping her golden tube of (always) scarlet lipstick and screwing three reckless but precision dashes onto her mouth—left top, right top, and bottom—all within a breathless blip of time. This inevitably led to an unmistakably asymmetrical design. I adopted this ritual for Madame D., and it, somehow, brought her to life at the eleventh hour."

Swinton had been obsessive about Rosamond Bernier for several years before Anderson invited her to play the fictional version. "Wes and I had drooled over footage of her. The example of her spanking and glittering and style got us going right off the bat. Milena Canonero presented us with a series of versions of what Berensen might wear. Being Milena, this involved the original design of exquisite silk printed with feathers of a variety of sizes."

Production designer Adam Stockhausen cites J.K.L. Berensen's "Berensen Lecture" as an illustration of how closely he, the director, the cinematographer, the art directors, the lead actor, and the costume designer (among other artists) have to work together to realize just one scene.

"With Milena, color becomes a key part of how a story is told, [but] often we will have to use very strong and specific colors within a confined palette," he said. "Look at the dress the character wears in the 'Berensen Lecture,' within the context of this very strong-colored auditorium."

"I remember fittings even quite near to our shooting with paper feathers pinned to

ABOVE: Tilda Swinton as Berensen, discoursing on Rosenthaler. Note the complementary hues of the background and Berensen's dress (which, like most of the character's clothing, is emblazoned or embroidered with a feather pattern). Since a decision had already been made to leave the space as it was rather than redecorate or repaint, costume designer Melina Canonero made the outfit to suit the work with the existing environment.

OPPOSITE: Still-frame of Rosenthaler (Benicio Del Toro) facing off against his future patron. (Note to readers: If you lift and lower this page, this image and the one on page 103 will create a shot/reverse shot effect.)

my collar—scale in the location, frame and details of lens specification being weighed up to the last," Swinton said. "We shot the scenes of Rosamond lecturing in the Upshur 'Maw' Clampette auditorium in the public theater in Angoulême. It was our first day of shooting, and we had the location for one single Sunday. As it happened, the color of the dress was magically in complete sync with the color of the theater seats. All that planning buys one a stroke of pure good luck, as is so often the way. The Meticulousness Bonanza! One detail that I was proud to contribute was the one wayward curl in Berensen's magnificent 'do. Like Madame D.'s wobbly lips, it brought a little history with it, and some spirit."

The fact that Swinton's life partner had created the paintings Berensen was describing made the experience sweeter. "Wes's original brief to my dear Sandro had been characteristically challenging," she said. "He needed the eponymous masterpiece to be a work that might have credibly changed the course of art. Not one of us felt that this had not been achieved on the day that the work was unveiled. I think they were still a little wet. But that was one proud moment under our roof."

## SHE WAS

At the same time that he worked with Kopp to create Moses's paintings, and Swinton to create Moses's biographer, Anderson worked with Del Toro to create Moses.

"Even when you talk about the inspirations, in the end, Benicio Del Toro is the inspiration for that character," said Anderson. "I've wanted to work with that guy for years, and I think he's been in my head ever since I saw him in a small role in *The Indian Runner*. He didn't have much screen time, but he managed to create this character who was peculiar and unique and totally authentic. He likes to do something that is a little bit 'out there,' but makes you feel as if you've seen a real thing. I don't know how you could do that when you're playing a character like the lawyer he plays in F*ear and Loathing in Las Vegas,* but somehow he does it."

Anderson then launched into a detailed account of a moment from Del Toro's performance in 2018's *Sicario: Day of the Soldado,* where his character, a DEA agent, goes to find and rescue a missing girl. The agent comes upon a farmer and converses with him in sign language. "He tells the farmer something like, 'I don't want to hurt you, I just need water.' The farmer says, 'How do you know how to sign?' and Benicio's character says, 'My daughter,' and the guy says, 'Is she deaf?' And he replies, 'She was.' And the way that you say that in sign language, you point your hand back over your shoulder. It's a really powerful scene. And it turns out that the sign language was Benicio's idea. It makes for a dazzling moment, and it's really unusual that it's based mainly on the actor's interpretation of what a scene could be. It's an idea that changes the scene."

Some ideas were more workable than others. When Anderson and Del Toro put their heads together to devise a montage showing all the different ways Moses manipulated paint, Del Toro said, "Wouldn't it be cool if I did something with fire? What if I were breathing fire?" So Anderson hired a fire-breather to teach Benicio Del Toro how to breathe fire.

"Finally the day came when the fire-breather was gonna teach Benicio how to breathe fire," Anderson said. "Not on camera—just the training part. The fire-breather arrived on set and did a demonstration for Benicio, and he had a beard, and his beard caught on fire. Our stunt guys were standing by and put the flames out. Benicio said, 'Okay, well—that's it for *that.*'"

## SON OF THE SON OF KONG

**F**OR Del Toro, playing Moses was another opportunity to explore himself by becoming someone else.

"I think that's the foundation of acting," he said. "To get to know yourself, or try to get to know yourself by drawing from your life, and in the process learning things about yourself—about what you are and aren't, you know? You learn many things about yourself when you become a character."

Del Toro said playing Moses let him explore his own insecurity, need for validation, and inability to accept compliments. "This guy doesn't feel that his work is that good. Even at the peak of his success, he's completely insecure," he said. "He still thinks it's not good enough or he could still work on it. I personally feel like that with most of the characters I work on, including this one. I always tell people that I never feel like I really have begun to truly understand a character until the last day of shooting. And then I'm like, 'Well, okay, that feels good—but it'd be nice if it wasn't happening on *the last day!*"

Del Toro wanted to be an actor before he knew what acting was. One of his earliest memories is of standing up before the congregation of a church in San Germán, Puerto Rico, and reading from a book—he doesn't remember the book, just reading from it—and thinking that he enjoyed how it felt when people paid attention.

Del Toro's mother died of hepatitis when he was nine. At fifteen, he moved from Puerto Rico to Pennsylvania with his father and brother, attending high school there and going to the University of California at San Diego to get an accounting degree. He took an elective course in acting, and the teacher told him that he had the talent to do it professionally; he just needed the training. Del Toro dropped out of UC San Diego, auditioned for the prestigious Stella Adler conservatory, and was awarded a scholarship there. This triumph made him feel as if acting had called to him. His studies at Stella Adler made him understand that "acting is a craft, that you have to have a foundation in certain basics to really do it well—that was a big turning point for me."

Del Toro worked his way up in the 1980s playing walk-on and henchman parts (he was in the James Bond film *The Living Daylights*), then shifted into second leads in the 1990s (he stood out in 1995's *The Usual Suspects* and 1998's *Fear and Loathing in Las Vegas*). Then he played Javier Rodriguez, an honest cop in a dishonest world, in Steven Soderbergh's 2000 drug-war epic *Traffic* and won an Oscar for Best Supporting Actor. Now he's the star of medium-sized films and a prominent supporting player in blockbusters (including *Star Wars: The Last Jedi*), and, thanks to the international success of the *Sicario* films, the kind of name that can help secure financing for a project. The mix of weariness, wit, and electricity that Del Toro brought to his best-known roles made him one of the great actor-stars of the century.

Anderson said his guiding inspirations when writing Moses Rosenthaler were the drifter played by Michel Simon in *Boudu Saved from Drowning* and the painter played by Nick Nolte in Martin Scorsese's episode of "Life Lessons" in *New York Stories*. Del Toro says he kept those two performances in mind throughout the shoot, but added bits of many others—in particular Zampano, the hulking circus strongman played by Anthony Quinn in *La Strada*. Simon and Quinn, said Del Toro, both had the ability to play characters who were "bigger than life, but also fragile like glass. In *La Strada*, Anthony Quinn is like if King Kong were a person. The son of Kong. Which would make me the [Son of the Son] of Kong. Or the son of Quinn! Anthony Quinn in *Zorba the Greek* or *La Strada,* he's that force of nature. And at the end of *La Strada,* he crumbles like a castle made out of sand, you know?"

The character's growl is a variation of the growl Del Toro uses when he's pretending to be the Wolf Man for his young daughter or reading her bedtime stories with animals in them.[2] He says that the director helped him devise a growl that was distinct to Moses. "In the end, I gotta give most of the credit for

TOP: Anderson gives notes during the filming of the Concrete Masterpiece riot sequence to Henry Winkler, Adrien Brody, and Benicio Del Toro.

BOTTOM: Felix Moati, Bob Balaban, Wes Anderson, and Henry Winkler stand in one of the spots where characters will be filmed looking at the Concrete Masterpiece for the first time.

OPPOSITE: Still-frame of Julien Cadazio (Adrien Brody) talking in a prison cell with Moses Rosenthaler

the growl to Wes," he said. "I asked him, 'How do you see me playing this?' and he gave me a growl reading."

Moses's barrel-chested purity contrasts with the relentless salesmanship of Julian Cadazio, a composite of Joseph Duveen and other legendary art dealers. Adrien Brody, another Anderson regular, slipped comfortably into the part thanks to his connections with the art world. The Oscar-winning actor is the son of painter and retired art professor Eliot Brody and photographer and regular *Village Voice* contributor Sylvia Plachy. And he is a painter himself. "Duveen's family was in an antiques business," Brody said, "and their story was a great influence on the film's presentation of the Cadazio trio, a nephew and two uncles, portrayed by me, Bob Balaban, and Henry Winkler. In doing the research for this part, I learned that Duveen had a great quote that kind of summed everything up, which is, 'Europe has a great deal of art, and America has a great deal of money.' Duveen soon turned that into amassing a fortune after figuring that there were plenty of industrialists in America who wanted the stature and refinement of Europeans and were willing to pay handsomely for it."

"Moses is doing it for the love of art," said Del Toro, "with what I guess is a very 'art for art's sake' kind of attitude. And the moment Adrien's character comes in and goes, 'Hey, I want to buy your work,' I think that Moses is very honest, saying his work is not for sale, and the art dealer almost accuses him of being naïve, saying basically, 'Every painter paints to make money, to make a living, or to show it." And Moses very much does not want that, and there's something very—I don't know if 'honest' is the right word, but certainly 'primitive,' about somebody who thinks that way. I think Moses very easily could have taken his work and burned it at some point. Ironically, the only thing that secures his place in art history is this money-grubbing art dealer, who turns right around and sells the work to the newspaper publisher, who puts it in a dedicated facility. Both characters are absolute in their positions, and I think Wes is clear in how he lays them out for the viewer."

2   At the time this piece was written, their favorite was *The Cat in the Hat Comes Back*, which Del Toro always looks forward to because it allows him to imagine what it would be like to play the title character. "My Cat in the Hat is not like any other Cat in the Hat. My version is El Gato."

Wes Anderson and Benicio Del Toro share a laugh during filming.

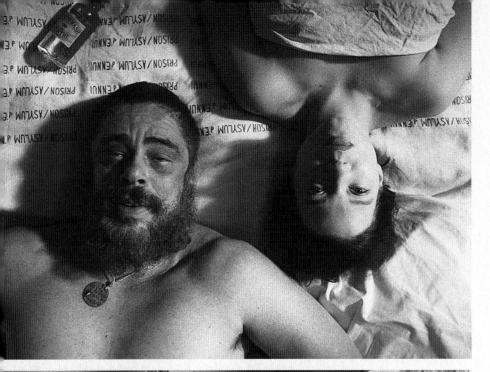

**Still-frames of a shot/reverse shot post-coital conversation between Moses (Benicio Del Toro) and Simone (Léa Seydoux), wherein the artist stares up at the ceiling and imagines new work**

## HANDS FOR CANDELABRAS

**W**ITH Del Toro playing his character as kind of a noble beast, it seemed inevitable that the beauty cast opposite him—French actress Léa Seydoux, of *Blue is the Warmest Color* and the James Bond films *Spectre* and *No Time to Die*—would characterize the characters' relationship as "a fairy tale for adults." Seydoux said one of her persistent inspirations—in many projects, not just *The French Dispatch*—is Josette Day's performance as Belle in the 1946 movie of *Beauty and the Beast,* directed by Jean Cocteau. "It is possibly my favorite film," she said. The affinity is so strong that Seydoux played Belle herself in the 2014 Christophe Gans film version of the tale. Seydoux compares Anderson's economical approach to spectacle with Cocteau's. "Sometimes special effects can be very complicated," she said, "and sometimes they can be very simple. You remember the candelabras on the wall in the Cocteau film? They're just hands coming out of a wall, holding candles. And it works very well. That's how Wes thinks."

Seydoux saw parallels to *La Belle et la Bête* in Moses and Simone's story—although, she points out, both transform into different people by the end of it. Moses starts painting again after a long period of paralysis and creates great work in a style once alien to him. Simone is a woman from a modest background who seems trapped in her job—imprisoned, in a way, although unlike her lover, she can at least leave the facility and sleep in her own bed. Simone cultivates multiple talents, becoming Moses's muse, critic, career advisor, and de facto (albeit secret) manager. She peers through the food slot of a jail cell during Moses's meeting with a would-be art dealer to make sure he doesn't get taken advantage of. She even gives Moses a tough-love pep talk when the pressure to create stymies him:

**SIMONE**
*I don't know what you know. I only know what you are. I can see you're suffering. I can see it's difficult. It might even get worse—but then it's going to get better. You're going to figure out whatever your problem is. (What's your problem?)*

**ROSENTHALER**
*I don't know what to paint.*

**SIMONE**
*You're going to figure out what to paint, and you're going to believe in yourself (like I do), and you're going to struggle—and then, in the spring, or maybe the summer, or possibly the fall, or, at the very latest, the winter: This new work will be complete. That's what's going to happen.*

Del Toro said Simone is "kind of like the foundation, she's the motivator. And I think that at that moment he feels someone has his back. The fear has dissipated."

Although Simone has self-interested reasons for exhorting her lover to develop his skills, she has genuine affection for him, and her pragmatic wisdom serves as a bridge between the painter's intractability and the more mercenary attitude of Brody's character, the art dealer.

"I wrote Simone specifically for Léa to play," Anderson said. "She's very charismatic, she's very skilled, and she has this something underneath it all that is really quite gripping. Rosenthaler is a guy who used to do one kind of painting. And then he has some breakthrough in this prison. He has a vision, and it's inspired by a person," he said, referring to the postcoital scene between Moses and Simone when he stares up at the ceiling and imagines art there.

"I think at that moment," said Del Toro, "the character feels that he is ready to dare, to take a chance."

Seydoux described Simone as a character who "has many variations, many layers. She's sweet, she's funny, she's touching, she's tough. She's full of colors." The character also represents a point of view on art and expression. That's why Seydoux was careful about trying to make Simone feel tough and earthy. She believed that in a story concerned with philosophical and economic aspects of art, a character like hers had to feel as real as possible, with the understanding that at the same time, she had to give the director everything he needed to make a Wes Anderson film.

"It's very abstract when you read [a film character] on the page," she said. "Even when you have a very detailed script, it's still abstract. It needs intonation. You have to fill in the part to make it your own, and it's a long process, with many steps, many levels. This is always true of cinema. Every aspect. Cinema is not a script. It is not made to be read. It's made to be watched. This is especially true with Wes. You have to bear in mind when you read his scripts that he has a tone, that it's unique, and that you're not going to truly understand who your character is, or what the story is actually about, until you're on the set acting the part, and much more so later, when you see it put together. I feel that with Wes, it has to go very fast or very slow. It's never in between. Acting is very physical with Wes. You have to have a certain pace. There is something in the rhythm, the way you walk in a room. With Wes, it's all about the rhythm. The way you talk—you can go very slow, then very fast, then very slow again, then very fast. Same thing with physicality. You run, stop, look right, look left. It's like a dance."

ABOVE, LEFT: **Benicio Del Toro, Tilda Swinton, Léa Seydoux, and Wes Anderson on set**

ABOVE, RIGHT: **Léa Seydoux and Tilda Swinton**

## THE BRAWL

THE riot scene was a dance of a different sort. The brawl between art-world denizens and convicts after the unveiling of Moses Rosenthaler's masterpiece is the largest set piece within its episode. It's *Guernica* by way of a *New Yorker* cartoon. As a camera on dolly tracks glides laterally across the combatants, viewers might initially think they're seeing a riff on the bullet-time process popularized in the *Matrix* movies. But there's just one camera rather than dozens, and the actors aren't properly freeze-framed: Rather, they're freezing in place, faces contorted by rage and exultation. It's as low-tech as a special effect can get. A "screaming" character is an actor holding an "I am screaming!" face.

Anderson worked with every actor in a freeze-frame scene to decide what their action would be. "It's a lot of fun for actors to do scenes like this," he said, "because you can give a talented actor a situation and they'll run with it and come back to you and say, 'What if I did this? And what if my face looked like this?' And then you get to see them do the face. They're such good actors that their choices are all very entertaining. Lois Smith, I think, is shooting somebody with a Derringer."

"This was an experience of true, hallucinogenic departure for everybody," said Swinton. "I can't imagine anybody didn't get a kick out of this bit. We were all suddenly active parts of a living cartoon from *The Beano*. The art department on Wes's films is always a magical treasure trove, producing dissected submarines and airplanes one minute, cornfields and the inner workings of grand Alpine hotels the next. But the props this particular sequence inspired were pure genius: champagne glasses pitched at an angle off silver trays strung together with invisible structures, projectiles suspended on fishing line. I had the honor of wielding a fire extinguisher disgorging a cloud of white candy-floss cotton wool."

"The bottles were made of sugar glass," said supervising art director Stéphane Cressend. "The liquid in the bottles was a special resin that we made."

Thanks to the frozen actors, said Kevin Timon Hill, "the scene didn't feel violent. It could've been a really violent scene and a different director could have turned it into something that way. But the way it was shot, as a big still tableau with the camera moving up and down, and puffs of cotton wool smoke and suspended hammers and glass, meant that what could've been a violent scene turned into quite a whimsical and fun thing to do."

"The ludicrousness of every object itself directed everyone handling them as to the degree of extremity with which to arrange one's face," said Swinton. "This was no moment for decorum." The hardest part, she said, was not blowing a take by bursting into laughter at the sight of another actor's rage face. "It's a pure miracle we managed to get the shot at all. We all tried very hard not to catch sight of the faces we were all

ABOVE: **Key grip Sanjay Sami (standing) looks on as cinematographer Bob Yeoman (seated) checks focus on a wheeled dolly shot of Simone (Léa Seydoux).**

OPPOSITE: **Two still-frame images from the sequence of freeze-framed art riots**

Producer, story collaborator, and pinch-hitting second unit director Roman Coppola does prep work.

**3** Stravinsky's ballet/orchestral concert work, done in collaboration with Sergei Diaghilev's Ballets Russes, premiered May 29, 1913, to hostile and even violent opposition within the audience. According to a BBC News article by classical music critic Ivan Hewett published exactly one hundred years later, "Dozens of witnesses left accounts of the evening, but they tend to say different things. According to some, blows were exchanged, objects were thrown at the stage, and at least one person was challenged to a duel."

**4** The default shape of movies until the 1950s, when images started to widen so that theaters could offer something different that people were getting on their similarly shaped televisions at home. The Academy ratio is 1.33 to 1, closer to a square than most subsequent shapes, which are more dynamically rectangular.

**5** 1924–2016; key cinematographer in the Nouvelle Vague movement; shot multiple masterworks by great French directors, including works by François Truffaut and Jacques Demy that Wes Anderson and Robert Yeoman have consulted many times during their partnership.

**6** A graduate thesis title waiting to happen.

**7** "The ship in *The Life Aquatic* is a real set," Anderson said. "The plane in this movie is a miniature. The only parts of it that are real-sized are the room where Tilda Swinton is, a little gallery, and a bedroom area."

pulling while the camera was rolling." "We actually do this thing twice in the story," said Anderson. "Once for the riot, and another time for a montage of all the different places where the painting caused a sensation and people went berserk because it was supposedly this radical thing, like *The Rite of Spring* or something."[3] Both the riot and the montage of the receptions were shot on the same soundstage. "We didn't shoot in the actual Hobby Room where we did other scenes," Anderson said. "We did a mural of the Hobby Room, which was partly just to take the moment out of reality—you can barely sense that it's a mural—and partly to control the distance, so that we could hold the background in sharp focus. We actually ended up having painted backdrops in each of the rooms in the montage of receptions, for that same reason."

The brawl scene and others like it turned out to be wildly complicated for Anderson the minute he realized how much science was required to execute them. Filmmakers have to have "a huge amount of light for shots like this, because there's a lot of depth of focus that's got to hold and you've got to set the distances of each performer in relation to the camera," he said. "There's hot lights stacked up like crazy. Having [actors] standing there for hours on end means you risk having them faint. Also, we shot this in the Academy ratio,[4] which is a more boxy, tall kind of frame, and there's quite a lot of vertical action. We're moving up and down as well as from side to side. Some people are standing on boxes and some are down on the floor. There's a whole range of depths and heights to this type of shot. It's all very complicated, so you have to prepare. Roman Coppola helped

me enormously with all of this. We had a whole team of people working on how to shoot these scenes, but it was Roman who was really in charge of getting everything tested and worked out in advance, with me paying occasional visits until it came time to actually shoot."

Bob Yeoman said that the key to lighting the shot was bouncing "a lot of light" off the ceiling, to create an all-over exposure of every person and object in a scene that had strange yet dynamic camera movements. "White [paint] on the ceiling gave a nice bounce to everything, which is really just us taking a page from the playbook of Raoul Coutard,[5] who shot a lot of the French New Wave films. We added a layer of diffusion underneath it all, to soften out the light and make it very even."

Dolly track was laid for the brawl with the inmates. Similar shots used the same soundstage and dolly track because they staged another shot in the same place and with similar-length track. Unusually for Anderson's dolly shots, they filmed the whole elaborate scene all the way through several times, then picked the best take. "I don't think there are many long takes anywhere in my movies where I don't cheat a little bit," Anderson said. "In my entire career, I don't think I've ever done a scene with a whip-pan between characters where there's not a cut somewhere. I feel like if you can kind of stitch things together and put the best parts of different takes into one take, why not do it?"

"Doing these sorts of *tableaux vivant* was a way for us to express these events in hopefully a fun way, a way that's consistent with a movie built around words," said Anderson. "All the stories in this movie have a lot of dialogue, voice-over, and on-screen text that goes with the images. This way of doing the [brawl] scene interested me because it was a different way of showing the action than you might usually get in a movie. Instead of a cacophony, instead you have silence, and there's somebody telling you about the action at the same time, or telling you about something else at the same time."

"Those scenes are the best examples of Wes doing hands coming out of walls for candelabras," Seydoux said.

They also escalate the film's unrealness, and the sense that anything could happen. Leading up to "The Concrete Masterpiece," there are segments that seem rather knowingly "not real," as when the waiter with the drink tray briskly climbs every stair in the *French Dispatch* building, closing distances far more quickly than he could in life; or when Sazerac stands in front of a construction site festooned with obviously miniature or cut-out buildings and machinery that could have appeared in *Fantastic Mr. Fox*. But the first full-length segment, "The Concrete Masterpiece," is a notable escalation. The unhinged young Moses's paintings glare back at him with wild eyes. When Upshur Clampette (Lois Smith) takes Moses's concrete abstracts[6] to Kansas, the film serves up one of the most fanciful "dollhouse shots" in Anderson's oeuvre: a cutaway set of a plane, reminiscent of the ant-farm shots of the ship in *The Life Aquatic* but with a curiously "illustrated" look, like something out of a Richard Scarry children's book.[7] Violence is expressed as a series of moving murals filled with bloodthirsty combatants. In a madcap cutaway during the brawl, the painter goes after the art dealer in his wheelchair, attacking him with every object he can get his hands on, the camera tracking behind him as in a third-person-shooter video game.

"I was the one pushing Benicio around in the wheelchair when he was chasing Adrien," said Sami. "There's a platform and a wheelchair rig on top of it that had to be strong enough to safely support Benicio, who is a massive and powerful man, probably 250 pounds. Benicio, let's say, got a little too into the scene. Adrien, like most actors, is rightly concerned about avoiding unnecessary injury, whereas Benicio, I think, is the kind of person you could stab with a knife onstage in the middle of a performance and he wouldn't even notice—he'd just finish the play. When he acts, he is a man possessed. He was just grabbing everything in sight and hurling it at Adrien, including an easel made of cast iron that was so heavy that I might have had trouble picking it up with two hands, and I'm a grip with a lot of upper-body strength. Benicio just picked it right up with one hand, and he might've flung it at Adrien like a discus if I hadn't done a hard stop with a dolly right there, rather than close the distance in a way that would've allowed him to really nail Adrien. If you're sold on the idea that the art dealer is in fear of his life, it's because there were moments where Adrien must have been wondering if Benicio was going to kill him."

**Directing the brawl that follows the unveiling of the Concrete Masterpiece.**
TOP: **Wes Anderson and Tilda Swinton;** MIDDLE: **Anderson and Adrien Brody;** BOTTOM: **Jérôme Lavaud and Henry Winkler**

TOP ROW, LEFT TO RIGHT: **Prisoners played by Christophe Robe and Antonio Da Silva (front and back view);** BOTTOM ROW: **Raphael Lagrue, Yoann Gaillard, and Grégory Sacriste**

OPPOSITE: **Cinematographer Bob Yeoman lines up the shot in which the inmates prepare to charge a bolted metal door separating them from the prison's high-society interlopers.**

## THE BROKEN NOSE

Among Anderson's favorite scenes in "The Concrete Masterpiece" are ones that put large numbers of people on-screen at the same time. The director was adamant that each face in *The French Dispatch* be striking [and close-up]. This ethos comes through most clearly in the scene where Moses is pushed to stand up in front of fellow inmates in the Hobby Room and talk about himself. As he speaks, the film cuts to the faces of prison inmates in isolated close-ups and small groups. All roughed-up by life.

One especially striking face is long and angular, with a nose that looks like a hammer smashed it. The nose belongs to Erick Dues, a social worker who teaches children with disabilities. He lives in Angoulême with his girlfriend and her eight-year-old daughter and fourteen-year-old son. Dues stands one meter and ninety-three centimeters tall. He has a shaved head. His skull is a bit bumpy because he's sustained rugby damage there as well. He has a thin, square face with somewhat sunken cheeks and a pointy chin. His nose is twisted to the left and smushed in from being broken more than once while playing rugby.

Dues was fourteen the first time he broke his nose. Another player ran straight into Dues's face with his head. "You know those wooden baskets that are used to carry fruits and vegetables at markets?" Dues said. "The wood is rather fine? The sound of the guy's head hitting my nose was the sound of the wood used in those little baskets being broken. Immediately after an impact like that, it hurts, and over time, it hurts less. Finally you're left with the nose you're left with. The woman in charge of casting said they were looking for people with especially distinctive faces to play the prison inmates. That is why I was selected."

Dues knew some of the other actors playing inmates because they, too, were rugby players who had been cast for their looks. He'd never met the others. By the end of the shoot, they were all friends.

Like most of the bit players and background artists cast from city streets, Dues had never been in a motion picture, much less a big one, and came away with a nonrepresentative experience. "It was great having Wes Anderson call me by my name and tell me

Tony Revolori as Young Rosenthaler opposite Wes Anderson, on the set where the character brutally kills people in a bar

where to stand or sit in a shot," he said. "I got to be around all these movie stars, and though I didn't have much direct interaction with them, they were all very nice. There was a time when I went to the hotel and Léa Seydoux and Benicio Del Toro and Roman Coppola and Wes Anderson all said 'hello' to me and asked how I was doing and how the shoot was going."

The filmmakers were so mesmerized by Dues's look that they kept giving him more things to do during the shoot. His feet doubled for Benicio Del Toro's feet in a close-up. Anderson also asked Dues to sit off camera and be Del Toro's focal point in the scene where Moses speaks to the crafts group.

"That was an incredible experience," Dues said, "to have Benicio Del Toro, one of my favorite actors, staring right at me, and feeling as if I'd gotten to witness him acting in private."

### "OH. IT'S ME."

**T**ONY Revolori, who played the young Moses, was just as starstruck by Del Toro. "I don't know how I can convey what a big deal Benicio was to me the entire time I was starting out trying to do this job," Revolori said. "He was the number one example that a guy like me can actually have an incredible career, and make good choices, and develop a style."

Before Revolori won the role of young Zero in Anderson's *The Grand Budapest Hotel,* he was a child actor for many years. His parents are Guatemalan immigrants Mario and Sonia Quiñonez, respectively a teacher and the owner of a tax-preparation business. Their family lived in Anaheim, California, six blocks from Disneyland. "We could see and hear the fireworks from the park every night," he said. Revolori's brother Mario is a professional actor, martial artist, and stuntman. The brothers went on auditions together growing up. Dad drove. The brothers grew up watching Del Toro's performances. They considered him a role model for actors of Latin descent who hoped to succeed in a predominantly white industry without surrendering their integrity. He was as important to them as Robert De Niro and Al Pacino had been to young Italian American actors in the 1970s.

Revolori and his brother took their stage surnames from their paternal grandfather, who died right before Tony got the lead role in *The Grand Budapest Hotel* (a part that Mario Revolori had also auditioned for). The actors' father was visiting the Guatemalan town where he'd grown up to bury his own father when Jeremy Dawson called on a busted-up public phone booth. He asked

TOP: After filming the scene where Moses Rosenthaler tries to kill Julian Cadazio, actors Adrien Brody and Benicio Del Toro embrace.

BOTTOM: Set photo of Del Toro and Léa Seydoux between takes of the scene where Rosenthaler attempts to describe himself to his fellow inmates in the arts and crafts room

permission for Revolori, then a minor, to fly to Paris for his final *Grand Budapest* audition. Tony Revolori's favorite scene in *The Grand Budapest Hotel* is the one where young Zero tells Ralph Fiennes's concierge M. Gustave about his family's experiences as refugees. Zero's story reminded Revolori of the story of how his father's side of the family arrived in the United States. "When my dad read that script," Revolori said, "he got to that part and said, 'Oh. It's me.' My father's side of the family was, we believe, Italian Jews, though it's hard to say for sure." He knew that they fled from Sicily to Portugal and then to Guatemala, changing their name at each new point of the journey, until they stuck with Revolori.

"And then there was a revolution in Guatemala," Revolori said. "There was a civil war. Guerillas went door-to-door in the villages looking for soldiers and making them enlist. My father was twenty-two, and my uncle was like nineteen or twenty. They were selected. And they just went to America after that, through Mexico, and then sent a postcard back to Guatemala saying, basically, 'We are in the United States now because we didn't want to have to join the army of the guerillas.'"

Revolori thought about those stories in the lead-up to shooting Zero's monologue. "I was thinking about how Zero got to be the apprentice to a master concierge at a great hotel, and how I'd gotten a similar opportunity by being cast in a Wes Anderson movie, and how rare something like that is for a guy who was as young as I was and who came from my background. That scene was a chance for me to be able to step up and tell my perspective a little bit. I treated the scene as a tribute to my family, and to any family that has had similar experiences. We did several takes. I completely lost it a couple of times. It was the first time I'd ever cried during a scene where I didn't intentionally try to make it happen. It just kept happening to me, naturally, as a result of saying those words. And to be honest, I didn't understand until years later why I cried playing that scene. I had to get some perspective on it."

It was also the first time that Revolori felt he'd been in a scene as dramatically powerful as some of his favorite scenes in the films of Benicio Del Toro.

For Tony Revolori, playing Zero was the culmination of a lifelong dream inspired by watching Del Toro. He never imagined he would one day play a younger version of his hero. To Revolori it was a sacred assignment, akin to the young Robert De Niro in *The Godfather: Part II* being cast as a younger version of the part Marlon Brando played in the original.

Revolori decided he would need to study Del Toro. *Really* study him. And he did. Film by film. Scene by scene. Even frame by frame.

"What I realized was that Benicio's facial expressions are always very calm, which is often the case with characters in Wes's films, but he can also have a sad-yet-also-angry quality, and I tried to work on those two things a little bit," Revolori said. "What helped me feel very in tune with him was body language. Shoulders: a little bit high and intense. Back: a little bit arched. Arms, kind of coming up a bit, in front, almost T. rex–like. A lot of fiddling with the thumbs and looking away when he's thinking. I never did any of that stuff in the film because when I'm on camera I'm always painting. But having done those exercises in advance was a good way to find my way into a performance that had the feeling of a Benicio."

Del Toro met Revolori for the first time at a screening of *Eternity's Gate,* a biography of Vincent van Gogh starring Wes Anderson regular Willem Dafoe. "Benicio said to me, 'So, I hear you're in the new Wes movie,' Revolori recalled. "I said 'yes.' Benicio said, 'Are you playing the young me?' I said yes, I was. He looked me up and down and said, 'Okay. Okay. We'll talk.' Then we made an appointment for a couple of weeks later, and we just sat and talked for four hours." They traded stories about their upbringing, Revolori telling Del Toro of how he'd decided to focus on athletics, music, and photography when his attempts to learn painting ended in frustration: "My hand-to-brain never got to where I wanted it, even after a year of study. It was a nice, strange kind of validation that I ended up in this movie playing a painter." They talked about how to make their performances consistent. "We worked on a certain way that the character would hold a paintbrush and made sure we both did it the same way. There were other things we tried as well. Benicio kept asking for my opinion. I told him at the beginning, 'I'm happy just to do whatever you do,' but he wouldn't accept that. He said, 'No—no small parts.' Which was incredible to me. I would've been happy just to be in the same movie with him, carrying out his instructions from a rooftop or window."

"The love goes both ways, to be honest with you," Del Toro said. "Tony is a great actor. I thought so when I saw him in *Grand Budapest.* I know how hard it is to try to be truthful in front of that camera. It's not easy, and I don't think there's a formula to it."

Their mutual respect gave a deeper resonance to the scene that ends the flashbacks to Moses's youth—the moment when Revolori hands over the role to Del Toro, along with a dog tag necklace.

The scene became a ritual of affirmation between acting generations: the acolyte acknowledging the master, and the master conferring respect by joining in the ritual.

"I know that the scene was bringing the past and the future together in a very unique way," said Del Toro, "and that when you do a Wes Anderson movie, you've got to be ready to do things like that, things that are outside the box, because that's the kind of cinema that he does. Wes has spent his career doing unusual things and getting away with it. I was an accomplice, you know? I don't think I was hesitant about it at all. Everyone who works with Wes is an accomplice."

Anderson always hoped the scene would feel different from anything else in the movie. "It did occur to me that I couldn't recall seeing anything like it before, which was a nice feeling," he said.

Notes from Del Toro helped Anderson get closer to his goal. "I like an actor who is mysterious just as much as I like an actor who is completely open about their process," he said. "You know, when I work with Jeff Goldblum, he's always saying, 'Tell me more, tell me more. What do I want? What am I doing here? What do I know?' He wants you to tell him anything he can. He's open to anything. And he's constantly rehearsing the scene itself, practicing it again and again and again, right next to you. That's quite different from Benicio. With Benicio, you don't really know what's going to happen until it's happening. There's something more opaque about it."

### A LITTLE POEM

THE opaque technique of Benicio Del Toro came through in the scene where he takes the character back from Revolori. The script laid out the moment simply: just a series of actions for actors to play with. Two actors, a chair, and a necklace.

"I thought, 'Wouldn't it be interesting if the older one and the younger one had a communication with each other because he knows what the kid is going to go through, and they share something,'" said Anderson. "They're the same person. His feeling for this younger version of himself is like, 'I know it's going to be hard, but there's nothing you can do about it. I'll take over.' I have no idea where the impulse to write the scene came from. It wasn't something I'd been thinking about doing for years or anything like that."

While the function of the scene was obvious, it raised questions. Was the elder Moses imagining the younger? Or was the younger somehow imagining forward in time and seeing his older self? Was the elder Moses thinking that the younger Moses would want him to be more forgiving of himself, and then rejecting the thought (perhaps not for the first time)? Who was replacing whom? Whose scene was it? What did it mean?

Said Anderson, "If you asked somebody like David Mamet 'How is this scene advancing the story?' I think he'd say, 'This scene doesn't do anything. You're not even changing anything with the character. You're just changing actors.' The way the actors performed it, it became a little poem."♠

# TO THE BARRICADES

**PART VI**

"T HE Children are Grumpy." So says graffiti glimpsed in "Revisions to a Manifesto," the second full-length story in *The French Dispatch*. And the children—teenagers, actually—are quite grumpy, with good reason. The alternate-universe France of Wes Anderson's movie appears to be embroiled in turmoil comparable to that of the real France circa 1968. That was a year of tumultuous protests in France, the United States, and other countries. The demonstrations—some pointed and purposeful, others inchoate in their rage—wanted, among other things, to end global imperialism fueled by corporate greed and individual indifference, a toxic stew of geopolitical forces exemplified by the US-led war in Vietnam. Also on the protesters' agenda: ending racism, sexism, neofascism, the nuclear arms race, and other societal ills. The under-thirtysomethings led the charge and reaped an outsized share of punishment. The student protests in "Revisions to a Manifesto" are rooted in more earthbound concerns—as Anderson has noted elsewhere in this report [and close-up], the wish to end gender segregation in dorms was based on a real movement in France—and the conflict between youth and the establishment briefly seems as if it could be resolved through a chess match, but then it degenerates into a riot, complete with barricades made of piled-up cars that evoke a steampunk variation of the iconic set from the musical *Les Misérables*. The protests, the crackdown, the aftermath, and the rest are presented by *French Dispatch* writer Lucinda Krementz (Frances McDormand) as a combination political analysis and "life of a city" article, modeled on "The Events of May, 1968," a two-part, diary-style piece by *New Yorker* writer Mavis Gallant.

Of course, Gallant, as far as anyone knows, never had an affair with a naïve young protestor[1] named Zeffirelli (Timothée Chalamet), a student activist who chafes against authoritarian rules, eager to take to the streets (though his political ideas are still, perhaps, evolving). And Gallant likely never exhorted such a young man to hook up with an exuberant and far more radical protester named Juliette (Lyna Khoudri), who is never seen in public without her compact and her motorcycle helmet, but has a far more vibrant worldview than her future paramour. Like "The Concrete Masterpiece," "Revisions to a Manifesto" is partly a story of women inspiring men to become their best selves. But unlike Moses and Simone's affair, the tale of Lucinda, Zeffirelli, and Juliette ends tragically, with the newly radicalized young man repairing a defective radio transmitter atop a

---

[1] Gallant did, however, write an equally famous 1971 piece titled "The Affair that Scandalized France," later published in book form as *The Affair of Gabrielle Russier*, about a thirty-year-old female teacher named Gabrielle Russier who had an affair with a sixteen-year-old male student named Christian Rossi, and was scandalized and prosecuted and ultimately killed herself. "Even her car might have belonged to an adolescent," Gallant wrote. "It was a small red Citroën called a Dyane, decorated with Pop Art flowers. On the rear window she had pasted 'make love not war!'"

Cropped still-frame image of Lyna Khoudri and Timothée Chalamet on the set of the student protest sequence

> *"Wes doesn't want to explain things like this. He's like, 'Do what you want, and think what you think.'"* —LYNA KHOUDRI

student-operated pirate radio station, getting electrocuted and, apparently, drowning, too, and becoming a commodified martyr. "His likeness (mass-produced and shrink-wrap packaged) will be sold like bubble-gum to the hero-inspired," Krementz writes.

"I always wondered, 'Where is the Mustard Region?'" says Khoudri. "I imagined it was a combination of something out of the Second World War and the student protests of 1968. I asked Wes, and he was like, 'In this movie, we are in France. I don't know where we are in France. If this guy is going to war, it's something connected to his country and what the government is doing.' Wes doesn't want to explain things like this. He's like, 'Do what you want, and think what you think. It's okay. Really!'"

It does seem clear from context, though, that this mid-twentieth-century France, like the actual France of that era, is a theoretically egalitarian but (in certain ways) reactionary country, with a history of wars and colonial action that can't be sustained without mandatory service. Mitch-Mitch's (Mohamed Belhadjine) play *Goodbye, Zeffirelli* is described by Krementz as "a poetic interpretation of his National Duty Obligation service." The Drill-Sergeant (Rupert Friend) in the scene boasts of catching "a bullet in the tail" in North Africa and ingesting "a rare, microbial, gut-parasite" in East Asia. The students sense that all this war-profiteering and imperialistic strutting is entwined with the spiritual death march of consumerism, even if they can't articulate exactly how it works. Their sloganeering can be comically overwrought and reductive: word salad from young people who appear to have skimmed texts rather than read them—see Juliette's tiff with Zeffirelli in the café over the acceptability of posting a photo of the entertainer Tip-Top, "a commodity represented by a record company owned by a conglomerate controlled by a bank subsidized by a bureaucracy sustaining the puppet-leadership of a satellite stooge-government. For every note he sings, a peasant must die in West Africa."

At the same time, though, an empathetic undertow implies that the students' anxiety and outrage are sincerely felt and rooted in real concerns. They're dire enough to drive Morisot (Alex Lawther), another recruit in *Goodbye, Zeffirelli*, into a depression so deep that he jumps from a high barracks window.[2] Before killing himself, Morisot tells his mates he wants to be "a protestor" because he can't face "that forty-eight-year period" between finishing his military service and retiring. What is Morisot protesting? All of it.

Asked what his personal politics are, and what he hopes viewers will take away from this story, Anderson is characteristically circumspect, offering only that "Revisions to a Manifesto" was inspired by then-recent news coverage of various international protests ("How could it not be?"), as well as his own awareness of how the political history of the 1960s and other decades got entangled with pop culture. (The argument over which musician's photo is politically appropriate for a student-frequented café could have occurred in any year that followed the invention of photography.) A cursory reading of "Revisions to a Manifesto" seems to mark it as more sympathetic to the students than the government, and more sympathetic to the radical students (led by Juliette) than to the more conciliatory, self-serving faction Zeffirelli runs with.

Anderson's own explanation of what drew him to the story aligns him with the writer who tells the tale: Lucinda Krementz. It might or might not be significant that Krementz is the only one of the star reporters in the film who isn't given a proper framing device. A brief shot at the very end of the segment shows Krementz seated at her desk in the *French Dispatch* office, indicating the finished manuscript to her editor, but that's it. Her work is her statement. There's nothing to add. Underneath all the reportorial detail and philosophical musing is a self-lacerating inquiry by a middle-aged writer trying to understand the passions of the young, and concluding that any discomfort they spark is her problem, not theirs.

"One thing is now finally clear," Krementz reads to us. "They are answering their parents. What do they want? To defend their illusions. A luminous abstraction." A moment later, she adds, "I am convinced they are better than we were."

"A lot of this story comes from my personal reaction to reading Mavis Gallant's work," Anderson said. "The thing I always liked about her is that she's such a complicated, interesting person. She has a high sensitivity for anything stupid or disingenuous, and so she sees a lot of bad faith on the part of the government, and a lot of pretense and muddy thinking on the part of the students. But what she doesn't see in the students is hypocrisy. She sees courage and sincerity. She sees that there's something real that they're trying to get, and that it's hard for them to express because when they do speak, they speak metaphorically. They know they want a different France, and the difficulty of articulating what they mean by that is funny, and maybe not in a lighthearted way. All I hoped to get across was a range of reactions to a situation like this one that also includes admiration for young people who take physical risks throwing themselves into this kind of cause."

Anderson wrote the role of Lucinda Krementz for McDormand, a two-time Oscar winner that he'd first worked with on *Moonrise Kingdom*. But although the actress's baleful intelligence anchors the piece,

---

**2**  The moment where Mitch-Mitch shows up at the café is the most temporally elaborate setup payoff in Wes Anderson's filmography. We've just finished watching a scene in a play that Mitch-Mitch hasn't written yet, translated into English by Krementz—i.e., a flash-forward. But because the scene explains why the playwright chose to reject his National Service obligation and burn his patch, it is also a flashback.

**Wes Anderson tests Zeffirelli and Juliette's moped in the background behind Frances McDormand.**

its momentum is fueled by the performances of the young actors playing the students (as well as by the music they love—specifically Christophe's[3] hit 1965 ballad "Aline," rerecorded for the film's soundtrack by Jarvis Cocker). Timothée Chalamet, Oscar-nominated for *Call Me By Your Name,* plays Zeffirelli, a lanky goofball with a chocolate-milk mustache. Although the actor's voice and demeanor radiate Americanness, Chalamet's slender face and lost-in-space expressions are suitably Gallic—and sure enough, his family is French. He speaks fluent French and holds dual French and American citizenship and has relatives who were involved in the 1968 political actions in Paris. "Because I have family members who were part of that student protest, it did feel oddly coincidental that I was cast in this part," he said, "and I was grateful that Wes let me play with the lines in French as well as English, although in the finished film I believe I'm speaking English exclusively."

Chalamet calls Zeffirelli "a deliciously complex role for me. I'm coming at it from the point of view of playing a self-realizing, self-stylizing young man who gets involved in a student revolution in France that's in full force—a young man who's trying to fight against the rigidity of old-school structures, just like members of the Chalamet family did in France in the sixties. Another thing that's fascinating to me is that Zeffirelli is going through things that I think a lot of kids are going through today, too, especially in the fights for climate justice and racial justice and economic justice that are happening everywhere. I hesitate to get into Wes's take on all that stuff or divulge any of the things we talked about with regard to the character. I'm not purposefully being coy, although some of that stuff is private. It's not out of pretension. I just feel that whatever an audience member takes away from this story is way more interesting and important than anything Wes or I might have to say politically."

Chalamet's counterpart is Lyna Khoudri as Juliette.[4] Born in Algeria, Khoudri was known to art-house viewers for her performance in *Les Bienheureux* (2017), about a family surviving in the aftermath of the Algerian civil war, the same conflict that her

[3] 1945–2020. French singer-songwriter whose music expressed a soaring yet melancholy romanticism. He died of causes related to COVID-19 a year and a half before *The French Dispatch*'s release.

[4] Filmmaker Franco Zeffirelli directed the best-known screen adaptation of *Romeo and Juliet,* released in 1968. Anderson assures viewers that there's no deeper meaning to his naming one character in a 1968 story "Zeffirelli" and the other "Juliette," other than that it's the way his mind works.

ABOVE: **Cover of the manifesto and its dedication page, from Zeffirelli to Juliette**

RIGHT: **Zeffirelli (Timothée Chalamet) and Lucinda Krementz (Frances McDormand) discuss writing.**

THIS PAGE: **Still-frame images from the confrontation between Zeffirelli (Timothée Chalamet, center, with Nicolas Avinée, right) and Juliette (Lyna Khoudri) at the Sans Blague Café**

OPPOSITE: **Mohamed Belhadjine as Mitch-Mitch, burning his service patch in protest of the government's intervention in the Mustard Region** OPPOSITE, INSET: **Mitch-Mitch's patch**

own parents came to France to escape. But by the time *The French Dispatch* had completed photography, she seemed on track for a Chalamet-like rise to stardom, having won a César award as Most Promising Newcomer for starring in another Algerian civil war drama, Mounia Meddour's *Papicha* (2019), about a fashion student named Nedjma who resists Islamic fundamentalism. The actress sees similarities between Juliette and Nedjma. "They both know what they want and are willing to take it to the end," she said. "They have a political conscience and defend the rights of those being oppressed. Nedjma's protest is artistic, while Juliette's form of protest is more direct, fighting against actual authorities."

The ranks of student protestors are filled out by new faces, including Nicolas Avinée as Vittel and Mohamed Belhadjine as Mitch-Mitch. Cast as kind of a comic relief team—a configuration that, as they both point out, has equivalents in every segment of the movie—they became close friends after realizing how many characteristics they had in common. The big one: Both became actors over their parents' initial objections.

Like Khoudri, Belhadjine is an Algerian-born actor whose mother and father—respectively, a school administrator and a construction foreman—came to France during the Algerian Civil War, settling in Essonne, a Paris suburb, around the turn of the millennium. Belhadjine grew up in a comfortable home, in a bedroom packed with comic books, novels, toys, and video games. The flat white walls were easy to project his imagination upon. From childhood, Belhadjine loved to play a game he called Joue Mohamed, or "Playing at Mohamed," where he would impersonate characters he'd seen in movies and on television. "I understood that by using my imagination, I could change the world around me at will," he said. "I was fifteen when I realized that my game was a little weird, and maybe somebody my age shouldn't be doing it anymore."

Belhadjine's love of playacting in his bedroom was replaced by an urge to act on stage and screen. He fell in love with stage acting in lycée, but had to agree to his mother's request to study communication at university along with the humanities. "It didn't work out," he said. "I didn't enjoy it." So he quit, worked for a while, saved enough money to take acting classes at a conservatory in Paris, and started auditioning for parts. Getting cast in *The French Dispatch* is the biggest thing that's happened to him.

Ditto Nicolas Avinée. His father is a cardiologist, his mother an ophthalmologist. Like Belhadjine, he grew up loving pop culture and video games and playing imaginative games, and was urged (along with his two older brothers) to study something more practical or lucrative. His eldest brother ended up studying architecture, while his middle brother is a doctor. Avinée got involved in theater at age ten during a family vacation on the shore of a Turkish lake. It was there that he acted for the first time, and also won his first acting award. It was a play about the French playwright Molière, who was played by another young actor. As Molière scribbled at a table, his creations came to life on other parts of the stage and acted out his stories. Avinée says he doesn't remember

much about the play except that his character wore a very long wig. Everything from the moment that the backstage crew put the wig on his head through the tumultuous applause he received at curtain call was blacked out of his memory. Avinée was declared the play's best actor and given a certificate to hang on his wall. "I still don't understand why I got the award," he said.

But the experience still inspired him to study acting for six years with a young persons' theater organization in Paris, then move into an adult theater troupe at an instructor's urging. (He was the youngest member of that troupe by a substantial margin.) Like Belhadjine, Avinée was told by his parents that he would need to concentrate on the sciences at university if he were to be allowed to study theater there as well. All told, Avinée studied theater for ten years before auditioning for *The French Dispatch*. He recorded his audition and emailed it to the casting department. Belhadjine did the same, but accidentally showed up to his callback audition one week early. Fortunately, the casting people were there that day, too. They found his bewilderment charming and let him read.

When the two actors were paired for a "chemistry read," it was obvious that they clicked. "The scene Nic and I did together involved our two characters overlapping each other, or speaking at the same time," Belhadjine said. "They had tried me out with other actors, but when they put me with Nic, that's when things started to get interesting."

"There was a moment," Avinée said, "where we both did our lines and then looked at each other, perfectly timed, and then we both looked at the camera at the same moment. Neither of us had planned to do that. We just did it. And afterward, we were both like, 'What? What is going on here?'"

"The really funny thing about casting Nicolas," said Anderson, "is that I had watched one of his audition tapes and said, 'I like this guy,' and told the casting director, 'This is one possibility,' and then I was in Angoulême doing some preparations, scouting and things, and then there he was! I saw him out of the window of a restaurant and thought, 'I know that one,' and then a few minutes later he's standing next to me, introducing himself. I was like, 'I knew that was you! You were the guy I just watched a video of!' He was there with a traveling theater company, putting

An overhead shot of one of the principal locations of the riot scene, at the Rue du Sauvage, as Lyna Khoudri's Juliette (lower center, motorcycle helmet) reacts to the "unauthorized allocation of funds for the mass-printing of this obtuse, ambiguous, poetic (in a bad way)" manifesto

on a show in the same room where we had just shot Tilda giving a speech. I was probably going to cast him anyway, but after that meeting, I thought, 'I might as well just do it now and make it official.'"

Even after reading the full screenplay, neither Avinée nor Belhadjine understood just how large the production would be. "Here in France," said Avinée, "a good-sized set will be maybe fifty people. On this shoot, it was not uncommon for there to be two hundred crew members and actors working, and sometimes as many as one hundred extras waiting to be on camera. It was surreal. It was inspiring."

Avinée and Belhadjine were taken with the communal atmosphere, with cast and crew at the hotel all mingling and eating and drinking wine and watching rough cuts of scenes. "One time Bill Murray got up and started doing a sketch, just improvising it, and it lasted ten minutes and delighted everyone," Avinée said. "It was treated by all as if that sort of thing was a perfectly normal occurrence." On a different day, Murray approached Avinée on the street outside the hotel and asked him to recommend a bar in the city. He suggested a place owned by a friend of a friend. Murray went there and bought whiskey shots for everyone.

"I was surprised by how hard people partied in relation to how hard they worked," Avinée said. "They worked much longer days than I was used to as an actor in France, and yet they were able to go to work the next day and be crisp and do good work after being out late."

Avinée was also surprised by how easy it was to become immersed in the world of Ennui-sur-Blasé, even though there were lights and power cables and clipboards and generators everywhere. "Even if you were just walking around Angoulême, you could see how the streets had been transformed into the aesthetic of Wes Anderson," he said. "I myself was completely transformed into a Wes Anderson character. I didn't look like myself. How strange it was, meeting other people while wearing that skin."

"I was so impressed by the ambience of this imaginary city," Belhadjine said, "and by the way that every corner had been set-designed, and how the movie kind of took on the life of the city, but also gave the city life. It was as if the city of Angoulême had gotten to act in a film also."

"The people of the city embraced us, and that helped us fill the screen up," said Anderson. "All the actors who are in the café

ABOVE: Still-frame from the flash-forward that depicts the production of Mitch-Mitch's play about his experiences in the Mustard Region. A spotlit Drill-Sergeant (Rupert Friend) holds the floor.

scenes are also in the barricades scene, which I felt worked for us. We figured that, since we had a large group of local teenagers involved in the shoot who had all invented their own characters to play while they were roaming around in the background, that meant if you saw the same faces more than once, it was because they were all part of the same little youth movement."

Anderson and his department heads had to solve logistical challenges to realize the segment's two blockbuster set pieces: the dance number and the barricades sequence. Both necessitated the fabrication of large, complex sets with custom-made moving parts, and choreography for dozens or even hundreds of extras, many of them nonprofessional actors and dancers, who all needed to be coached so that their carefully rehearsed actions would come across as spontaneous.

The scenes were, by their nature, less controllable than the rest of the shoot. Most of "Revisions to a Manifesto" consisted of scenes where every shot had been mapped out in advance, in keeping with the director's animation-influenced process. "Individual shots become individual sets now with Wes," said Adam Stockhausen, "which is different from the [default] method of filmmaking, where you dress or build a set that's intended to be shot from a variety of angles. That process started to disappear on *Moonrise Kingdom*, which Wes made after *Fantastic Mr. Fox*. Now we're at a point where, with certain exceptions, each shot is a set and each set is a shot."

"The way Wes works is not exactly real," said Bob Balaban, veteran of multiple Anderson productions, "but it creates a world."

The death of Zeffirelli is a vivid example: It's shot on a forced-perspective set where the scale of the foreground and background elements is notably (and purposefully) out of whack, to the point where it seems to echo the construction site in the Sazerac prologue and the bare-bones, borderline abstract set from Mitch-Mitch's play. "That moment when Zeffirelli is hanging off the light tower and everything that led up to it and followed it moves me," said Chalamet, "and it moved me when we were shooting it, and it moved me even when I read it on the page. When somebody doesn't let their naïvetée presuppose their potential, their ideas, or their way to contribute to the world, it's moving, particularly when it ends in premature death, and it so often does in Wes's movies." When the electricity strikes, the bolt is so not

> "It was as if the city of Angoulême had gotten to act in a film also."
>
> —MOHAMED BELHADJINE, AKA MITCH-MITCH

real that it might as well have been drawn by Chuck Jones.[5] The sense of inconsolable loss is conveyed by Alexandre Desplat's score, Christophe's song "Aline," the narrated scrap of his poem to his two lovers, the image of Zeffirelli's parents riding silently in the back of a taxi, and the glamorous, even more stylized shots of Zeffirelli and Juliette riding her motorbike at night.[6]

None of these elements, alone or in combination, is sufficient to overcome the innate skepticism of viewers who need for everything in a movie to "feel real"—whatever "real" means. But Anderson's films aren't aimed at such viewers. The target audience is people who can use their imaginations to fill cracks that are normally filled by money.

"It probably sounds strange, considering that he was so much more overtly political, but there is a sense in which Wes's films remind me of Luis Buñuel's," said filmmaker Nicolas Saada. "The mundane presentation of powerful events in Buñuel's films provokes anguish in the audience, because they are recognizing things that are not recognizable."

## LE SANS BLAGUE

The Sans Blague Café is the epicenter of student life, activist and otherwise, and the location of several key moments: the burning of the patch, the chess match, and the dance number that channels *The Umbrellas of Cherbourg* by way of the long-running RTF series *Discorama* (1959–1975).

The Sans Blague Café set was built entirely in the Felt Factory, including the exteriors of buildings that are visible through the windows when the camera is inside looking out. "I've never worked on a film that had so many painted backdrops," said Kevin Timon Hill. "There weren't green-screens, there were amazing painted backings. Every time there was a window, another director might have just put up a green-screen, but we did these beautiful forced-perspective backings in nearly every perspective where you're inside looking out."[7]

"When we were looking at the set [after it was built], Wes said, 'Wouldn't it be great if the walls could move?'" Yeoman said. "I think the result is one of the most fun parts of the movie. You're looking at the exterior of the café, and then suddenly the wall just opens up and Lyna Khoudri comes down the steps. And then at the very end, Lyna and Timothée are by the jukebox and the walls open up and the scooters go driving by in the background. I love doing stuff like that, where you break with reality."

"Wes wanted to add the front of the café opening, and have it be open during shooting, and [dolly] through the wall as it opened," said Stéphane Cressend. "I went to see the construction and figure out how we could do it and found a solution very quickly. The wall in front of the café would slide open suspended on a rail. I went to the set that day and saw that Wes was shooting through it."

Cressend appreciated that camera movement, because it meant that Anderson was cheerfully acknowledging that the audience was seeing a set, not a preexisting location: a thing that was built to be filmed. "It was an homage to the crew's work," he said.

## THE RAWNESS OF THINGS

For the barricades scenes, Anderson focused on covering as much narrative ground as he could with as much momentum as he could. One part of the mission statement was honoring the films of the Nouvelle Vague movement, which were relatively inexpensive but made with so much verve that they had a certain swagger. Anderson consulted his colleagues to figure out how to make this segment edgier than the others. Shards of cinema verité would contrast nicely against the gliding dolly shots and pop-up-storybook sets. Yeoman noticed that Anderson was doing things he didn't ordinarily do, like letting him film actors in harsh sunlight without bounce cards to soften the image, and urging him to shoot scenes with a handheld 35mm movie camera without getting hung up on creating perfect frames. "Several movies ago," Yeoman recalled, "we were talking about light, and Wes said, 'You know, you can shoot everything at magic hour and it's beautiful, but it gets boring after a while because everything is perfectly lit.' Wes said, 'Sometimes you have to embrace the rawness of things not being perfect.' I agree with him on that. Sometimes for a movie, it's better if it's not perfect."

One fleeting example, Yeoman says, is a shot of Zeffirelli and his friends playing chess. "The sun is hitting them pretty hard there. My inclination would have been to soften it up a little bit, but we went with what it was, which was very contrast-y, and in the end, Wes was right. It gave that shot a character that was different from the other sections of the movie, and there are a lot of shots like that in this section of the

[5] 1912–2002. Longtime animator and cartoon-short director for Warner Bros. (and later, United Artists). Killed da wabbit.

[6] The first scene that Chalamet and Khoudri shot together.

[7] The exterior of the café as seen in an establishing shot (with scooters zipping through the foreground) is an existing Angoulême corner with period-specific facade elements fitted over it. "We did that shot during preproduction because it was such a big, wide shot and we didn't need any actors for it," said Yeoman.

TOP: The breakaway Café Le Sans Blague set that was built on an interior soundstage in the production's local studio; MIDDLE ROW: Composite showing how the built exterior matches up with the existing Angoulême location; illustration of the controversial entertainer Tip-Top (actually *French Dispatch* soundtrack contributor Jarvis Cocker) by Molly Rosenblatt; overhead shot of "vintage" pinball machine, actually a refurbished older model game (note the wooden interior) with graphic overlays and tweaks created by the art department; BOTTOM ROW, LEFT TO RIGHT: A menu, a coffee cup, and a flyer

OPPOSITE: Still-frame of Mohamed Belhadjine, Nicolas Avinée, and Lyna Khoudri outside of the Café Le Sans Blague

movie. I was kind of concerned that all during the shooting of the story about the students, the sun was kind of in the wrong place for me a lot of the time. But that gave all that footage its own feeling, and it suited the story."

The barricades sequence was a chance to apply that episode's roughened aesthetic to a large-scale action scene. The sequence was pushed off to the end of the shoot because it had so many actors and extras and had to be shot at the same time on a real outdoor location, Rue du Sauvage. "I always refer to the big protest sequence as 'the outdoor sequence,'" says Chalamet. "It was out in the open air, in sunlight, which made it feel different from the stuff we did in the studio that they made out of the abandoned factory, where even if we were supposed to be outdoors we were shooting on an indoor set."

Juliette and Zeffirelli's escape on Juliette's motorcycle was achieved with a mix of different kinds of shots. Some required stunt riders or stand-ins, while others used Chalamet and Khoudri. A chunk of the budget for the sequence went to the designing and building of the barricades, respectively made of discarded Citroën automobiles. Each barricade was made from glommed-up piles of metal maneuvered into place with flatbed trucks and cranes, then locked together like puzzle pieces. A fused infrastructure prevented the auto carcasses from collapsing under the weight of actors, stuntpeople, and crew members. "You could get from one side of a barricade to the other quickly by opening a hinged door that had been welded and bolted inside the scrap," Yeoman said.

Yeoman said Anderson's decision to embrace a handheld shooting style encouraged the crew to work as fast as they could, prizing energy over perfection. One can see the results of that approach in the scene at the barricades where Krementz, Zeffirelli, and Juliette have it out over the Krementz/Zeffirelli affair, Krementz's parasitic "neutrality," and the substance of Zeffirelli's manifesto. The dialogue and actions are as meticulously conceived as elements of a stage play, but the shooting style is in the vein of a mid-twentieth-century documentary—or a drama with camerawork inspired by documentaries.

"It was a very long scene with a lot of dialogue between Frances and Timothée and Lyna and other

THIS PAGE: Still-frame image from the film's account of the students' anti-gender-segregation-in-dorms protest action against the government, expressed through a chess match

OPPOSITE: Wes Anderson directs the shots of the chess sequence.

> "The way Wes works is not exactly real, but it creates a world." —BOB BALABAN

TOP: The in-progress build of the street around the Sans Blague Café set in the Felt Factory

LEFT AND ABOVE: A collection of student protest signs fabricated by the graphics department

characters," said Yeoman, "and Wes wanted to sustain the energy that the actors were going to be generating, but we were shooting on [35mm motion-picture film]. You can use a four-hundred-foot mag, which runs out after roughly four minutes, or you can use a thousand-foot mag, which can go for roughly ten minutes. But to hold a thousand-foot mag is very heavy and awkward, so traditionally and generally, people shoot with four-hundred-foot mags whenever they shoot handheld. When the actors are in a zone, Wes likes to keep the energy going. He's like, 'Okay, let's go again! Let's go again!' Four minutes can go by rather quickly, so rather than wait two whole minutes while [the camera team] takes a mag off and puts another mag on and resets it, Wes decided to try a different plan."

"We did this thing where we shot handheld and used smaller cameras with remote focus and all of this gear," Anderson said. "We had two of those cameras. When one was being used, the other was being reloaded. Which meant that whenever Bob, who likes to operate his own cameras and is very good at handheld work, finished shooting a roll of film, somebody standing nearby could just hand him a new one, as if he were a fashion photographer. These were not even sync-sound cameras,[8] and so they were noisy."

"Wes picked up the camera and shot sometimes," said Chalamet, "like a guerilla filmmaker shooting a run-and-gun sort of thing. But then when you watch the movie, even though this segment has a little bit of an edge that makes it feel different from the others, it retains that Wes Anderson spirit—that framing, that sincerity, that structure.

"There were times where, because we were doing so many takes in a row, Sanjay Sami operated a little bit, and I might have done a shot or two, to give Bob a break. But really, this sequence is Bob's. And the thing about Bob is, he's a superb camera operator.

"What was so thrilling about being outside, after so much of watching Wes directing indoors on built sets, was that he made use of the elements, just like indie filmmakers would," said Chalamet. "What I mean by that is, like, the wind blowing the smoke off the grenades that were thrown, the effect of fireworks, you know, all of that stuff just does what it does, and Wes turns it into part of the scene, drawing from the atmosphere of the moment in the same way that he does that scene in the film with Willem Dafoe, the one where he's just kind of standing outside: The texture and movement of the snow [are] so important to that shot."

"It was a lot of work to get it all done," Anderson said, "and we were racing along the whole time, shooting straight through the day without stopping, but it worked out really well. I think the actors appreciated being able to get into it and stay in it."

"I was working and having fun at the same time," said Khoudri. "It was magic."

**8** A film camera with a sound recording element built into the camera itself, recording location sound onto a magnetic strip. A non-sync camera is just recording a picture. Sound has to be recorded externally, to a separate device, with a slate providing a common marker. Non-sync-sound cameras are noisier. On a lot of lower-budget films shot on celluloid with non-sync cameras, you can hear the rattle-clack of film being pulled through gears by its sprockets.

A section of barricade made from items that could have been seized from classrooms, such as desk chairs, file cabinets, and globes

les ENFANTS

LEFT: **When Zeffirelli and Juliette make their escape on a moped; these shots were filmed on a soundstage in Anderson's take on the style of Cinema du "Look."**

OPPOSITE, TOP: **Zeffirelli steels himself to climb up the transformer tower.**

OPPOSITE, MIDDLE AND BOTTOM: **A martyr is born.**

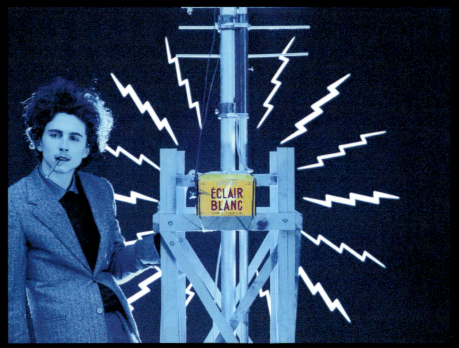

## MILES OF TILES

**T**HE last grace note added to this sequence was the domino display/race. Even though it would only be seen for a few seconds, Anderson wanted it to make an impression. So he hired the domino champion of France, Thibault Lesne.

Lesne has been playing with dominoes since he was five years old. He became obsessed with dominoes while watching the competitive domino series *Domino Day* (1998–2009), which was produced in the Netherlands. He used his sister's dominoes, which were "tiny," until his parents bought him a proper set, "maybe because they knew I loved dominoes." Then he went through a period of many years when he put his dominoes away and joined a human pyramid team, competing for prizes and suffering injuries. "We fall, and sometimes some people hurt themselves, like arms broken," he said. "But it's not really dangerous, you know? In twenty years of pyramids, I broke a bone just one time."

Dominoes eventually called him back. Lesne now holds the French record for the display utilizing the most dominoes. Previously Lesne's record had been seventy thousand dominoes; when interviewed in spring 2020, he had just attained a new record: ninety thousand dominoes in a single display. Realizing that goal required a team of forty people working in teams of ten, eight hours a day, for a week.

Lesne also holds the record for the biggest field of dominoes in France (in terms of area). His biggest displays concentrate on using dominoes in storytelling rather than to create acrobatic patterns and collisions. One of his displays reenacted the forty-five minutes in a Parisian bank robbery between the time when one of the tellers managed to trip the alarm and when the police arrived.

"I did a lot of events of dominoes falling in France and in Belgium, and this summer I went to the Netherlands to join the Dutch domino team," he said. "They call me the French expert just because I'm the main one in France, I think. But in the dominoes world, no, I'm not really famous. There are many people in the world far more accomplished than myself." The world record for the largest number of dominoes, he says, is four million, by a team out of the Netherlands in 2009. "It took eight weeks with ninety builders," Lesne says with admiration.

Lesne visited the *French Dispatch* set twice. The first time, he instructed the crew on the best way to do an elaborate domino display. But when the director saw the footage, he wasn't happy with it, so he brought Lesne back to personally supervise another go. It wasn't a complicated display compared to what Lesne has done elsewhere (although he was struck by the fact that Anderson wanted to use playing dominoes with dots on them; Lesne uses smooth dominoes for his displays).

Co-producer Octavia Peissel found Lesne on Facebook through the page that he maintains for his art. He came away impressed with the production—particularly with Anderson's interest in every detail, including the domino display. He confesses, however, that he made an embarrassing mistake during the first detailed conversation he had with the special effects department. "The head of the department called me and said, 'It's a Wes Anderson movie. Do you know who that is?' And I was like, 'Oh, yeah, I love him. I love *A Nightmare on Elm Street*.' And he was like, 'You're thinking of Wes Craven,' And [I] said, 'Ooops! Sorry!'"♠

ABOVE: Domino choreographer Thibault Lesne arranges tiles during a competition.

OPPOSITE: Max Dalton rendering of the final moment of Zeffirelli's short life

## PART VII

# DEATH COMES FOR EVERYONE

"I was flat on my back with the camera so close to my face that I was looking at my own reflection in the lens," said Stephen Park. "I was shivering."

It was an icy day in February 2019. Stephen Park was lying on a gurney, locked in the mind of the chef Nescaffier, who would have been the focus of the final segment of *The French Dispatch*, "The Private Dining Room of the Police Commissioner," had the latter's adorable son, Gigi, not been kidnapped by the Chauffeur and his criminal gang. On a chair beside Park was Jeffrey Wright, *Westworld* star, stage and screen actor, and the segment's protagonist and narrator, Roebuck Wright. Nescaffier had just regained consciousness following a near-death experience brought on after serving radishes dusted with toxic salts to the Chauffeur's criminal gang, surviving "thanks to the extreme fortitude of his almost superhuman stomach." The denouement of the movie's most action-packed story, this scene is literally an afterthought, enclosed by two framing devices: Roebuck Wright being edited by Arthur Howitzer, and in the 1970s being interviewed by a talk-show host (Liev Schreiber). But in the fullness of recollection, the moment feels like the key not just to that segment, but to the film: a celebration of the loner who leaves his homeland and reinvents himself abroad. Roebuck—as he'll be henceforward referenced, to avoid confusion with the same-surnamed actor—had originally turned in a draft that gave Nescaffier just one line of dialogue, but is persuaded by Howitzer to restore a bit he'd previously cut. After reading it, Howitzer pronounces it "the best part of the whole thing" and "the reason for it to be written."

No pressure.

"It was cold, and that was helping me," Park said. "My character was near death in the scene. I felt completely open."

**Nescaffier (Stephen Park) contemplates eternity after surviving his self-poisoning.**

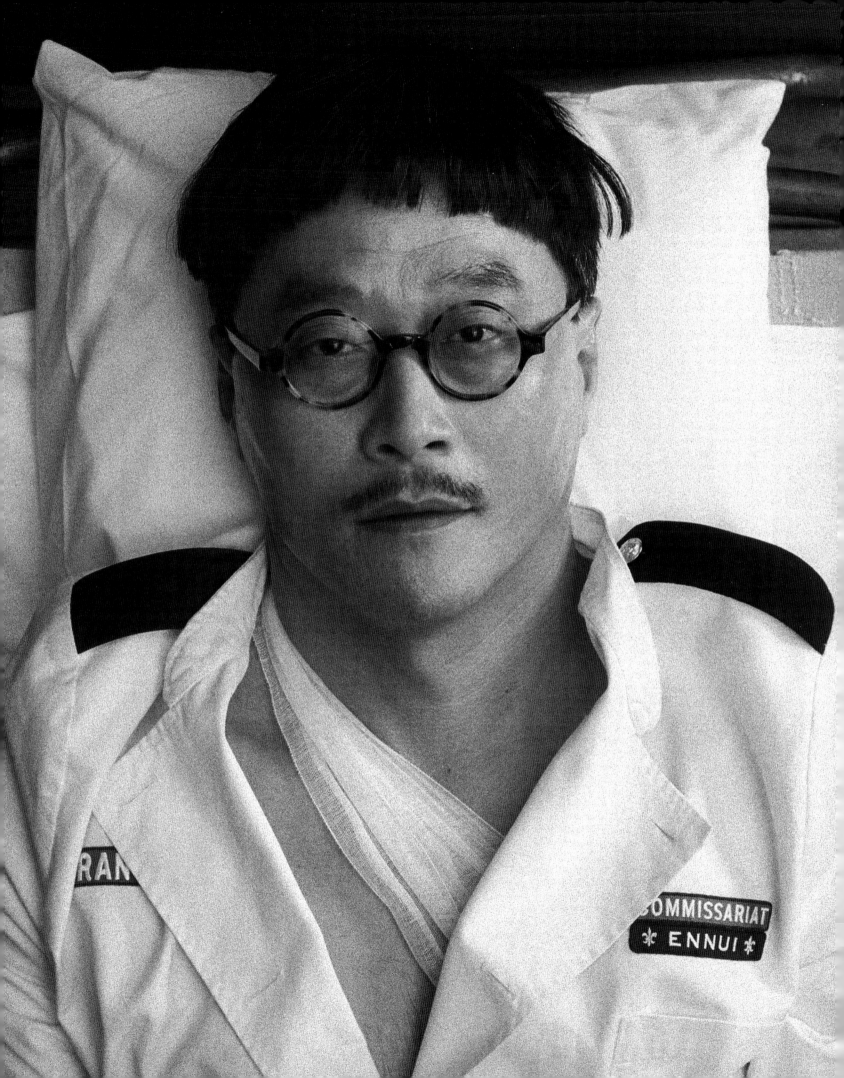

ABOVE: Still-frame image showing digitally multiplied Nescaffiers engaged in virtuoso displays of culinary skill

Between them, Park and Wright had logged about 150 film and TV credits, in careers that could do double duty as surveys of the mediums' evolutions over three decades. They booked their first roles within the same twelve-month period: Wright as a prosecuting attorney in the 1990 Alan J. Pakula murder mystery *Presumed Innocent,* opposite Harrison Ford; Park as Sonny in Spike Lee's 1989 drama *Do the Right Thing,* an immigrant Korean grocer whose impatience with the neighborhood's Black clientele gives way to solidarity following a fatal act of police brutality. Since then, each actor had played an array of roles that revealed fresh aspects of their talent.

Park had been in the repertory company of Fox's pioneering sketch show *In Living Color* and played a detective in the Michael Douglas urban-decay potboiler *Falling Down,* a PT boat captain in *Sgt. Bilko,* Fuyu in Bong Joon Ho's *Snowpiercer,* the hapless but duplicitous Mike Yanagita in the Coen brothers' *Fargo,* and the aptly named Mr. Park in the Coens' *A Serious Man,* who advises the spiritually befuddled hero to "accept the mystery."

Wright was generously awarded for his roles on the New York stage, became an indie film sensation in 1996's *Basquiat,* and then went on to create a gallery of scene-stealing supporting characters in such projects as *Ride with the Devil, Hamlet, Shaft, Ali,* the remake of *The Manchurian Candidate, Broken Flowers,* and TV's *Boardwalk Empire,* as well as the Daniel Craig incarnation of the James Bond franchise, in which Wright played CIA officer Felix Leiter five times. Wright also won an Emmy playing the dual role of Belize/Mr. Lies in Mike Nichols's HBO adaptation of *Angels in America*—a distinction atop a distinction, as Wright was already the only member of the show's Broadway cast to reprise his role on television.

Although Park and Wright hadn't worked together prior to *The French Dispatch,* each had followed the other's career and was looking forward to meeting in person. The weeks that they shared on the sets of *The French Dispatch,* not to mention the communal dining room at the hotel, cemented a mutual admiration society that long predated the shoot. In interviews, Wright described Park as "a marvelous actor. . . . a man of kindness, sensitivity, and a phenomenal work ethic," while Park said Wright was "... such a regular person, and with a very strong intuition. I immediately felt connected to him."

Part of the connection, Park said, came from the feeling of having been singled out by Wes Anderson, who wrote both roles with these performers in mind and gave each actor the sort of direction they were known to prefer, leaving the self-contained, free-floating Wright mostly to his own devices, but making himself constantly available to Park, a prodigious researcher and planner who travels to the set with research material, including books, mood boards, and journal entries—and who loves to ask questions.

By the time Park lay on the gurney in the Felt Factory, he was so deep into Wes Anderson's world that he'd entered a trancelike state. He'd watched the crew build an alternate universe around the cast: a knowingly cartoonish yet often lyrical mind-space that combined a hybrid of James Baldwin and A. J. Liebling defying racism and homophobia to become a literary rock star; a boy-genius crime-solver getting kidnapped by crooks who slice a piehole in a ceiling like the thieves in *Rififi*; gangsters and cops unleashing enough firepower to reinvade the beaches at Normandy; and a chase scene combining precision driving, an underground foot chase, and death-defying flips by a circus strongman in tights.

And now it was time to shoot the segment's paradoxically subdued finish: a locked-down close-up of an actor delivering a monologue about a near-death experience.

"Wes was physically very close," Park said. "The set was quiet because he wanted it that way. He was whispering as he was directing me. It was very intimate to hear Wes in my ear, whispering. It felt great, because we understood each other so well by that point in the shoot that every time he was saying something, I knew exactly what he wanted. It was great to have that connection with him and feel, at that moment, so unified with him, and connected with Jeffrey."

There was another bond between Wright and Park as well, deeper than their status as one of Wes Anderson's special projects. It had to do with being actors of color who'd spent much of their careers simultaneously trying to get cast and avoid typecasting. Park, who was born in New York and raised in Manhattan and upstate, came into acting after an aborted attempt to become a doctor to please his parents. He'd grown up being a class cut-up, acting in school productions, and making Super 8 movies with his friends, and had loved every minute of it, but he nearly left it all behind to become a doctor because his parents had made him believe that "acting was not that noble of a profession" and that school was "for learning responsible subjects, like math and science." He studied premedicine at the State University of New York, Binghamton, and became so depressed that he decided to drop out. His then-girlfriend urged him to take some electives only for pleasure, as sort of a going-away present to himself, and Park gleefully overcompensated, filling up his schedule with theater classes, including acting, voice, movement, and mime.

It was mime that seized Park's imagination, because it connected him to the primordial core of acting, the transformative impulse, bypassing culture. As a Korean American, it wasn't always easy for Park to find a way into a play written by an Anglo-American regionalist like Sam Shepard (*Fool for Love*) or Tennessee Williams (*A Streetcar Named Desire*), but he got a nearly electrical thrill pretending to balance on the edge of a skyscraper or incarnate an animal, an element, or a pun, because it was a pure problem-solving exercise. "Race was always in my mind as I studied acting, because I was cognizant that I was usually a minority in any situation I was in," Park said. "Usually as an actor I was entering a white world as an Asian person and trying to feel like I belonged in that space. Something that resonated for me about mime was that race was not typically an issue, whereas playing in *Fool for Love*, it was." Park's teacher was a Japanese-American graduate student named Takeo. The experience of learning and performing mime was meditative and athletic, a performance and a challenge. Sometimes it reminded Park of the martial arts classes he took back in middle school, studying karate with a master who wore a gold kimono and used to dazzle visiting parents by balancing an apple on a colleague's neck and chopping it in half with a katana. Self-discipline and self-knowledge were key, but there was also an outer-directed element: a sense of showmanship, and pride in mastery.

Nescaffier is described in Roebuck's prose/narration as a man with creative powers and physical skills verging on the superhuman. Anderson said the initial idea for Nescaffier came from reading *The Power Broker*, Robert Caro's classic biography of Robert Moses, the master builder who transformed (some would say mangled) New York City during the post–World War II era. "Because all of his money came from tolls, not from government funding, Moses was able to create his own kingdom, and that included a private dining room on Randall's Island, and we had this idea of a police commissioner in our movie with his private dining room above something like Quai des Orfèvres, which is the old police headquarters on Île de la Cité in the middle of France—this massive building—and that somewhere in these labyrinthine quarters was a wonderful little kitchen, and it was run by this one incredible guy, and that guy needed to be played by Steve Park." As written, Nescaffier is as much of a virtuoso in his fiefdom as Roebuck, a euphoric prose stylist with a typographic memory, is in the world of letters. A lateral tracking shot across Nescaffier's kitchen reveals three Nescaffiers packed into the same space, cooking in multiple timelines like some culinary X-Man.

The role was a perfect fit for a variety of reasons, starting with the fact that Park has spent much of his career being the sort of actor that connoisseurs appreciate but whose life is never vexed by paparazzi. Soft-spoken and modest even when promoting a film he co-starred in, Park described his family history as

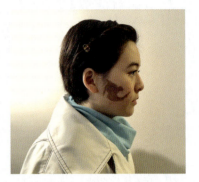

ABOVE: Photos from Stephen Park's moodboard, which helped inspire his performance as Nescaffier. Left to right: Filmmaker Bong Joon-Ho (on the night of his Oscar wins for his film *Parasite*, Bong dined with a group that included Park. When Park told Bong about Nescaffier, he mentioned that the character's bowl haircut was based on one of Park's photos of himself as a child. "[Bong] told me I looked like his grandfather," Park said, "and he pulled up a photo of his grandfather on his phone and showed me, and I took a picture of it and shared it with Wes"); Park as a young man; Park's daughter Eliza with the birthmark Saoirse Ronan's character wore in *The Grand Budapest Hotel*; Eliza as a crewmember of the *Belafonte* in *The Life Aquatic with Steve Zissou*

BOTTOM, FROM LEFT: Anderson, Park, Dafoe, Wright, and Yeoman on set

"a typical immigrant story," then proceeded to narrate a tale that was anything but: an epic comedy-drama of assimilation and generational change, packed with so much detail that listening to it was like watching a film unreel on a giant screen.

"My father got a medical degree at Seoul National University in Korea," Park said. "He did his residency in the US. Back then [the late 1950s], the US was getting a lot of people with medical degrees from other countries. There was a story about him taking a cab to Cumberland Hospital in Brooklyn, where he did his residency; he didn't have enough to pay for the cab, so he gave the cabdriver his camera." Born in 1962, Park spent his early childhood with his sister in Clinton Hill, Brooklyn, a tough neighborhood back then. "There was urine in the elevator. There were stabbings in the lobby. One time a woman came and knocked on our door and asked if she could be let in and stay for a while—a domestic violence–type situation." In the late 1960s, Park's father got a residency at Memorial Sloan Kettering hospital in Manhattan. As the family car pulled away from the old apartment building, Park saw that there were armed guards ringing the block. "Something had happened. I don't know what. But I remember a guy with a rifle."

A couple of years later, the Parks relocated to upstate New York, and Park graduated from high school, went to college, traded premed for theater, and tried to make a go of it as a stand-up comic for several years before realizing "very late in the game that stand-up comedy really wasn't for me." Park now lives in Brooklyn again with his wife, Kelly Coffield Park—also a former *In Living Color* cast member—and their two daughters, one of whom is a Wes Anderson superfan who dresses up as his characters on Halloween.

The experience of playing Nescaffier opposite Wright as Roebuck—and being part of the ensemble of a film that is, at least in part, a consideration of what it means to be "from" somewhere—caused Park to reflect on his parents' experience, and his. He says that, for him, the film captures a sense of what it means to feel like a part of a place while also standing apart from it. Park has wrestled with those contradictory feelings all through his life, whether he was protesting discriminatory casting practices in college in the 1980s, drafting a 1997 "mission statement" from the set of *Friends* asking the entertainment industry to offer better roles for Asians, or figuring out how to make a character like Sonny in *Do the Right Thing*—a minor part in a panoramic ensemble—seem more complex without making a famous auteur feel as if a day player was rewriting his script.

Park has always been adept at the second thing. He is especially proud of improvised touches that added subtext to his characters, such as the moment in *Do the Right Thing* where Sonny establishes political solidarity by telling one of the cornermen, "You, me . . . same," and the little behavioral touches in *Fargo* that suggest that Mike Yanagita, who deceives a police officer into believing that his wife died of cancer, might be mentally ill.

Nescaffier was a bigger role than Park often got—big enough that he finally received his first "starring" credit on a poster[1]—and that meant he had a bigger sandbox to play in. There was enough room to make a statement, should he choose to go that route—and he did. Reading early drafts of pages from the Roebuck segment, then the whole, finished script, Park realized that many of Anderson's characters were high-achieving creatives who had voluntarily relocated to unfamiliar terrain to reinvent themselves. The emigrant's tension—between being *in* a place but not always feeling *of* a place; between feeling pride in the new self they created and sadness at the parts that had to be suppressed or jettisoned—connected to Park's experience, and inspired his prep work. Before shooting began, he created a mood board to develop his notion of Nescaffier as a guru or shaman, but one who kept his own counsel and communicated with others mainly through his creative work as a chef. Park's collection of inspirational images included everything from photos of Jeong Kwan, the Korean-born Seon Buddhist nun who became famous via Netflix's *Chef's Table*, to a stock photo of a stopwatch (symbolizing the character's precision and sense of timing) to a snapshot of young Park in the sixties with a bowl haircut like Nescaffier's.

Park was particularly interested in evoking a "spiritual" quality through his performance. This goal was largely inspired by his study of Jeong, whom he describes as "the mother of everyone she's feeding" and "a person who wants to spread joy through food." Park also drew on his own spiritual practices, which include extensive meditation, reading, and studies with the likes of Don Miguel Ruiz, author of *The Four Agreements*. His notes include a reproduction of "The Four Reminders," a set of Buddhist prompts meant to serve as a reminder of what is real:

**1**
Maintain
*an awareness of the
preciousness of human life.*

**2**
Be aware
*of the reality that life ends;
death comes for everyone.*

**3**
Recall
*that whatever you do,
whether virtuous or not, has a result;
what goes around comes around.*

**4**
Contemplate
*that as long as you are too focused on
self-importance and too caught up in thinking
about how you are good or bad, you will suffer.
Obsessing about getting what you want and
avoiding what you don't want does not
result in happiness.*

---

[1] "I had no idea until I saw the poster that I was going to be on it," Park said. "I came home after I found out and told my wife, 'I feel like I've been anointed.'"

Wes Anderson directs Park in the kitchen set.

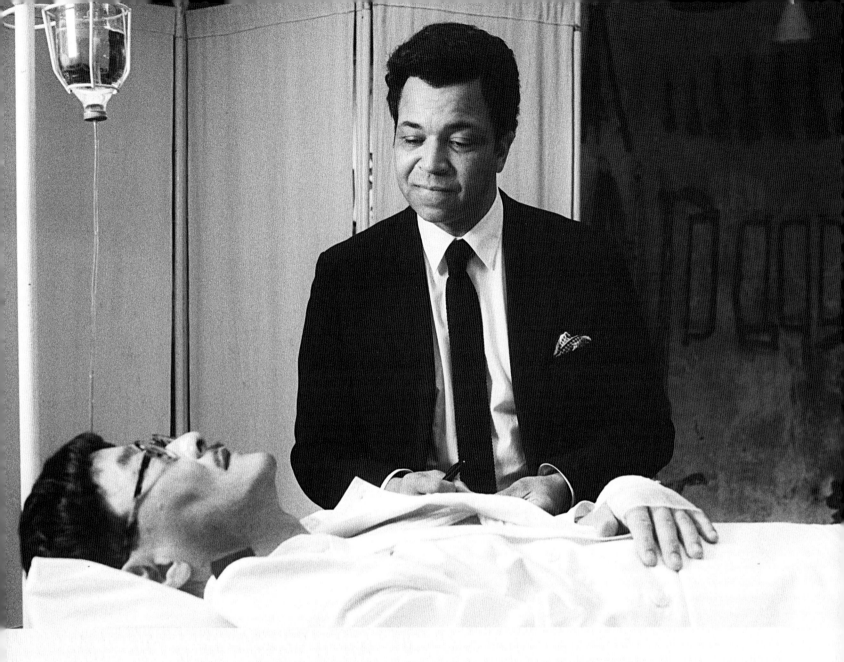

ABOVE: Still-frame from *The French Dispatch*: two expatriates, Nescaffier (Stephen Park, prone) and Roebuck Wright (Jeffrey Wright), find common ground.

OPPOSITE: Wright preparing to begin his guided tour of the police station

Park also spent many hours with a professional chef who taught him to look like an expert in the kitchen. "He showed me how to sharpen a knife. That was the main thing: I wanted to do it like him. He did it so fluently and so fast. I had three or four knives in my [hotel] room. I practiced and practiced. *Click click click, chww chww chww,*" he says, imitating a knife-sharpening sound. "The kind of performance that Wes likes, and the kind of performance I was after, was very much like a dance, so I wanted to perfect my actions as a chef and do them as economically, fluidly, and gracefully as I possibly could, to try to convey that dancer-ly feeling."

All this work was in service to a character that, in the end, would occupy a few minutes of screen time. But Park says he's never daunted by the imbalance between the labor required to make a thing and the thing itself, because you can sense the former in the latter even when the artist doesn't draw attention to it. The resulting performance feels like a summation of everything Park has done to date—including the sense that, like Roebuck, and like Steve Park, Nescaffier still bears a bit of the immigrant or expatriate or model minority's psychological burden, a faint sense of dislocation even when things are going well, coupled with an anxiety that he has to be better at his job than every other person in the profession if he's to be treated as an equal.

"Nescaffier has that kind of spirit, a feeling of being somebody who is just wanting to spread joy through his food. But there is also this quality that is depressed, because of all that weight he carries," he said. "In the end, he says he's not a hero—he just didn't want to let everybody down. I saw him as living kind of a monk's existence. I wanted there to be a feeling of loneliness, or aloneness. For Nescaffier, as for so many of the characters in the film, there is a humility in knowing that he's an immigrant here. And honestly, that's how I survive, too, making sure that I'm at the top of my field and doing the best I can possibly do."

"That scene with Nescaffier and Roebuck Wright was one that I was looking forward to seeing these actors play," Anderson said, "because I think it gets to the heart of a lot of what interested me about so many of these characters. It's significant that Roebuck Wright shares that moment with Nescaffier where they're talking about being foreigners, and what it means. There's something a bit sad about it, but also something inspiring. You need two great actors to get it all across."

## THE RHYTHM OF THE WORDS

"**I** WANT music," said Jeffrey Wright, scrunching into a wingback chair in his New York apartment many months after returning from filming *The French Dispatch*. "That's what I look for on the page. I tend to view language as musical. And I even see storytelling as musical, in that there are rhythms and there are melodies within, and there is timing that allows certain things to happen. And there are tacit moments, moments that are crescendo, and all that stuff. More than anything else, it is the music of language and story that I love, that really touches me, and there's poetry and imagery and allusion and wit and all of those things inside of it. All of those things, for me, make up notes in a song that I try to play. All of these matters are expressed in how Roebuck Wright speaks, and in how he writes. The writing and speaking are extensions of each other—or the same thing expressed by different means."

All of this, dear reader, was Wright's answer to a query: "How did you end up acting in *The French Dispatch*?"

Can't you hear Wright saying it all in his low-tide baritone, finessing each fully formed thought just so? Every syllable that he uttered had that mellifluous, hyperfocused, yet improbably casual Jeffrey Wright quality, which just happens to sound like Roebuck Wright. The actor was not in character that afternoon, but you could hear the fictional writer speaking through him. It was easy to see why Anderson conceived the role for him, and wrote it in a manner that he imagined would play to his strengths.

Wright is a superstar character actor in the vein of Gene Hackman, Robert Duvall, Michael Kenneth Williams, Philip Seymour Hoffman, and Gary Oldman: not sleek or glamorous, but so imaginative and magnetic that it scarcely matters. Anderson has been a fan of Wright's since the nineties, when he saw him in *Basquiat* and Suzan-Lori Park's play *Topdog/Underdog*. He became enraptured by Wright's spellbinding control over dialogue, and kept his name on a mental list of actors that he hoped to work with someday.

In summer 2018, when Wright was finishing work on season two of HBO's *Westworld*, Anderson arranged to meet him at Café Select in New York to ascertain his interest in joining the cast of *The French Dispatch*. Anderson told the actor that Roebuck Wright was an amalgam of several legendary writers—"a lot of Baldwin, a bit of Liebling, a dash of Tennessee

Arthur Howitzer (Bill Murray) does "last looks" on Wright's piece as a character identified in the credits as Cheery Writer (Wallace Wolodarsky) stands by.

Williams in there"—but warned that he didn't have script pages to show yet because he was "still tweaking it." Then he flew to Paris, and a couple of weeks later the tweaked pages landed in Wright's email inbox.

"He sent me the scenes that were set inside the office of *The French Dispatch,* and he sent me Roebuck Wright's story," Wright said. "How do you describe it? I could tell you that reading this material was like hearing a song on the radio for the first time and having the melody immediately sear itself into your brain. It was just such wonderful music, of the sort that I enjoy listening to and playing. I was hypnotized by the words on the page. It was just meticulously crafted, as expected, and so detailed, down to the placement of each comma. Of course I said 'yes.' At that early stage, my interest was entirely about the language and about the words, which I think is fitting because *The French Dispatch* is a story about those things. I was trying to craft in my head a body that those words could inhabit. The initial preparation process was focused on the narrative, the paragraphs, the sentences, and the structure."

In retrospect it seems odd that it took this long for Anderson and Wright to find each other, so complimentary are their aesthetics. Both have a strong affinity for the stage—from *Rushmore* and *The Royal Tenenbaums* up through *Moonrise Kingdom, The Grand Budapest Hotel,* and *The French Dispatch,* Anderson's films are packed with plays and allusions to plays, while Wright, for all his feature-film experience, still prefers to approach roles as if they were stage creations, inhabiting sets that get finished in the spectator's mind (which, truly, is what soundstage sets are, especially on Wes Anderson's productions). Wright speaks of Anderson's directing as a "cinematic proscenium that allows him to create worlds and contain them. That allows actors such as myself who are experienced on the stage to easily step inside them. But it also means that we are more likely to be drawn into them in the first place, because they are framed in a way that makes them innately alluring to us."

And then there's the temperament thing. Both Anderson and Wright stay laser-focused on minutiae even as they try to keep the big picture in mind. Both treat creative expression not just as an intellectual exercise but a logistical challenge. Who better to anchor a narration-heavy film's most narration-heavy segment—a nesting-doll contraption in the spirit of *The Grand Budapest Hotel* that unfolds across four time periods and makes space for flamboyantly unreal touches, including direct address, expressionistic

Anderson directs the dinner at the home of the police commissioner.

> "You can be a stranger in a strange land, and you can be a stranger in a strange land in your own land."
>
> —JEFFREY WRIGHT

lighting changes, breakaway walls, and animation—than a stage-trained film actor who has, time and again, proven himself at ease speaking sentences as long and convoluted as the one you just read? Wright's characters from *Boardwalk Empire, Westworld, The Manchurian Candidate, Angels in America,* and *Boycott* (where he played the Reverend Dr. Martin Luther King) are all, to borrow Roebuck Wright's words, "typographic creations," enclosed by a nimbus of language: written, spoken, dreamed. This new character was another wizard of words, formidable even when wounded.

Wright did wonder, based on those tweaked-but-not-finished pages, whether he, Anderson, and the cast and crew could answer all of the questions he still had. "My first question was, 'Who is this guy?'" Wright said. "I mean, aside from the literary touchstones that Wes might have used to craft him, who is this guy as a character? Why has he escaped his country and found himself in Ennui? What things drove him away from his home country, and what things drew him to this new place? The character as I found him was very much about that journey, and also—like all the other writers—about being an expat. And yet, specifically for him, as a Black, gay man in his mid-to-late fifties when he arrives, I just needed to know more. Chiefly, what are the things inside him and what are those things outside of him that bring him to where he is when we find him at the start of this story? All those questions needed to be answered. And they were interesting ones for me to think through, because they were already hinted at in those pages. They were hinted at in how Roebuck Wright comports himself and how he speaks, as well as in all the other externals that he had to craft in order to exist in the new world that he had chosen after having fled the world into which he was born. It was clear that this was going to be a fascinating journey for me, and for Wes as well."

Anderson hadn't thought that far ahead when he considered casting Wright: Mostly, he just wanted to work with him. Anderson confesses that initially he "approached [the character] mainly from the point of view of somebody who has chosen to live abroad, and who has had to come to terms with the fact that when you do that, you've consciously chosen a life that is isolating in some way."

Anderson imagined Wright ". . . doing the scene where Roebuck, who writes about food, talks about the solitary feast, and about being alone in a foreign country and going to dinner on his own, because that's something that I think I understand, and it's something he shares with so many characters that I think of as possibly lonely figures, especially Lucinda Krementz."

"This city is full of us, isn't it?" Roebuck asks Nescaffier. "I'm one, myself."

"Seeking something missing," the chef replies. "Missing something left behind."

"Maybe, with good luck, we'll find what eluded us, in the place that we once called home," the writer concludes.

Anderson says the actor's imagination helped refine Roebuck Wright as a Black man who identifies as "homosexual" (the nomenclature of the era) and is persecuted for both characteristics; who still feels inescapably American, even though the hatefulness of America drove him to France; and who, at the time of his first meeting with Howitzer in jail, was starting to accept that when it comes to those sorts of attitudes, France is no paradise, either.

The challenge for Anderson, as Wright saw it, was "being appreciative of the limitations of his own experience and research while at the same time infusing the gaps with as much craft and outside input as he possibly could. That's what actors do as well, and this part was written in such a way as to allow me to fill in whatever gaps I thought existed. For instance, while I myself am not an expatriate gay man, I like to think I have a compassionate heart and an understanding of sexual fluidity and the expat mentality, and there was plenty of historical precedent for that sort of character that was readily available for me to draw upon. So I did. And of course," he says, drawing himself up to full height and cracking a mischievous smile, "I have personal experiences of my own as a Black man in America and all the shit that potentially dredges up, and I was more than willing to bring them into play!"

What unified every aspect of the film for Wright was the sense that the major characters were all in a sort of "self-created limbo" that "hopefully will speak to a lot of people, in America and other countries, at this moment in time. You can be a stranger in a strange land, and you can be a stranger in a strange land in your own land, if you know what I mean. Given all that, the question then becomes: Where does one find, or take, solace? *The French Dispatch* offers a partial answer. The magazine's writers are all misfits who, to some extent, have found shelter in this place that allows them to do what they love, which is write and create, and to have permission to do so. A lot of Wes Anderson characters have this predicament in common—including, if I may be so bold, Wes Anderson himself," he said, laughing. "In that respect, the legitimacy of Wes's observations seems to me undeniable."

ABOVE, LEFT:
Mauricette Couvidat's street casting photo

ABOVE, RIGHT:
Still-frame image of Couvidat in full costume and makeup as Maman

## "THE BIG VEGETABLE"

In the eponymous private dining room of the police commissioner, actually a soundstage at the Felt Factory in Angoulême, Mauricette Couvidat, aka Maman, felt as if she'd gone Hollywood.

She liked it.

It had been several months since the Angoulême native was interviewed in a drugstore on the basis of her foghorn voice and hand-drawn-doodle silhouette (see page 68). Prior to being cast as the Commissaire's mother, Couvidat had appeared only in one other production, an "amateur movie made by friends" titled *Adieu, Dino*. Strangely, her character was named Gigi, just like the boy in Anderson's film, and there was a kidnapping plot: Couvidat played a member of a pedophile ring that abducted the daughter of a drug dealer. She did not consider herself an actor at the time, and still doesn't.

"I mostly did [the other movie] to have fun," she said. "It played three times at the cinema in Espace Franquin. The filmmakers advertised it and people came to see it, some of them because they knew me. So when Wes Anderson's people asked me to do this one, I said 'yes' right away. Why not? It was a really great experience because they were professionals. It was completely different from the other movie."

She thought about how different during the shooting of the sequence where the gang abducts Gigi (Winsen Ait Hellal) while Nescaffier (Park) cooks for Roebuck Wright (Wright), Maman, the Commissaire (Mathieu Amalric), and his oldest friend Chou-fleur (Hippolyte Girardot), who "looks like a corpse." The main job that day was a high-speed, low-angled tracking shot that circled the table as the diners sipped a beverage described in the script as a "lilac-colored" aperitif (the color proved unimportant anyway, as this particular shot ended up being in black-and-white). Key grip Sanjay Sami pushed cinematographer Robert Yeoman around a circular piece of dolly track on a platform. Off camera, Anderson read Roebuck Wright's voice-over narration to help time the words with the movements of the camera and the actors. "The drink, a milky, purplish aperitif, ferociously fragrant, overtly medicinal, ever-so-faintly anesthetizing (and cooled to a glacial viscosity in a miniature version of the type of vacuum-flask normally associated with campsites and schoolrooms) cast a spell," Anderson intoned, as the camera circled and circled, the dolly wheels going *whirrrrrr* on the tracks, "which, during the subsequent sixty-second interval, was to be mortally broken. On three overlapping dramatic timelines, the following events came to pass . . ."

"I didn't really know Wes Anderson before this, because I've never seen his movies," Couvidat admitted. "But people started telling me about him, and I learned that he's very good at what he does." She now calls him Le Grand Légume, which roughly translates as "the big vegetable," like the Anglais honorific The Big Cheese.

"On set, everyone was very attentive with me," Couvidat said. "I was treated like a princess. I felt completely comfortable. I kept calling Wes Anderson 'Monsieur Anderson,' but he asked me to call him Wes. It felt strange because he's Le Grand Légume, such a bigwig, so I wanted to be respectful. All the technicians, no matter what their job was, were also very nice to me. So I'll have a very good memory of this. There was the one who played the cook, Stephen Park, and there was Mathieu Amalric, and Hippolyte Girardot, who played the friend, and Jeffrey Wright, and they all asked me who my agent was. And I said, 'I don't have an agent. I'm nobody. I take care of the elderly for a living.' Everyone thought I was a real actress. But I'm not! I'm just a simple and normal lady."

Couvidat was initially most intimidated by Matheiu Amalric, a character actor/movie star/producer/national treasure in his home country, on par with an American star like Robert Duvall in the 1970s or Tom

ABOVE: Wes prepares for the post-poisoning tracking shot from "The Private Dining Room of the Police Commissioner" segment.

OPPOSITE: Wes Anderson and Mathieu Amalric on set

Hanks in the 1990s. She had been a fan of his for years. She stayed mostly quiet on the first day of shooting because she was so overwhelmed by the scale and proficiency of the production and so daunted by being in the same room with Amalric and all of the other career performers, and didn't want to embarrass herself.

"It's humbling because you're surrounded by professional actors, who rehearse, work on intonation, gestures," she said, "but I just followed instructions, doing whatever Wes asked of me. Mathieu often wanted to hang out with me because I had a lot of funny stories, so we had a lot of funny moments together."

By day two, Couvidat had settled into the job and was more relaxed, trading chitchat and anecdotes with the other performers, sprinkling profanity into her language, then escalating to filthy jokes. "For somebody so salty, Mauricette was extremely respectful and gentle and well-mannered on the set," said Anderson, "even though Mathieu and Hippolyte would tell me later that their private conversations were extremely obscene! She was telling them wild stuff! But her manner on the set was immediately impeccable and everybody loved her."

"Of course she didn't speak much English, but she was so authentic and had a great voice," said Park. "Everything about her makes you think, 'My God, I can't believe this woman wasn't a movie star.'"

Not only did Couvidat never imagine this sort of experience for herself, but she simply considers herself fortunate to have survived the hardships in her life and to have emerged in one piece. Compared with everything she's been through, performance anxiety on a film set is nothing.

"I'm a widow," she said, pouring a glass of wine and leaning back in a creaky chair at her kitchen table. "My husband is dead. He committed suicide. I lived in Bordeaux before, then I moved to Angoulême. I have two sons. One is forty-three years old and the other forty. I don't have anyone in my life. I'm single. But I'm fine with it. I enjoy my freedom and I work a lot, too. I work with the elderly, who are in the last phase of life: terminal. Most recently, one of my charges had a stroke and died in my arms. Of course that sort of thing happens often. But let's just say it suits me and I like what I do, because I like the elderly, I love people. None of that prevents me from going out.

"I lived in Bordeaux from 1973 to 1984," she continued. "I still have a sister who lives in Bordeaux, so I go there often. It's a city I know well, and it's very pretty. While I was there, I worked at the Poudreriem in Saint-Médard-en-Jalles, a historic weapons manufacturer that started out making cannon fodder in the eighteenth century. My husband was a jealous man,

and he loved alcohol. He was cheating on me, and I told him to leave, but his mistresses didn't want him. Or maybe he didn't want to be with them. But I told him I have my dignity. It's one thing to be *cocu, battu,*[2] but at some point you can't ignore it anymore, and you get your things and get out."

She decided to make her escape after a long period in which her husband had been beating her regularly. She warned him that if he ever hit her again, she'd leave and take their sons with her. There was a period of no violence. Then one night they got into an argument over the house—he wanted her to sign it over to him, and she refused. She finally signed under duress, and he hit her anyway. "And I said 'Enough, I'm not married to these walls,' and I packed my suitcases and I left with just the kids." They took a train to her parents' house in Angoulême, where they stayed for fifteen days. Then she and her sons moved into a domestic violence shelter. She interviewed for jobs, found work, and moved into a new apartment. She's lived in Angoulême ever since.

"You can't save someone who's sick, you know?" she said. "But what saved me is my character. If I hadn't had character, who knows what would have happened? I had two boys, so I had to think of them. It's not easy raising two boys alone, because they're boys, but I don't let people take advantage of me. So I left Bordeaux to get away from my husband, and he didn't accept the divorce, so he killed himself. But please don't feel bad. I was relieved. I was a happy widow. It's not something you're supposed to say, but it's the truth! I landed in Angoulême because I'm originally from Angoulême and I knew the city. I've been here ever since. Like I told my lawyer and notary: I'm not married to walls. I can rebuild my life. With people like my husband, I'd rather be single. Don't worry; I've had adventures. I didn't escape to a convent. But now I'm nearly seventy years old. My sons come over every night for supper because I love to cook. And they're happy to come over for a meal at Mommy's."

She fell silent for a moment.

"When I left my husband," she said at last, "I was like a butterfly. I was so happy. I felt so good about myself. I can't live with dominant people. I want to be respected. I respect others and I expect the same."

Then her demeanor brightens and she begins talking about Matheiu Amalric again.

"One time, while we were eating, Mathieu lost his fake mustache. With the light of his cell phone, he looked for it on the floor. I told him, 'My poor Mathieu, you won't find your mustache there. You'll find it tomorrow when you go to the bathroom.' And everyone laughed. Mathieu never did find his mustache. The makeup artist had to make him a new one." ♠

[2] Roughly, "cheated on, beat up."

# ON RAILS

PART VIII

"IF I didn't tell you what I did, you'd never know what I did."

That could be the motto of a great stage magician—but it's a line from Wes Anderson's key grip Sanjay Sami, an illusionist of a different sort.

Anderson and Sami have a unique relationship: Sami's the person who figures out how to pull off camera moves that the director has been warned are impossible. *The French Dispatch* would prove to be the culmination of their decade-plus partnership, which spans four features and multiple commercials. In addition to all the sinuous camera moves scattered throughout the other segments of *The French Dispatch*, Anderson had written a spectacular, showstopping, can-you-even-believe-it dolly shot that followed Roebuck Wright through police headquarters as he described the place in voice-over. On paper, it read like a more controlled and hyperkinetic version of the crane shots in *The Life Aquatic* that followed Steve Zissou and company throughout the bisected *Belafonte*.

Anderson told Sami that he wanted the camera to move laterally, seeming to pass through walls as it followed the narrator through the building; suddenly shifting direction by ninety degrees in order to walk in front of him; resuming lateral motion; and so on.

This would have been manageable (after a half day's rehearsal or so) were Anderson willing to film the scene with a Steadicam, a motion-stabilized handheld camera employed by many a virtuoso director. But he didn't want to use a Steadicam. He wanted everything done on dolly tracks because, as Sami put it, "there is a level of exactness to Wes's dolly shots that cannot be achieved with a handheld camera, even a Steadicam. The precision Wes demands is so great that you have to put the camera on tracks to get the effect that he wants. The stability, the rigidity, of a dolly is what makes it a Wes Anderson shot."

Sanjay Sami, Grip Olympics contestant and camera department engineering wizard

Anderson and Sami on the set of *The French Dispatch*

The big challenge was how to get a dolly shot on rails to switch direction by precisely ninety degrees without lifting the camera off the track or otherwise "cheating" in some manner. Anderson wanted the entire scene to unfold in one continuous motion: a zig and a zag, smooth and tight. There seemed to be a consensus going into the production that the shot could only happen if Sami built something that no filmmaker had ever used before.

Sami was game. This wasn't the first time Anderson had asked him to work a miracle. He'd done it several times already. You might even say it was the basis of their friendship.

Based in Mumbai, Sami has been a key grip for nearly thirty years. He worked in Bollywood at first, then branched out into international productions, amassing more than eighty credits on feature films, TV series, music videos, and commercials, and working for Martin Scorsese, David Fincher, the Akhtar siblings, Tarsem Singh, Mira Nair, and other filmmakers of note.

Sami is famed for his ingenuity. He's part filmmaker, part mad scientist, going into a workshop and creating rigs, tracks, and other contraptions that will allow directors to execute shots that normal commercial equipment won't permit. It's bespoke filmmaking that matches the mentality of Anderson, who wears custom-made suits, builds sets to match hand-drawn animatics, and brings an animator's sensibility to live action (and vice versa).

Sami's association with Anderson started with *The Darjeeling Limited,* which was shot in India. The director came to Sami with a daunting challenge: He wanted to follow the actors up and down train corridors at a variety of speeds, stopping and starting on a dime; they couldn't, however, capture the graceful movements Anderson wanted in the default way, by following the actors with a handheld, smooth-gliding Steadicam, because Anderson was determined to shoot on an actual train, not on a soundstage with rear-projected backdrops, and the passenger cars they'd selected had hallways the width of a grown man's shoulders. In addition, *Darjeeling* was to be shot on 35mm film, in anamorphic wide-screen format. That meant the cameras were big and heavy and could barely fit into the hallways of the passenger cars, much less dance through them.

They were deep into preproduction when Sami devised a solution. The train's ceilings had been ripped out and the inner skins of the corridors removed by a team led by production designer Mark Friedberg. Friedberg was getting ready to redecorate and repaint everything with a team of local artists and craftspeople. Sami looked at the gutted ceilings and realized that if they embedded a very long track in the middle, running the entire length of the car, they could then add a sort of makeshift tripod mount, embed it onto the track, and attach a 35mm motion-picture camera to the mount. Then they could drag or push the camera forward and backward along that single piece of overhead track. Easy-peasy.

Anderson, Bob Yeoman, and Friedberg endorsed Sami's concept, but Friedberg worried that the track in the ceiling would need to be disguised—otherwise it might be identifiable as camera track. Anderson wasn't worried. He believed that almost no one watching the film would be looking for clues as to how they did the shot. "And if they do notice the track," he said, "they'll think it's part of the ceiling."[1]

"And so we got ourselves a die maker," Sami said, "and we paid to have a custom extrusion of aluminum made." The extrusion, designed by Sami, was inspired by the narrow, strong beams that allow for the delicate movements of cranes and other equipment in factories. The camera mount fit snugly into the groove of the track. With just a little lubricant, they were able to move the camera forward and backward through the hallway, so smoothly and quickly that sometimes the result looked as if it had been achieved with a miniature version of a Steadicam, or one of those "flying" Skycams that cover sports and concerts. Friedberg told him later that if he hadn't come up with the overhead rig, the camera wouldn't have had as much freedom of motion, and audiences wouldn't have been as able to appreciate the beauty of the passenger train interiors.

On *Moonrise Kingdom,* Sami didn't have one main challenge that was immense and project-defining, but he was handed numerous smaller ones that all required ingenious, low-tech solutions that wouldn't blow the production's modest budget. An outdoor shot from the point of view of a running dog was accomplished by attaching a lightweight 16mm motion-picture camera to a stick, holding the lens at dog height, sprinting with it, then checking the dailies from the lab the following day to see if they got any usable footage.[2] A shot from the point of view of a flying arrow proved more vexing. They tried swinging the camera from a rope, but it looked like they were swinging a camera from a rope. They ended

---

1   By this point in our story, it should be clear where Arthur Howitzer's maxim "Try to make it seem like you did it that way on purpose" comes from.

2   Film cameras usually have video monitors that produce an image by inserting a video "tap" into the lens housing and feeding the signal into a nearby monitor by way of a length of cable. The *Moonrise* crew couldn't use monitors to check the dog POV shots because the additional equipment would have added weight to the cameraperson's load, restricting their speed and range of motion.

> *"When you stop the camera, or slow it down and speed it up again, it's all punctuation. It's a comma, it's an ellipse, it's a full stop."* —SANJAY SAMI

up mounting a lightweight camera to the front of a motorized dirt bike.

"Our attitude about all of that kind of stuff was that if we just kept doing it over and over, one of the shots would be right," Sami said. "That's always Wes's attitude about getting results. He always says, 'We'll know when it looks right.'"

The dolly shots on *The Grand Budapest Hotel* needed to be "a level up" from *Moonrise,* Sami said, because Anderson had achieved most of the goals he set for himself on *Moonrise* and wanted a new challenge. The *Grand Budapest* crew was "undaunted" because they knew Anderson was once again applying the lessons of animation to live action. All they had to do was figure out how to make the shots look like Anderson's animatics.

"Everyone is there, ideally, to execute a vision that they can all see because it was crystal clear in the storyteller's mind to begin with, and because he communicated it to us visually by actually *showing* us what we're supposed to try to do," Sami said.

"That is not to say that Wes plans everything or accounts for everything, and we just execute, and that's it," he clarifies. "There's always an element of mystery. The process of execution is not clear to him. But the picture that he has of the end result is clear, and that helps us achieve the goals that he sets for us. And that's good, because Wes is well aware of the obsessional nature of these sorts of shots, as well as the ingenuity and labor that they require of others. One time he confided in me, 'Sanjay, I think my condition might be getting worse!'"

Sami theorizes that Anderson's fine-grained visual style came out of his writing, which is similarly exact. There's not much room for verbal improvisation in a Wes Anderson picture because the dialogue is written to mirror, complicate, or intensify Anderson's filmmaking choices. Every ellipsis, comma, colon, semicolon, exclamation point, parenthetical, and period in a line of dialogue complements the camera movements, lighting, visual effects, sound effects, and music. It's all of a piece. Filmmaking is screenwriting, screenwriting is filmmaking. All is text. The discrete shots are phrases, sentences, or paragraphs within the larger manuscript of the film. Words matter. Punctuation matters. Sentence length matters. The longer, more elaborate camera moves in a Wes Anderson picture could be compared to a monologue in the theater, or a run-on sentence in an essay or novel that keeps going and going till it finally stops.

"To me, a stop in a dolly move is a form of punctuation," Sami said. "When you stop the camera, or slow it down and speed it up again, or do whatever, it's all punctuation. It's a comma, it's an ellipse, it's a full stop. It could be the equivalent of underlining or italicizing just one or two words. I like to think that what happens in the filmmaking process when you're working for Wes is somewhat like the process that happens when an actor takes dialogue on the page and performs it, tweaking it a little bit every time until, as Wes would say, it *sounds* right. That's what happens when we're shooting one of these complex moves that stops and starts and changes direction. Going into the shot, Wes knows in a general way how he wants the camera to move, but he doesn't know exactly how to *punctuate* it. We have to figure all of that out as we go along. We have to discover how to make it sound right. It usually takes Wes six or seven takes to get one of these shots to the point where we can all see what the shot is actually going to be, and at that point, we can kind of let go and concentrate on perfecting it. Up until then, it's like we're rolling [film] during a rehearsal."

Anderson's commitment to shooting his live-action features on film intensifies everyone's focus, Sami said. "Your commitment to a shot becomes much more intense when you can hear the film running through the camera's gate." The number one rule is: *Don't stop.* Especially when you're walking in front of a camera rig that's mounted on a dolly. "Sometimes I'm moving a [camera rig] that weighs half a ton right behind an actor, at high speed, with the expectation that I'm going to follow along very closely all the way through the shot," said Sami. "I tell the actors, 'If you blow a line, if you stumble, if you do whatever, just keep going. Don't stop. Go off course or something if you have to, but keep going. Because it's not easy for me to stop this thing! It weighs half a ton!'"

Anderson doesn't get flustered if it takes a long time to get a tracking shot right, Sami said; he's gotten to the point where he's accepted that certain things are controllable and others have to happen ". . . organically and gradually. Wes tells everyone, 'We'll know that it's right when it's right.' We know that we finally got a shot that Wes is happy with when he says something like, 'Now we're gonna do one more for the fun of it,' or 'Let's do one more for the love of it.'"

Even so, Sami knew that the police station tracking shot would test everyone's patience. It was the most difficult shot in the film, and it had to be just right.

"It's the most complicated shot I've ever worked on in my life," he said. "When I got to that part of the script, I thought maybe I was reading it wrong, because there was no way you could do a dolly shot that long and that elaborate without a cut. I wrote an email to Wes and said, 'It looks like one shot.' He said, 'That's because it is.'"

Still-frame from the filming of the H&M Christmas TV commercial in which Sami first deployed a version of the 90-degree switching dolly track.

## "THE MANGALORE RIG"

Luckily, Sami came into *The French Dispatch* having already solved a similar (though less monumental) Wes Anderson challenge.

It happened on the set of a Christmas-themed 2016 ad that Anderson directed for the clothing retailer H&M titled "Come Together." Adrien Brody starred as Ralph, a train conductor who regretfully informs his passengers that their double-decker train has been subjected to snow delays that will "interfere with many of [their] holiday plans and celebrations." Ralph eases their distress by throwing an impromptu Christmas party on the moving train, complete with hot chocolates and a tree.

The first shot in the ad is a medium-wide image of Ralph in his conductor's compartment, the edges of the window creating a frame within the frame. As Ralph speaks into the train's public address system, the camera advances closer to him, backs away, tracks right, rises to reveal the upper level, tracks left, then moves down, returning our gaze to Ralph's window. Each directional shift is exactly ninety degrees.

Anderson insisted that the entire shot be done on dolly tracks because that was the only way to achieve the effect he wanted. "A Steadicam would never work for the level of precision that Wes requires—that thing where you're moving pretty fast and then suddenly—bang!—you do a hard stop and go back the other way," said Sami. "That motion is characteristic of a Wes Anderson shot. You can only achieve it by putting the camera on rails."

Sami went into his workshop and custom-built pieces of dolly track just for that shot. They were linked together in the manner of the wooden toy train sets manufactured by the Brio toy company. Brio train sets consist of straight and curved track pieces of varying length that join together like jigsaw puzzle pieces, and can be arranged in any configuration that the railroad builder desires.

Then came the masterstroke: Sami invented a two-tiered system of dolly track and found a way to switch between the tiers, in the way that real trains switch from one track to another at a full-sized real-world railroad yard. Now Anderson's dolly shots could move in a grid system, going forward and backward, then left or right, in a continuous, smooth motion.

The H&M setup consisted of long, solid pieces of track joined at perpendicular angles to a third piece of track. At each end of the third piece were breakaway segments of track with wheels affixed to the bottoms—basically, these were second dollies that were joined to that third piece of track but could be released by removing a small pin. Once the pin came out, the now-detached end piece of track was free to wheel along the piece of track that it was already sitting on. The dolly platform containing the camera and the camera operators was suddenly carried along atop the detachable, wheeled end pieces. Basically, Sami had figured out a way to put a dolly platform on top of another dolly platform. That second platform was actually a breakaway piece of track that you'd never know was detachable until an assistant cameraperson pulled the pin that set it free.

It was weird-looking, but it worked. And the result was a Wes Anderson dolly shot—a specific kind of shot that Sami loves to describe because his engineering genius made it possible.

"There is a rigidity to Wes's dolly shots that is reminiscent of shots in animation," said Sami. "And of course this was inevitable: I think at this point it's clear to everyone that Wes has dived deeply enough into animation that the style has begun to spill over into his live-action films. Our main job now is to match Wes's cartoons, and make the result feel seamless. The only reason such a thing is even possible is because Wes has done all the preparation and given us the clearest instructions that we could possibly get. He's shown us the shot before we've done it."

Anderson was overjoyed when Sami showed him the sketches. Sami's creation looked like something out of an as-yet-unmade Wes Anderson film about a brilliant, toy-obsessed kid who grows up to become a key grip.

Anderson told Sami, "You need to name this," so Sami dubbed the contraption "The Mangalore rig," after the region of India where he happened to be working while he and Anderson planned the H&M ad over the phone.

The Mangalore rig would never be used again. None of the contraptions that Sami creates for Anderson are ever used again.

"Each one of these things is a prototype," Sami said. "It's a prototype built for the day of the shoot, to suit the requirements of the shot and the set. And we build it knowing that once we've used it, it's done."

Sami went through the same type of creative process while planning the police-station shot. But it was more intense because the shot was supposed to last four minutes and cover a lot more ground. Anderson told Sami that they could use the Mangalore rig as a starting point. But the problem was, there was a lot more ground to cover, and a lot more changes in direction, some of them quite dramatic.

Anderson briefly considered building the police station interior at the armory where they'd shot many of the prison scenes but changed his mind and decided to create the entire thing from scratch at the Felt Factory, leaning on their old friend plywood. Four weeks elapsed from the moment that Anderson decided to build the set to the day they finally shot the scene.

"That included building the set, designing that set, dressing it, creating it," said co-producer Octavia Peissel, "and it was the length of one entire, crazy stage. The camera move itself had three ninety-degree direction changes in it, and dollies stacked on top of dollies. You could look at a diagram of how it was done and still not understand it. But the really amazing thing about it was it had to be so choreographed. Guys had to be boxing in the gym at the exact right time. Guns had to fire at exactly the right time in the shooting range. Everybody had to bustle through as Jeffrey walked in the space at exactly the right time, and everything else around them had to work out."

Art director Kevin Timon Hill calls the police station dolly shot "the single hardest thing in the shoot," and the scene that he and other crewmembers are proudest of. "We'd gone so quickly to get that set made, and everyone put in 150 percent," Timon Hill said. "The relief of seeing that camera move down the track, and seeing how Sanjay did all these amazing direction changes—I loved seeing all that come to life! We tried to get the whole dolly with all the direction changes in one go, through seven sets and three corridors."

**Special effects team members on ladders ready the "shooting range" portion of the police station set as Sanjay Sami prepares to push the dolly down an enormously long track.**

TOP: The Commissaire in the disguises room, dressed as a priest, presumably in preparation to go undercover

RIGHT: Recruits hone their pugilistic techniques in the gymnasium.

OPPOSITE: Signage, graphic elements, and a city map featured in the police station sequence

| | | | | |
|---|---|---|---|---|
| ABANDONED VEHICLES | 5ᵉ ét. | 6ᵉ ét. | PERSONNES DISPARUES | |
| CRIME LAB | 4ᵉ ét. | 5ᵉ ét. | NIGHT CRIME | |
| BRIGADE ANTI-BOMBES | 2ᵉ ét. | 3ᵉ ét. | MILIEU TASK FORCE | |
| FAUSSES ALARMES | 3ᵉ ét. | 2ᵉ ét. | PERMIS | |
| COMPTABILITÉ | Aile A | Ss-s. | MOTOR POOL | |
| BEAT COPS | 2ᵉ ét. | Aile D | STUPÉFIANTS | |
| DISPATCH | 1ᵉʳ ét. | 3ᵉ ét. | URGENCES | |
| OPÉRATIONS DE TERRAIN | Rdc | Rdc | PAYROLL | |
| FRAUDES | 1ᵉʳ ét. | Aile C | NOISE COMPLAINTS | |
| HITS AND RUNS | 3ᵉ ét. | 1ᵉʳ ét. | LABORATOIRE PHOTO | |
| FUGITIVE RECOVERY | Aile B | 4ᵉ ét. | PSYCHIATRIE | |
| HOMICIDES | 3ᵉ ét. | 5ᵉ ét. | HYPNOSE | |

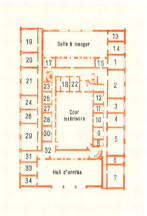

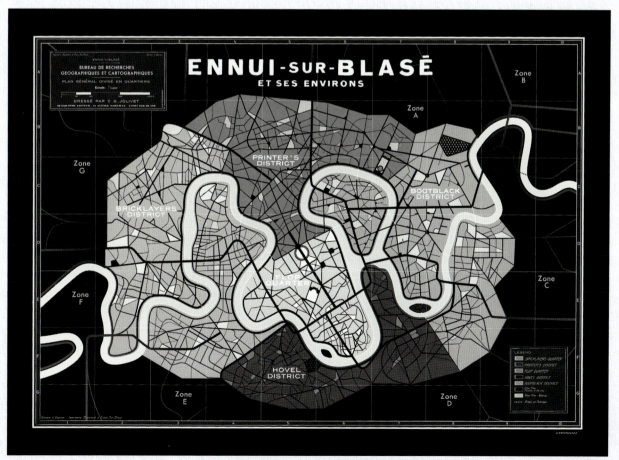

**CRIMES-IN-PROGRESS MAP**

For Wright, the shot was an opportunity to test theories of characterization and performance that he'd developed during the run-up to the shoot. These mainly had to do with Roebuck—a triple outsider thanks to his nationality, race, and sexual orientation—asserting control over his life and career by acquiring a virtuoso's mastery of language. The whole segment is presented as a recollection by Roebuck on an early 1970s talk show. The host—played by Liev Schreiber—questions, prods, and cajoles him between commercial breaks. Roebuck's account jumps around in time, touching on his early years in Angoulême, his first meeting with Howitzer, his thoughts on being a stranger in a strange land, and the physical experience of going to the police commissioner's private dining room to profile a legendary chef only to end up covering a violent kidnapping.

The tracking shot through the police station is the moment where all of the exposition that got us to this point starts to recede in the film's rearview mirror, and the segment morphs into a comedic action thriller—at times a borderline caper flick in the vein of Steven Soderbergh's heist pictures, or the heist genre's French granddaddy, Jules Dassin's 1955 classic, *Rififi*.

"My feeling was, Roebuck is not a guy who avoids affectation necessarily, you know?" said Wright. "So there's something in him when he comes [to France] that informs how he presents himself, something that reflects a tension between assimilation and freedom. When we first see him, he has—obviously in age, but also in aesthetic—evolved from the man we see at the beginning of his story, that broken man in that solitary cell known as the Chicken Coop. He has changed as he's lived, but he's also changed as the times have changed, in terms of how he presents himself to the world. The way he speaks, the way he carries himself, seemed to me like a way for me to comment on the balance between the Europe that the character chooses as his home and his Black American–ness."

The police station tracking shot, said Wright, allowed him to take control of the segment and Roebuck's story in the manner of a stage star taking the spotlight and delivering a dazzling monologue while executing a series of difficult actions with seemingly offhand grace.

"It's an act of incredible boldness and confidence, shooting the scene the way Wes shot it," Wright said, "and I think it shows Roebuck Wright at the peak of his confidence in the story, reciting from memory, and word for word, passages from his best-known magazine piece, for a rapt audience. Most delightfully, he turns the police station, a place that tends to be inhospitable to men such as himself, into a set, almost a playground, that Roebuck Wright is completely in control of. He has total freedom of movement in that shot, and no one else in the place acknowledges him or impedes his progress, because that's not actually *him* there in the station. He's there, but he's not there. He's revisiting the station in his memory, verbally painting us a picture of what it was like, taking

OPPOSITE: **Cinematographer Bob Yeoman walks through one length of Sami's dolly track.**

THIS PAGE: **A few of the areas that the camera travels through; from top: gymnasium, strategy room (featuring the map seen on page 167), and shooting range**

Cutaway set that reveals to audiences how Nescaffier's kitchen abuts the Commissioner's workspace, and the Locksmith's set opposite the kidnappers' lair, to which the Commissioner and his team decamp once the abduction has taken place.

**THIS SPREAD:** Detail images exploring the police station set. Clockwise from top left: Exterior of the photography department; the strategy room; list of disguise accessories made available to undercover police; an assortment of mustaches; the many wigs of the disguise room; sketches of alleged perpetrators

us through all of the different rooms and areas and so forth. The shot ends at the Chicken Coop, that solitary cell, the site of his abject humiliation, his brokenness. But because we've just seen a demonstration of his mastery, the moment doesn't bring us down, or even sting. It's poignant."

"[First assistant director] Ben Howard asked me after about twenty takes—when we were essentially finished with the shot—if he thought it might be a good idea for Jeffrey to deliver the dialogue directly to the camera rather than as voice-over," said Anderson. "And I said, 'Uh. Yes.' And Jeffrey said, 'I think I can.' And he could."

"I wish everyone reading this could have been there," said Dawson. "Jeffrey was incredible. And the boom operator [Damien Luquet] was just as impressive. I have a vision of him sort of dancing backward, in and out of camera range, to keep up with Jeffrey, with the camera moving constantly and everybody breaking a sweat."

"The ambition and absurdity of these shots [are] something that you have to get used to," said Sami. "I remember all of these moments on *Grand Budapest* where Ralph [Fiennes] was called upon to do ridiculous, undignified things in the name of getting the shot Wes wanted. One time Ralph was asked to sit on the back of this ridiculous contraption with Tony and pretend they were riding a motorcycle. Because he's so English, he was never shocked by anything, including requests that anyone who has never worked with Wes would be shocked by; but even so, you could tell that there were moments when Ralph looked at Wes and thought, 'Okay, this director is obviously an unpredictable, erratic, insane person, so let's just do what he asks and see what happens.'

"Universally, all of us, even the ones in Wes's inner circle, still sometimes have that reaction to Wes. There are moments where we're like, 'That's it—with this request, he's lost his block.' But you just have to accept that Wes is right. Even when he's completely mad, he's right. Even if you don't think he was right on the set, when you finally sit down to watch the full cut and you get to one of those scenes, you invariably think, 'Oh my *God*—he was right.'"♠

**Still-frame image of Roebuck Wright alone in a hallway at the police station**

A talk-show host (Liev Schreiber) interviews Roebuck Wright about his most famous *French Dispatch* article.

# THE COVERS OF THE FRENCH DISPATCH
## of the LIBERTY, KANSAS EVENING SUN

...

ILLUSTRATIONS BY
JAVI AZNAREZ

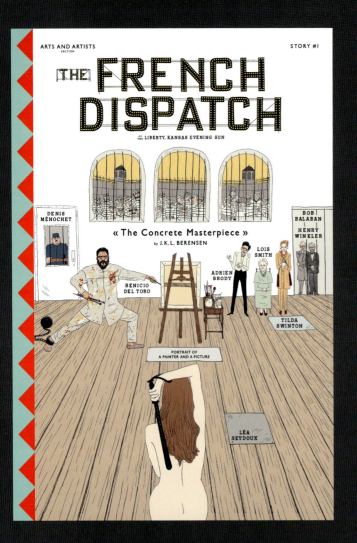
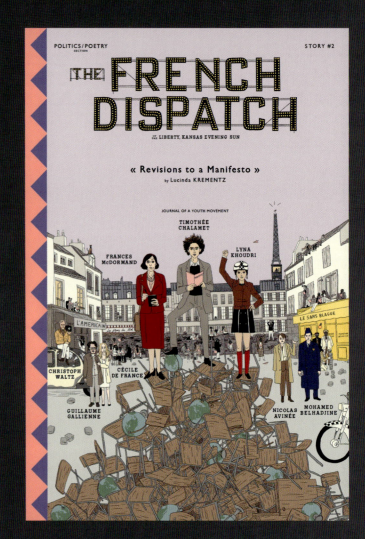
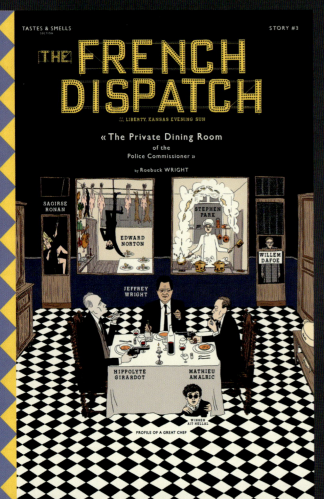
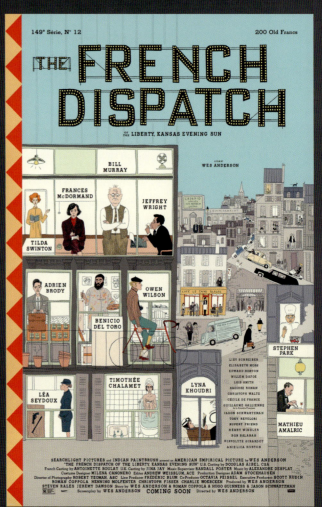

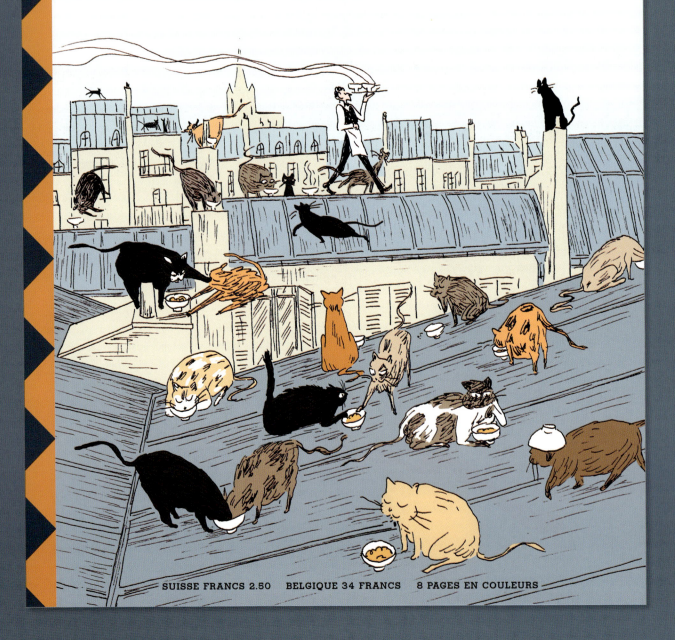

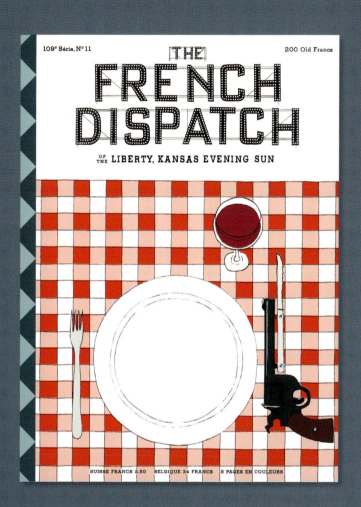
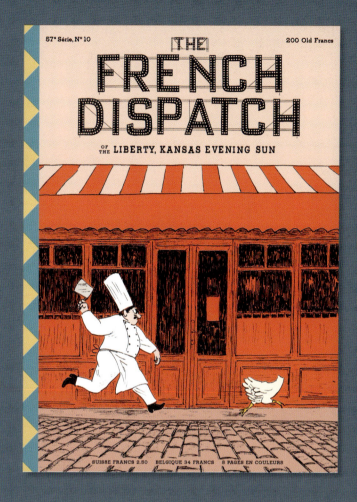
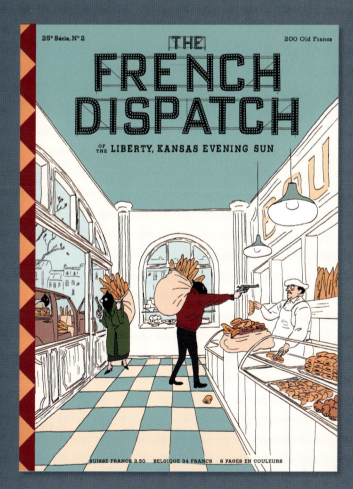
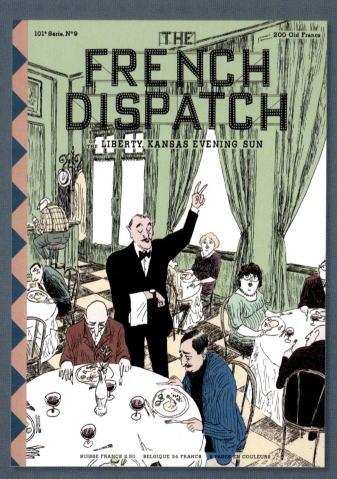

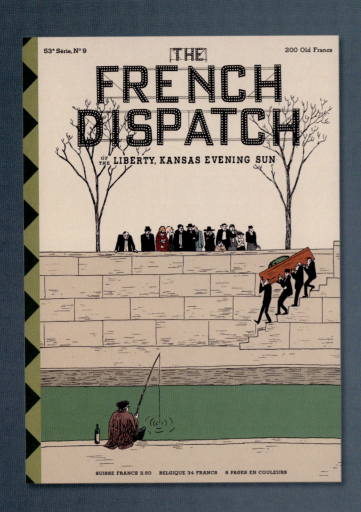
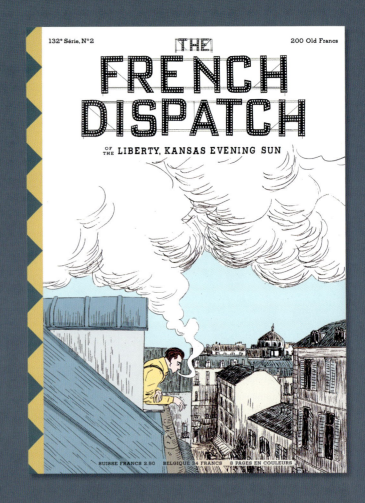
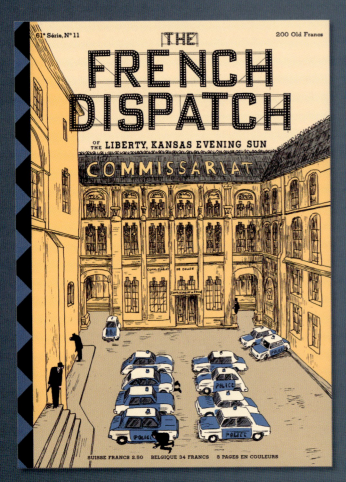
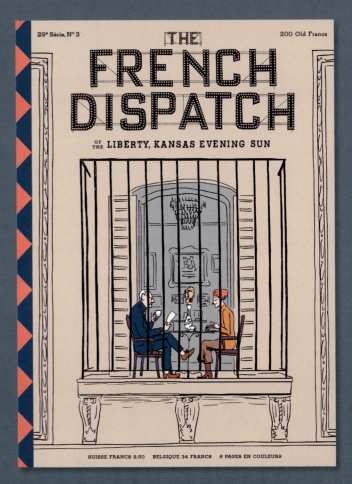

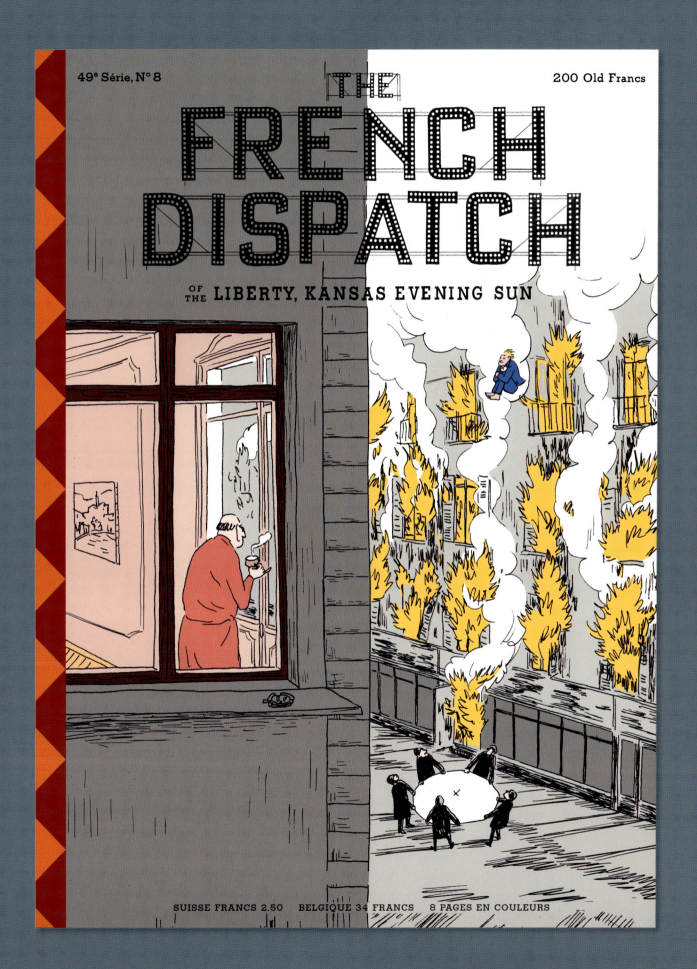

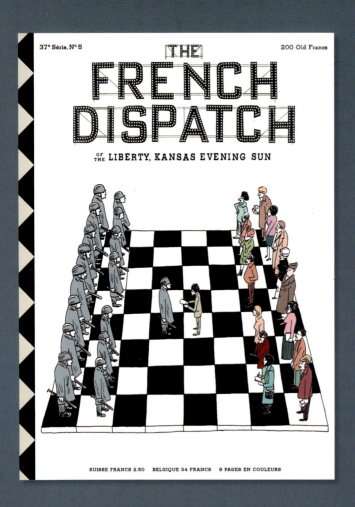
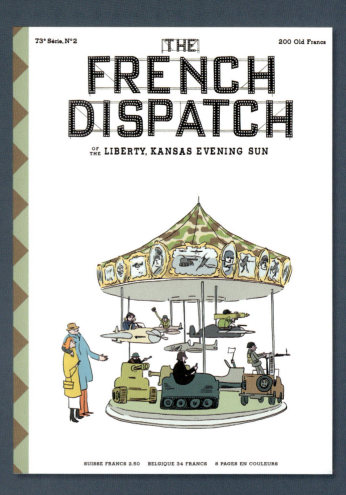
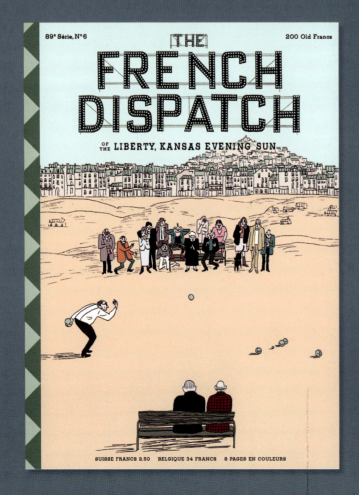
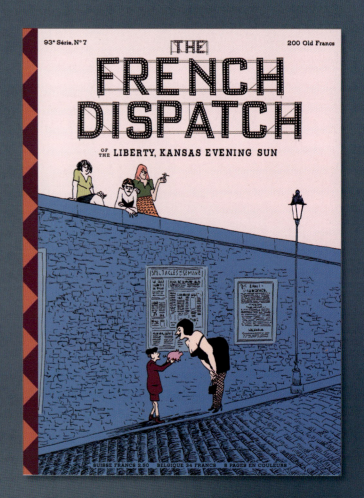

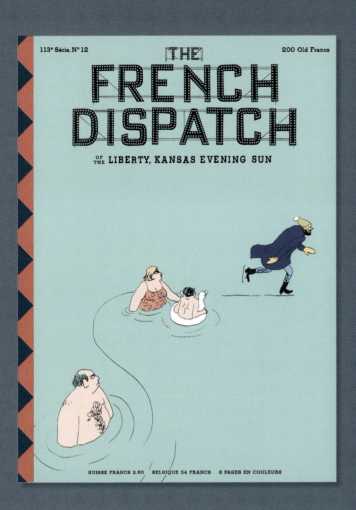
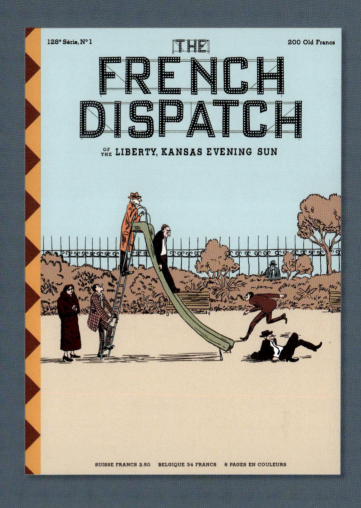
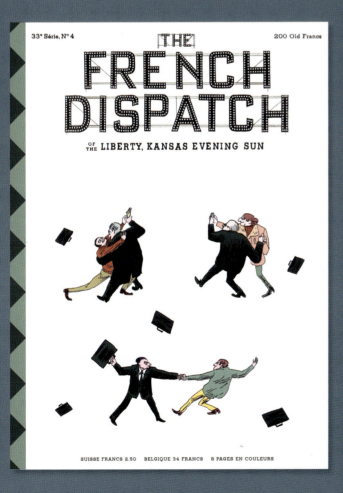
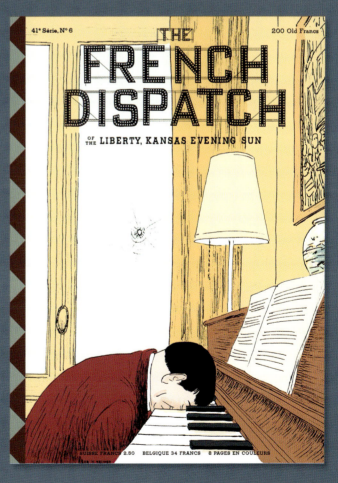

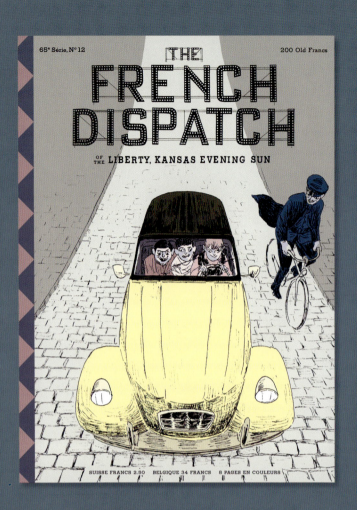
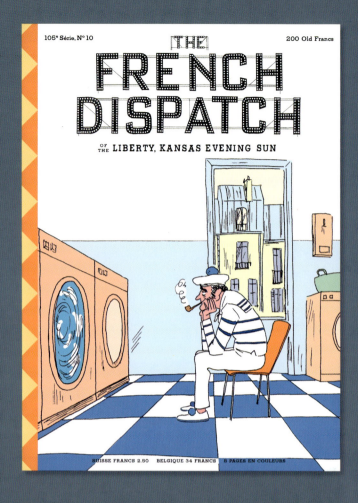
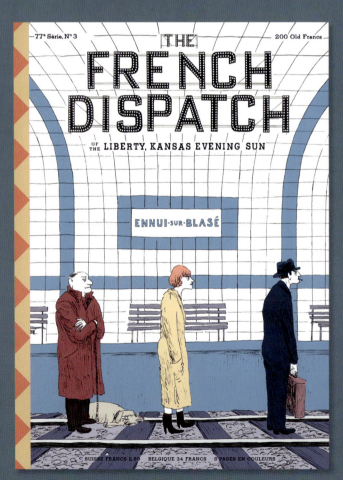
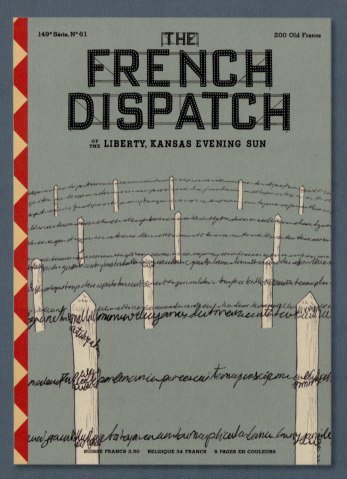

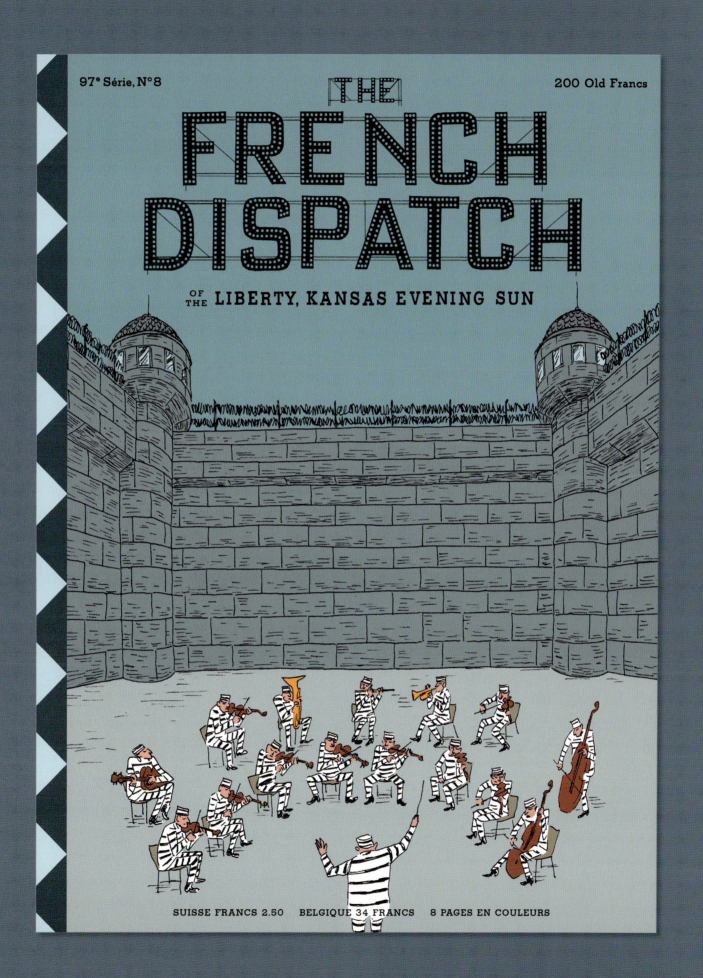

149ᵉ Série, Nº 12

# THE FRENCH DISPATCH

of the LIBERTY, KANSAS EVENING SUN

1925-1975

SUISSE FRANCS 2.50   BELGIQUE 34 FRANCS   8 PAGES EN COULEURS

# THE ROSENTHALER PLATES

**1**

**2**

**1**
*ABSINTHE BOTTLE*
22 × 22 CM
OIL ON PAPER

**2**
*A PERFECT SPARROW*
12 × 12 CM
BURNT MATCH ON PAPER

**3**
*SELF-PORTRAIT*
50 × 40 CM
OIL ON WOOD

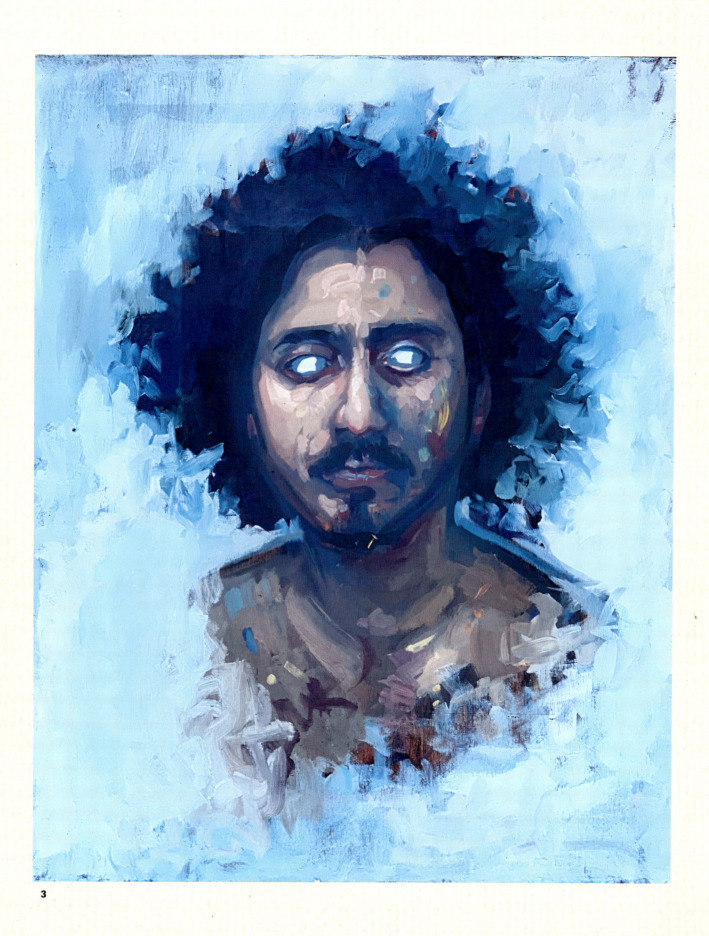

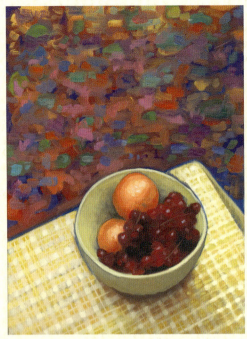

4

5

6

**4**
*STILL LIFE*
30 × 40 CM
OIL ON SACKCLOTH

**5**
*FOOTBRIDGE*
50 × 40 CM
OIL ON CARDBOARD

**6**
*BOXCAR*
50 × 40 CM
OIL ON SACKCLOTH

**7**
*SIMONE, NAKED, CELL BLOCK J HOBBY ROOM*
50 × 60 CM
OIL ON SACKCLOTH

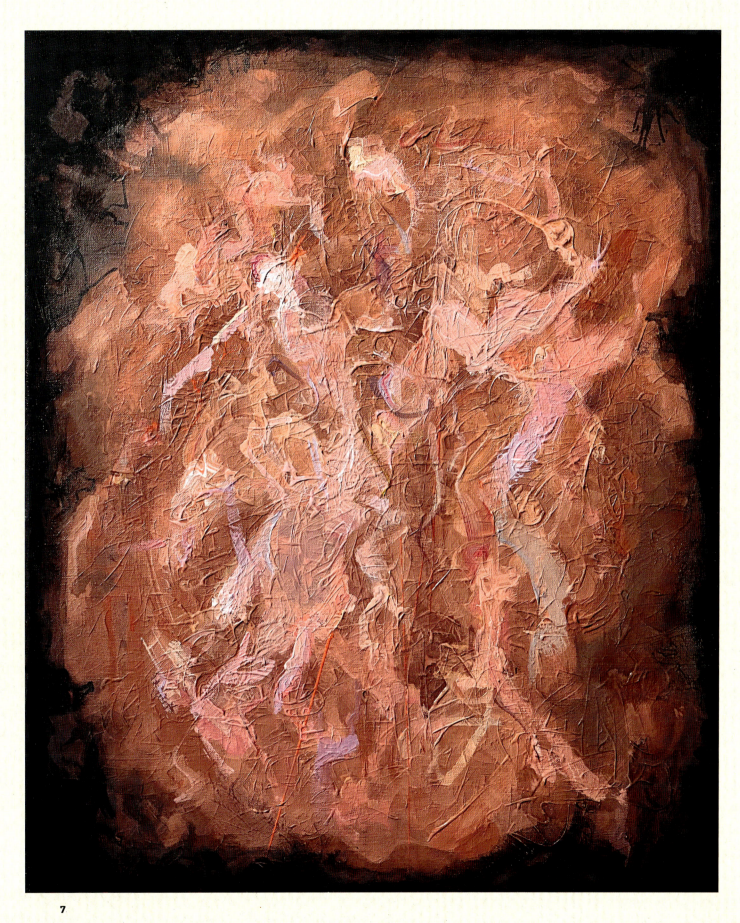

7

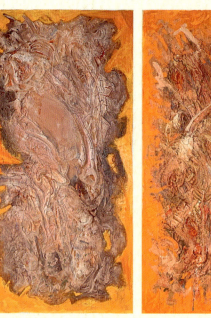

*TEN REINFORCED CEMENT AGGREGATE*
*(LOAD-BEARING) MURALS*
150 × 300 CM EACH
OIL ON CONCRETE WALL

*TEN REINFORCED CEMENT AGGREGATE*
*(LOAD-BEARING) MURALS #9 (DETAIL)*

# MUSIC

*for*

# THE FRENCH DISPATCH

{ MUSIC }

**COMPOSER**
*Alexandre Desplat*
ON
The French Dispatch

**My name is Alexandre Desplat;
I am the film composer of** *The French Dispatch.*

Each time Wes Anderson contacts me for a project there's what I call "a sparkle." This time the sparkle was something that we'd call Dadaism. You know, Dada? Because when I read the script, it was so unpredictable, impolite, provocative. The movies that Wes Anderson had done before were not as strongly oriented that way. First of all, the screenplay is three different stories linked by a thread.

Wes and I always try to talk about the storyline, but of course on this film we quickly began to speak about the music and how it would play. What kind of sounds could the stories bring?

From there, we went very quickly into the details of instrumentation, and that's where we started.

The first big question was: This is a triptych, a set of three stories with some linking material, so what do we do with that? Do we link all of the stories together musically? Or are there separate, kind of, um ... tones?

Instrumentation is always a very important decision to make. On *Fantastic Mr. Fox, Isle of Dogs, Moonrise Kingdom,* and *The Grand Budapest Hotel,* each time we had very strong but limited amounts and types of instruments, and that immediately gave a color to the score.

Now here, again, we had to find something that belonged to *The French Dispatch* and that had nothing to do with Wes's other films, which is something that I love doing: trying to stay in the same aesthetic musically because I think that there's a real continuity from *Mr. Fox* through now, but at the same time explore other territories. We needed to make sure the audience feels that there is something that vibrates only with these new images that they are watching. If it's a new story, it should be a new kind of music. Otherwise it would be like if Bill Murray was dressed the same way or Tilda Swinton had the same hairdo in every film. It would be horrible. Each time Wes makes a film, he takes his theater troupe—you know, his company of actors—and, as if by magic, changes them into somebody new each time. That's what I want to do with each new score. Do something new, but keep the same face, the same silhouette.

The first and third stories have a score. The second does not. It's songs.

The first story is about a painter. There's a flashback to a moment in the past where this painter, Moses Rosenthaler, killed a couple of other men. He's put into prison, and in that prison he starts painting. Very early on we see that his model, Simone, is a beautiful woman who happens to be a guard at the prison. The story has an ironic point of view about the art market and how an art dealer who is also in the prison wants to represent Moses's paintings and tries to create an exhibition of his work in the prison. Money comes into the equation as well. But the core is this weird relationship between two characters, a prisoner and a guard, who become a painter and model, so that they're doubles of themselves. They have double personalities!

Wes and I decided very early that each of the three stories should have a score with its own sound. In the first section about Moses and Simone, played by Benicio Del Toro and

Léa Seydoux, we decided to have mainly solo piano performed by Jean-Yves Thibaudet—which is a very strong decision to take, you know, on a third of a film, to have only piano as the score! But that choice gave us very quickly an intimacy, a precision, and a poetic, strange dimension, all of which pulls us away from the prison, where this painter is creating these strange paintings.

Anyway, there is also a gangster or thief story, with a kidnapping and ransom—that's the story with Jeffrey Wright as the journalist and Ed Norton as the gangster and Mathieu Amalric as the police commissioner. And here the music is more—a bit more jaunty, I would say. Maybe more related to some of the earlier scores we've done, in terms of rhythm? Not in terms of instrumentation, because the instrumentation is very strange! There are some bassoons, piano, and tympany. It's very strange. It's nothing like what we've done before in terms of the combination of instruments.

One thing that is important, maybe, to say here is that the way Wes uses the score is always by stripping the individual elements. The accumulation of elements in the score to his movies can change and reorder. The individual elements may not appear in the finished film exactly as I had written them into the score. Sometimes a piece could start with a piano, and then a full orchestra would play. Wes might instead go into the recording of the full orchestra and take only the tracks of the bassoons, for example, and only play those at the start of the scene. And then the piano that was originally meant to start might come in a bit further along. Or the harps. Or the recorders. Whatever instrument we've used! It's all very sophisticated and meticulous in combination. You know, his movies are Swiss clocks. They're really so precise and detailed. It's the same for the music. The score for a Wes Anderson film is not just a wash or a flow of music. It's full of changing colors, stopping at the most unpredictable moment. ♛

INTERVIEW WITH
*Jean-Yves Thibaudet*

(BY MZS, JUNE 2020
IN LOS ANGELES,
BY PHONE)

(MZS)   I DISCOVERED YOUR RECORDINGS THROUGH YOUR ALBUMS OF JAZZ COVERS, *CONVERSATIONS WITH BILL EVANS* AND *REFLECTIONS ON DUKE,* AND I TREASURE BOTH OF THOSE.

(JYT)

A lot of people started knowing my work through the *Bill Evans* album. That's always very touching to me, because it's a very special album that I did with probably more . . . I don't know how to explain this! It's not that I don't put my heart into every album, but this one, because of the content, being jazz and being different from what I usually did, I think I give more of my own, I think, of what's *inside* me, you know? It's a very personal, very intimate album, which I don't think I can do with Chopin, where you just have to play what is there.

Maybe it's stupid, what I'm saying, but I feel that I've given that one more of my complete, own insights than any other record I have made. And people feel that, and it's really interesting to me to see how, after that, they get to see me play some other things or whatever. That album really has done that. All over the world, I see people who just come and say, "Oh, we didn't know you, but then we listened to that and we saw you." That's very touching for me.

{ The French Dispatch }

**WHEN DID YOU FIRST START PLAYING PIANO?**

I was five when I started, and I entered the conservatory for my formal first class when I was six.

**IS ANYONE ELSE IN YOUR FAMILY A WORKING MUSICIAN?**

No, there are no professionals. But my father and mother are amateur musicians. My father played the violin, and my mother played piano. They were not necessarily in the profession, but music was very present and very important for us at home. We had a piano in the living room, which meant I was also attracted to it. So all of this music was at my disposal, so to say, and they were there to help me, but it was not a profession for them.

**DO YOU HAVE ANY BROTHERS OR SISTERS, AND IF SO, ARE THEY MUSICAL?**

Yes. Again, they are . . . everybody learned music in the family, but none of them is a professional musician. One of my sisters is a musician, perhaps more so than the others, in the sense that she's played piano, cello, all kinds of things, and what she still does is sing in a chorus. She loves it. Music is part of her life.

**WHAT WAS IT LIKE GROWING UP WITH TWO PARENTS WHO PLAYED? DID YOU PLAY WITH THEM?**

No, I'm telling you, they knew how to play, but I never heard my mother play the piano. I think she stopped even before she was married. I'd never seen her or heard her play. I know she studied piano when she was young. I think every girl from a good family in Europe is part of that thing where the parents get them lessons, and I think she played piano. But I don't think it was much more than that.

That being said, when I was having my lessons at the beginning, my mother would come with me, and I think she

{ MUSIC }

would understand what was happening, and at home she would have me practice. So that was good.

My father, I did hear, many times. And we did perform together at home. Not concerts, but we did play together. He would take his violin out of the box, and he liked to play it. It was one of his recreational activities. He was very busy, and he liked to play music to relax. Sometimes the two of us would do things with my sister. She might play cello and we'd do a little trio. But all of that was very low-key.

**CAN YOU DESCRIBE WHAT IT WAS LIKE TO LEARN HOW TO READ MUSIC? WAS IT SOMETHING THAT CAME EASILY TO YOU? WHAT WAS THE PROCESS?**

That's a very interesting question. I learned to read music before I learned to read the alphabet!

**THAT'S FASCINATING.**

Yeah. I was able to read music before I was able to read words. Music was very easy for me. We had that amazing class in kindergarten in France that had a part—I don't know if it was every week?—but it was called "Awakening to Music." So that's what we were doing for one hour each week. The teacher would have music playing, and we would either dance in the class or clap, and she had all kinds of instruments that we'd play. Someone would blow into a flute, someone would do percussion; it was basically anything to just get you acquainted with music and with rhythm. And then the first thing we did was learn to read the notes, so that's how I learned how to read notes way before I could read the alphabet. It was so funny.

I think it's beautiful because it just makes you learn music and makes you aware of music and what you can do with it. And then after that, at age five or six, I started to really learn the lessons. But I already knew how to read music, no problem.

**WHEN YOU PLAY MUSIC, AND WHEN YOU THINK ABOUT MUSIC,
DO YOU PICTURE NOTES IN YOUR MIND'S EYE?**

That's a good question. I'm not sure.

**IS IT A VISUAL PROCESS, TO ANY DEGREE?**

Yes, it's visual. I can see the score, and I think it's important that when I memorize something, I can see the score and see the notes on the page. I can see exactly where they are, like on the page when I turn it, and where the next phrase is. This is completely visualized just because you practice so much, you learn, you see the music, you look at it for hours and hours and hours, and it gets imprinted in your head. Then there's certainly auditory memory, the memory of the ear. Of course, a lot of people can't hear something. But then there really is photographic memory—I have it, at least—where I can see all my notes.

Now when I read a score, even if I sight-read something for the first time, it's like reading a book for me. It's like, I just don't think, "Oh, this is the thing." I just read it. In my brain I process it and I play it. It's like reading a book. The only difference is that instead of words it's notes, and the notes translate to my fingers to play the piano. It's a completely natural process.

**WHAT ASPECTS OF MUSIC, OF PERFORMANCE OR
INTERPRETATION OR COMPOSITION, CAME NATURALLY TO YOU?
AND WHICH ONES DID YOU STRUGGLE WITH?**

Honestly, I don't think I had a struggle with anything. I mean, I had wonderful teachers and they made me really love everything I was doing, so it was never something I was pushed into or something I was forced to do. It was always a real pleasure and a fun, playful thing for me, which makes a real difference. I always enjoyed it.

{ MUSIC }

I want to say, because I think it's just the truth: Some people are born with a gift, and I think I was very lucky and privileged to be born with a lot of gifts. I mean, sight-reading is, for me, something that is very easy, and that I was always extremely good at. I know a lot of fabulous, completely professional, great musicians/colleagues, who struggle with it.

Sight-reading for me is so easy. I can just read pages of music and play, play, play. Also, I have a very good memory for the ear. I have what we call absolute pitch—

**PERFECT PITCH?**

Yeah, but we call it absolute pitch. I can remember anything in my life that has to do with notes or music. Again, it's just not something I think about. You play something, like F, and I don't think, "Okay, what is this?" It's just like seeing red and you go, "Oh, this is red," but instead it's like, "Oh, this is an F, this is a G." I'm not trying to be prideful about any of this. It's just there. I'm lucky. I think it's a gift.

**WHEN YOU'RE LEARNING A PIECE, ARE THERE PARTS OF THE PROCESS THAT ARE MORE FUN THAN OTHERS?**

I mean, I would like to say everything is fun. Sometimes memorizing some pieces that are very complex is a little bit frustrating, and I think that process does get [harder] with age. I think it's easier to memorize when you're very young than when you get a bit older, but that's true of everything in life, unfortunately!

Probably the most difficult thing for me, I would say, is to memorize a complicated modern piece, or something that is not really matching your ear, where you have to kind of force yourself, spoon-feed yourself, every single note that you have to remember, and in the right order, if possible!

{ The French Dispatch }

**DO YOU REMEMBER THE FIRST TIME THAT YOU PERFORMED FOR AN AUDIENCE THAT WAS NOT PEOPLE WHO YOU KNEW?**

Oh yeah. It was when I was seven. I've been speaking a lot about it lately for some other projects. I was seven, and it was during a holiday in Romania with my family. We were there with my sister, my father, my mother, and suddenly we were in a place that had this lovely casino, and they had a piano and a little concert hall there. And I don't know how I decided . . . everybody knew I played the piano, and my mother and father, we had friends, and they said "Oh, let's do a little event," some kind of special celebration or something, and they said, "Let's have Jean play a little concert." I played for about half an hour, which is a lot when you're seven, with my prodigy pieces. It was all my repertoire then, probably!

I went to visit that place again a few months ago after God knows how many years. It's still there, the piano's still there, the little stage is still there, and it was quite remarkable to remember.

**WHEN YOU WERE YOUNGER, DID YOU EVER PLAY WITH A BAND OR GROUP OF OTHER PEOPLE YOUR AGE?**

Yeah! We had chamber music classes, absolutely. I loved that. My God. You know, the piano can be a very lonely instrument, because as a pianist you can always practice, and just play by yourself, and have your life happily organized. A violinist cannot. A violinist needs to have a piano, because usually everything written for a violin needs the pianist. They need to be accompanied all the time. The cello as well. Cellists don't always play alone—rarely, anyway. So for me, my only occasion to be discussing music with other musicians is to be playing chamber music. There were groups at the conservatory where you can do sonatas, trios, quartets, quintets, whatever. And also we were playing for each other and for showing what we could do.

**IN CLASSICAL MUSIC, WHO WERE SOME OF THE PEOPLE YOU LOOKED UP TO, EITHER PIANISTS OR OTHER SORTS OF MUSICIANS?**

There are so many! I always say Arthur Rubinstein, because not only did I admire him as a pianist, but I was also lucky to meet him twice when I was a kid. He just had that very incredible love of life, and happiness, and joy and pleasure of playing the piano.

The second time I saw him, I spoke with him after the concert. He asked me, "What do you want to do when you grow up?" and I said, "I want to be like you. I want to be a concert pianist, I want to play piano, travel all over the world and play concerts for people!" And he said, "Okay! Good luck! You have to practice." He was really my idol. The joy that comes out of this guy, it's unbelievable! Just unbelievable!

**ITZHAK PERLMAN HAS THAT QUALITY AS WELL, I THINK.**

Exactly. Those people always love everything. They like to drink good wine, smoke good cigars. They just love life in general, and all of the pleasures that go with it, and music is one of them. They're just bon vivant, and I think you have to be. If you're born, if you come into this world, you try to be happy. We should all be happy.

**WHAT WAS IT LIKE PLAYING PIANO FOR AN ALEXANDRE DESPLAT SCORE, FOR A WES ANDERSON FILM?**

What I find incredible with someone like Alexandre is that he is able, in every movie that he writes, to be somebody completely different. I mean, he is like a chameleon! He writes completely. Whether it's the score for *Godzilla* or *The Shape of Water* or *The Grand Budapest Hotel*, each score has completely the right elements.

{ The French Dispatch }

**I WOULD LIKE TO KNOW ABOUT THE INPUT WES GAVE YOU, AND THE COLLABORATION YOU HAD WITH HIM.**

I think of the word "superfluous," meaning what is nonessential, what you don't really need, and I think for him it is the same thing. He is so gifted, he has such a strong vision, that he doesn't need to have all those whistles and bells and all these things come together. He has good actors and he knows exactly what he wants, and he brought the same attitude to the music. I've worked with quite a few directors, but it was very, very impressive to see how intensely he worked with me, and how he knew exactly what he wanted. He was able to explain it to me and to make me do it, and until he had what he wanted, he would do it again.

It was remarkable to see how he would explain to me not just a scene and what was happening, but just a feeling. He was very good at talking about it and giving me that inspiration that I would go to the piano, sit, I'd play it, then he'd send me more things, and finally we'd look at each other and say, "We got it." We listened, that is, the moment you put the music with the image on the monitor, you put it together, and then you realize that it works. There's magic. And you say, "Okay, we got that scene. Let's move to the next one." But it was amazing to see how the vision evolves, and how passionate and knowledgeable his understanding is of what the music would bring or add to that scene, its strength, all the feelings. It was incredible how he could articulate all that.

**WAS IT A COMPLEX OR DEMANDING PROCESS?**

Actually, we worked very fast. It was unbelievable. We wrapped all the parts where I play in maybe two or three days. It was done very quickly because he knew exactly what he wanted.

**IT'S INTERESTING THAT WES WAS PRESENT FOR YOUR RECORDING OF YOUR PIANO PART, BECAUSE AS YOU KNOW, A LOT OF DIRECTORS DON'T GO TO THAT LENGTH. THEY ARE NOT ACTUALLY DIRECTING THE MUSICIANS AS WELL AS THE ACTORS. MOST OF THEM WOULDN'T KNOW WHAT TO SAY BEYOND VERY GENERAL COMMENTS BECAUSE IT'S JUST NOT THEIR AREA OF EXPERTISE, EXCEPT FOR THE ONES WHO KNOW A BIT ABOUT MUSIC, OR WHO HAVE WRITTEN OR PLAYED MUSIC.**

That's exactly my point. That's exactly what I wanted to say. That's why I really appreciated Wes's input. He knew what he was talking about.

And of course, knowing him as a person . . . I mean, I've been a big fan of his work for many years. On my side, what happened was, I thought, "Of course he works with Alexandre Desplat, they have a very good relationship with *Grand Budapest* and all the other things," and Alexandre and myself have worked together before—the last movie we did before that was *Extremely Loud and Incredibly Close*, and I really enjoyed working with him. He's an old friend and I love his work. Then one day he just called me out of the blue, like at the end of a summer. He said, "Hey, I'm doing this movie, we are really thinking of you," and I said, "What is it?" and he told me, "Wes Anderson," and I said, "Wow! That would be fun!" And he said, "He wants to do some music in the style of [composer] Erik Satie, and he thought you would do that really well," and I said, "Okay, I'm in!" I hope this isn't too much information!

**NO, IT'S ENJOYABLE! THE WORK OF CREATIVITY IS INTERESTING TO ME.**

Well, then, I want to say once again that it was incredible to see the involvement of Wes in the making of the music for this film. It was clearly very important for him. Very often we would watch a scene, then he'd explain to me the context, and then I would go to the piano and start working. He was there all the time with me. All the time.

{ The French Dispatch }

I felt like I was an actor. That's what was so beautiful about it. I felt like I was an actor who was playing music, and he was directing me on how he wanted the music to sound, as if I was giving an actor's performance in the character of the film, if that makes sense?

**IT MAKES PERFECT SENSE.**

This is what I like about playing for movies, something that is so different from what I normally do. Usually when I perform, I do whatever I want. I'm my own director. I can play a piece differently, I can interpret it and do whatever I feel. But now, suddenly, working for Wes, I become an instrument, being played by someone who knows what he wants. It's fascinating.

**WHAT SORT OF DIRECTION DID WES GIVE YOU THAT CHANGED HOW YOU WERE PERFORMING A PIECE?**

There are so many examples. Before almost every take, he would tell me something. Mostly it would have to do with expressing feelings or atmosphere, or storytelling, or those kinds of things. He didn't get into technical, pianistic things. But sometimes he would talk about the sound. If he found that something I was doing was too loud or too Hollywood, he'd tell me. Or he might say something like, "I want this to be very violent here."

**WHEN YOU ARE SURRENDERING TO SOMEONE ELSE'S VISION AS OPPOSED TO BEING IN CONTROL OF YOUR OWN VISION, HOW DOES IT FEEL DIFFERENT? WHAT ASPECTS OF YOUR TALENT COME TO THE SURFACE THAT MIGHT NOT NECESSARILY BE AS STRONG IF YOU WERE TOTALLY IN CHARGE?**

You have to be very flexible, very available. You have to open all your antennas and be there watching and then gauging what's going on or what the person wants. It becomes very different from anything else I do.

I think as artists we all have, somehow, some kind of ego inside of us, somewhere. And I think it's normal. If you do something like that, then suddenly here, you become really a servant. I mean, we musicians are always the servants of the composer. That is how I see myself. When I'm playing Chopin, I think I'm there, for example, to play Chopin's music. I can, of course, put my interpretation on it to a certain extent, but I am mainly there to serve the beautiful music that he wrote. In a movie, you have beautiful music written by great composers like Alexandre, but that's just one half. The other half is what that music has to do, and how it fits together with that image, and that moment in the story. I like to work on that.

But you have to forget about everything that you think, or that you might want to do. You have to serve the director and the composer and the movie.

# fondu enchaîné

THE Nº1 ENGLISH-LANGUAGE CINEMA MONTHLY FOUNDED IN 1962

Dispatches on THE FRENCH DISPATCH

**34 pages** on Wes Anderson's latest

*Bringing* America *to* France *to Bring* France *to* America

# WES ANDERSON EN FRANÇAIS
## "Or: An American in Ennui"

## WES ANDERSON'S "Framerica": A New Antiterra

**MARK CERISUELO**

From the outset of *The French Dispatch*, French cinephiles find themselves in familiar territory, and recognized. Wes Anderson's homage hits home: A waiter steers himself toward the (as yet unknown) offices of the film's eponymous magazine. The wide, fixed angle reveals a building at the end of a public square. The café server, dressed in a suit, is making his way toward it. We follow his vertical progression up each floor as he appears through the windows, which have been conveniently left open. This shot is a tribute to—or even better, a retracing of—its equivalent in the celebrated Jacques Tati film *Mon Oncle* (1958). Tati showed his character M. Hulot ascending the floors of a building on foot, and the viewer accompanies him right up to his apartment, nestled beneath the rafters. It's an extraordinary expenditure (both artistically and financially) from Anderson, who offers a tribute—that likely goes unnoticed by many—for the sole pleasure of expressing his appreciation. Recall Erich von Stroheim, who

TATI / HULOT

VON STROHEIM

MON ONCLE

demanded that for *Foolish Wives* (1921), we hear the phones ringing at the Paris Hotel in Monte Carlo (meticulously re-created in Hollywood), while the production was, of course, a silent film. . . .

But it would be wrong to assume, at least in Anderson's case, that this can be chalked up to artistic whimsy, for two reasons that are tied to France. The first relates to Tati's film, a wonderful meditation on France's transition to modernity and its subsequent refusal of this transition. The ultramodern house of M. Hulot's sister (and the house that also inspired Blake Edwards's *The Party*) is the opposite of the title character's home, while the film's new neighborhoods are a stark contrast to the bucolic and charming suburbs. Automation is contrasted with a slower lifestyle, as the automobile to M. Hulot's way of life. Through its resistance to inevitable progress, France is a country whose roots are on display and whose past is like a geological section, perceptible even in the present.

FRANCE

Wes Anderson imagines France as a country that ages without changing. A series of split-screen images illustrate the absolute continuity between the city of Ennui-sur-Blasé (Boredom on Blasé) in the past and today. Under Tati's influence, the fiction of *The French Dispatch* shows as never before a Wes Anderson split between two worlds, countries, and languages. Both the filmmaking and the dialogue are bilingual. Just as French critic Jean-Louis Schefer saw Tati's films as being less about laughter and more about "living together."

ZOLLER SEITZ

It is by no means insignificant that Matt Zoller Seitz's publications dedicated to Wes Anderson are designated a "collection." And the first in the series is introduced by Michael Chabon, a Nabokov-like writer who discerns the influence of *Pale Fire*'s author on the filmmaker. *Ada, or Ardor*, Nabokov's last masterpiece, was without a doubt a source of inspiration: *The Royal Tenenbaums* evokes its incestuous plot, and *Moonrise Kingdom* its happy lovers' pure youthfulness. Moreover, Wes Anderson's universe takes up Nabokov's double action of assembling through collecting on one hand while prolonging the existing world on the other. The Tenenbaum home on Archer Avenue or New Penzance from *Moonrise Kingdom* could be imaginary extensions of a real place. Similarly, the strange marine specimens that populate *The Life Aquatic* are unknown species inspired by known ones. *The French Dispatch* pushes its own logic to the limit by weaving unprecedented links between an America exemplified by the flatlands and flatter accents of Kansas, where the magazine is headquartered, and France, which

NABOKOV

ROYAL TENENBAUMS

KANSAS

has been distilled to one city, Ennui-sur-Blasé, which conflates the actual city of Paris with the history and geography of the old country as imagined by outsiders.

Wes Anderson, who has been a resident of the Left Bank for several years, is not the only American-born filmmaker with Gallic affinities; there are numerous examples of Paris's magnetism in the work of Noah Baumbach, Greta Gerwig, and Sofia Coppola; and Bill Murray spent a year at the Sorbonne and the French Cinémathèque incognito, following the box-office failure of his adaptation of *The Razor's Edge* (1984). In 2001, Anderson's friend and regular collaborator Roman Coppola directed the brilliant *CQ* in Paris, and the the student revolt article in *The French Dispatch* owes that film a huge debt. Coppola plays the eponymous magazine's manager; he knows exactly what he's getting into when he collaborates with Anderson on his journey to Framerica.

**A RAZOR EDGE**

The work is in-depth, and the Tati/Anderson pairing gives way to a Nabokov/Anderson duo. Indeed, the Framerica map that the filmmaker draws owes much to Antiterra. The Franco-American country is certainly not a planet—revealed to be the place of action in *Ada*, but we tend to forget this. Nabokov the magician lures his reader in with a cold region known as "Estotiland"—which could be mistaken for Quebec (East Estotiland or "French" Estoty)—at the Arctic extreme of Siberia (West Estotiland), or Alaska (Lyaska). And it's not difficult to recognize Montreux, where the writer lived, behind the name Mount Roux in Aniterra's Switzerland. Ennui-sur-Blasé is a similar invention.

If we believe Heidegger's "fundamental affective tonality" (*Grundstimmung*), boredom is at the heart of Anderson's internal map. It's also the boredom of youth that produced the events of May 1968. *The French Dispatch* delivers an offbeat version of the latter, but it's still disturbing to read the pediment of an uncertain Sorbonne (i.e., University of Paris) renamed University of Boredom. In this wonderful moment dedicated to anti-establishment youth, Anderson builds on a precedent: *CQ*, the first manifesto of the Parisian "dandy generation" in which Jeremy Davies plays a young assistant director newly arrived in the French capital during the *Barbarella* (1968) era. Coppola might have left his mark on the youth of Ennui-sur-Blasé via the character of Juliette, a revolutionary student played by Lyna Khoudri.

**L'ENNUI**

**COPPOLA**

The connection between French cinema of the 1960s and Anderson's personal inspirations are presented here for the first time in an unabashed but indirect way, in a sort of black-and-white reverie, where immaturity becomes the filmmaker's top value because one must never grow up. The viewer will also note a subtle (because it's indirect) return of the parent couple from *Moonrise Kingdom*: Frances McDormand "handles" Parisian events in her own special way for *The French Dispatch*—her "manifesto" writing rivals that of her young lover—and Bill Murray proves to be a particularly understanding editor in chief. It would be quite risky, nonetheless, to juxtapose images of May 1968 with Anderson's film, and to forget the relationship between the American artist and French cinema.

**MAY 1968**

**VHS**

The French New Wave gave Anderson an idea of film. As a philosophy student in Austin, he discovered film by reading the books of Peter Bogdanovich (on Ford and Hawks) and watching films on VHS at the University of Texas's video library. Forty years after Godard, Truffaut, Rivette, Chabrol, and Rhomer's experiences at Henri Langlois's French Cinémathèque and other Parisian movie houses, and forty years later, Anderson and the Wilson brothers re-created that process of self-education in Austin and Dallas. The future director of *Bottle*

*Rocket* never had to go through in-classroom filmmaking critiques, but an education through films (and not film school) nevertheless allowed him to grasp the essentials

CINÉMATHÈQUE

by devising his own way of doing things and getting his own band together—all lessons learned from the French New Wave.

THE 400 BLOWS

SHAMELESS PLUG

The profound impact of Francois Truffaut's debut feature, *The 400 Blows* (see *The Wes Anderson Collection*, page 312) can be seen in his attention to the child characters and the recurrence of certain devices, such as the use of letters read in voice-over to the viewer. (French filmmaker Arnaud Desplechin often uses the same processes.) But Anderson's personal tastes don't bind him solely to the French New Wave of *Cahiers du Cinéma*. One of Anderson's favorite French filmmakers is Louis Malle, whom he appreciates for his cultural position at the crossroads of diverging paths. More so than *The River* (J. Renoir, 1948), James Ivory's Indian films, or even Satyajit Ray's masterpieces, it's Malle's documentaries about India (*Calcutta*, the television series *Phantom India*) that revealed India to the future artist behind *The Darjeeling Limited*. Malle is the codirector of Jacques-Yves Cousteau's *Le monde du silence* (*The Silent World*), whose importance for *The Life Aquatic* is well established.

MALLE

INDIA

There is also Malle's *Murmur of the Heart* (1971), a literary film (it resembles a roman à clef) that addresses a difficult topic: mother-son incest. Invited to the French Cinémathèque in 2016, Anderson chose to program this unjustly forgotten title. Louis Malle, married to Candice Bergen, crossed the Atlantic in the opposite direction of Anderson and lived in the United States for twenty years until his death in 1995. However, he shot *Au revoir les enfants* (1987) in France, which brought him a form of final reconciliation with his homeland. This celebrated film, based on real events experienced by the artist during the German occupation of France, charts the tragic destiny of two Jewish children hidden in a Catholic middle school. It forms a sort of diptych with Malle's *Lacombe, Lucien* (1974), cowritten with Patrick Modiano (Nobel Prize, 2014).

BERGEN

AU REVOIR LES ENFANTS

Keeping this in mind, it's of great interest to follow the winding route of Anderson's increasingly backward-looking inclinations since *The Grand Budapest Hotel*: in an indirect way, as far as politics, he lays precise groundwork for Stefan Zweig's concept of the "world of yesterday," Central Europe before totalitarianism, and the more current ecological concerns that color *Isle of Dogs*. *The French Dispatch* gives the impression of a stylistic high (of "pure" Anderson, as if referencing a drug without flaws) and an intense search for one's place in the world. Yet again focused on the grief associated with the loss of a father figure and structured according to the "Frenchness" of certain realms of thought (arts, politics, cuisine), *The French Dispatch* never falls into repetition or clichés.

A WINDING ROUTE

THREAD

By following the thread of his two previous films, Anderson's Framerica provides a utopic version of a habitable world—joining Jacques Tati's endeavor with *Mon Oncle*—but one whose horizon isn't really clear for generations that have a harder and harder time imagining their future.

**MARK CERISUELO** IS A PROFESSOR AT THE UNIVERSITY OF PARIS-EST MARNE-LA-VALLÉE, WHERE HE TEACHES CINEMA AND AESTHETICS. A CRITIC FOR *La Quinzaine littéraire*, HE REGULARLY CONTRIBUTES TO *Positif* AND *Critique*. A FILM THEORIST, HE IS INTERESTED IN THE LINKS BETWEEN LITERATURE, PHILOSOPHY, AND CINEMA, IN THE WORK OF JEAN-LUC GODARD, AND, ABOVE ALL, IN AMERICAN CINEMA. WITH CLAIRE DEBRU, HE PUBLISHED IN 2013 WITH CAPRICCI *Oh Brothers! On the Trail of the Coen Brothers*.

# The Real and Imagined WORLDS of Wes Anderson

### SIDDHANT ADLAKHA

You know a Wes Anderson film when you see one, though it's usually easier to pin down what it looks like than why it works (thematically, narratively, and/or emotionally). His distinct pastels and symmetrical frames evoke children's storybooks, yet he constantly flirts with adult themes like paternal abandonment and adolescence left behind. He also evokes nostalgia for places you have never (and could never have) been, creating fantastical worlds born from the deep recesses of cinematic memory.

DOUGHNUT

APPLE PIE

Anderson is an American filmmaker the way doughnuts and apple pie are American—that is to say, uniquely and definitively, despite their heavy European influence. They're familiar and comforting delicacies, sugary sweet enough to satisfy, yet so ravishing to the eye that you crave even more. *The Royal Tenenbaums* is one such film, introduced to me as the quintessential Anderson shortly after I moved to America but before I'd had a chance to experience his body of work. It was his first foray into what would soon become a signature approach to time and place:

AMERICA

NY-NY LAS VEGAS

The film's New York City is composed of streets and locales plucked from some fictional realm, an uncanny, dreamlike New York where the details felt both alien and familiar. I was a newcomer to the real New York when I watched the film, and it seemed to evoke unspoken truths about the city's characteristic whimsy and the way it could mask that signature New York stench of isolation. It was like his images had been wrapped in colorful pastry boxes by Sprinkles or Magnolia, or any of the aromatic Manhattan confectionaries that caught my attention as I passed by and pictured what awaited inside. I dreamed and experienced New York all at once; I imagine Anderson takes a similar approach to his cinematic settings.

MAGNOLIA

A few years after *Tenenbaums*, beginning with *The Life Aquatic with Steve Zissou*, Anderson's work would offer entire fictitious histories and geographies that deepened with each passing film, moving gradually from background to foreground as his career progressed. Half of *The Darjeeling Limited* unfolds in a storybook version of an Indian train car with the real India just outside, while all of *Fantastic Mr. Fox* is an actual storybook brought to life through stop-motion. By the time one arrives at *Moonrise Kingdom* and *The Grand Budapest Hotel*, his films become subsumed by their own fictional worlds—for better in most cases, though some would argue for worse in the case of *Isle of Dogs*, whose fictitious Japan has more to do with "the insides of Anderson's brain than it does any actual place," according to American critic Alison Willmore. "It's Japan purely as an aesthetic," she wrote, in her essay "Orientalism Is Alive and Well in American Cinema" for BuzzFeed, which helped contextualize the larger cultural conversation surrounding the film in an age of increasing racial awareness. However, Japanese-born essayist Moeko Fujii noted in *The New Yorker* that she found the film—cowritten by Japanese writer Kunichi Nomura—to be rife with recognizable detail and a familiar use of the Japanese language, which places "the onus of interpretation solely upon the American audience."

INDIA

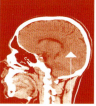
BRAIN

While Anderson's films often gaze backward in time through precise, albeit often whitewashed lenses of French and American cinema canon—the fictionalization in his work can be read as over-simplification—their emotional impact is always surprising, arriving as if out of nowhere after hiding behind the idiosyncratic and the seemingly juvenile. *Isle of Dogs*, while a hodgepodge of Japanese imagery in service of a quaint story of canine companions, is ultimately a prescient film about mismanaged viral disease, deportation, and confinement, and the ease with which human beings compartmentalize the horrors they enact for political gain. Though one might ask: Is its fiction backward, since it projects a tale of American nuclear atrocity onto Japanese society, going so far as to invoke the image of a mushroom cloud? Undoubtedly. But does its childlike aesthetic also reveal the bitter pill that is human cruelty? Undoubtedly, too. A double-edged sword cuts deeply either way.

JAPAN

MUSHROOM CLOUD

Anderson, a man who didn't leave the United States until he was in his thirties, has a penchant for grafting a distinctly American outlook, both as a filmmaker and as a traveler, onto unreal places sketched from real-world locales. By all accounts, I ought to dislike *The Darjeeling Limited*—as I'm from India, the film was often recommended to me with trepidation, lest I take offense to its uncanniness—but despite the titular locomotive existing in some fantasy realm, I found myself ultimately drawn in by Anderson's curiosity, as well as his seeming desire to take a place and turn it into a living, breathing celluloid fairy tale (or, in this case, a coffee-table book on wheels). The train, on which much of the film takes place, was concocted not from the real India, which Anderson was exploring at the time, but the India that existed in his cinematic imagination, via the films of Satyajit Ray.

Never has this starry-eyed approach been more apparent than in *The French Dispatch*, a delightful film about a print magazine

RAY

inspired by *The New Yorker*, which Anderson read as a teenager. Only the publication's characteristics, both visually and journalistically, have

THE NEW YORKER

been projected onto a small French town that, while it draws from elements of real French history, seems to exist outside of any known time or place. Exploring its corners, as does journalist Herbsaint Sazerac (Owen Wilson, playing a version of *New Yorker* writer Joseph Mitchell), feels like traipsing through an elaborate dollhouse.

MITCHELL

*The French Dispatch* is the logical live-action successor to *The Grand Budapest Hotel*, a filmed narration of a fictitious book (written about an interview, itself about another interview), about a snow-globe version of Europe circa World War II. Where *Grand Budapest* uses the fictional country of Zubrowka as a spoonful of sugar for backgrounded elements of Nazi persecution—alas, another relevant tale—the artifice of *The French Dispatch* is the film's central focus. The wryly named town of Ennui-sur-Blasé is its very reason for being, and it represents Anderson's storybook worlds ceasing to be mere backdrops. Through segments recalled by journalists exploring the town's art, food, and politics, this world advances to the very forefront Anderson's artistic intent, as if his films, rather than merely featuring fictional places, have become entirely about them, acting as cinematic documents of an imagined history.

SNOW GLOBE

This approach to the almost-real was always on the tip of Anderson's tongue. In his 1998 coming-of-age film *Rushmore*, Max Fischer (Jason Schwartzman) displays an obsessive affection for his private high school, the prestigious Rushmore Academy. While based on and filmed at Anderson's picturesque alma mater, the St. John's School in Houston, the fictitious academy is a world unto itself, in which Fischer attempts to spread his wings across an infinitude of extracurricular activities, dedicating himself to the school in a way that betrays a form of arrested development. Fischer doesn't seem to want to grow up and graduate, though he's eventually catapulted into adulthood when he begins romantically pursuing his teacher, Rosemary Cross (Olivia Williams). In Anderson's films, characters are constantly trapped between childhood comforts and adult harshness, a theme literalized through his production design, which stretches and contorts conflict into something resembling taffy. The result is a particularly delectable form of denial.

HOUSTON

NEW YORK TIMES, 1999

Fittingly, Anderson told journalist Laura Winters, in a 1999 *New York Times* interview, that he pictured Fischer's story as a children's fable akin to Roald Dahl (the author of *Fantastic Mr. Fox*). *Rushmore* was Anderson's first film in which characters are replications of children's storybooks, introduced in isolated vignettes, like the opening pages of a young readers' story, while his later films would finesse this method by using actual pages and chapter titles. Each person's narrative isn't just a familiar comfort, but one waiting to come apart at the seams (usually in the rare moments Anderson's tightly controlled camera flies off its dolly). *Rushmore* was also the first of several Anderson films in which characters would sand down the edges of macabre real-world events through an artistic medium, like theater—as if the director were zeroing in on his own instincts to sanitize real-world barbarity.

VIETNAM

For Max Fischer, this instinct takes the form of a sprawling school play about romance set against the Vietnam War, a bloody event that forced a generation of young men to grow up far too quickly. In *Moonrise Kingdom*, the story of a troubled tween couple's premature elopement, a retelling of Noah's Ark coincides with an oncoming deluge, while each room the camera enters is blocked and framed as if it were a stage of its own. And in *The French Dispatch*, a soldier attempts to process his trauma by writing a reflective stage play in the wake of the film's version of France's May 1968 period of civil unrest (during its second segment "Revisions to a Manifesto," based on *The New Yorker*'s coverage of the real revolt titled "The Events in May: A Paris Notebook," by Mavis Gallant).

NOAH'S ARK

GALLANT

By fictionalizing this unrest, Anderson grants himself permission to film it with a romantic gaze—or rather, a journalistic gaze that he in turn romanticizes—going as far as to name the young couple in the story Juliette (Lyna Khoudri) and Zeffirelli (Timothée Chalamet), a pair who flirts, frolics, and explores each other sexually before leading the revolution. One gets the sense that Anderson wishes these events could be as glossy and pristine as Franco Zeffirelli's 1968 film *Romeo and Juliet*, a formative depiction of young romance in European cinema.

ROMEO AND JULIET

Making palatable the horrors of history might seem dishonest at first, but Anderson's sprightly camera rarely shies away from what lurks beneath his vivid exteriors. In the candy-colored *The Grand Budapest Hotel*, the fictitious nations of Zubrowka and Aq Salim al-Jabat bear the hallmarks of a real history recalled, perhaps even passed down orally. We see Zubrowka on-screen as an ostensibly real place in 1968, while an author based loosely on Stefan Zweig (Jude Law) interviews Zero Mustafa (F. Murray Abraham), the hotel's elderly owner. During their conversation—set against the backdrop of an actual stage, no less—

ZWEIG

Zero recalls the painful events of his youth in the 1930s, where he's played by Tony Revolori. The events that upset him most during these recollections, however, are barely portrayed on-screen, while the events we do see are presented in a colorful, fun-house version of the resplendent lodge, itself housing a greater, interconnected history with other grand hotels (The Society of the Crossed Keys).

The film, rather than retelling the worst parts of Zero's traumas, focuses instead on his rosy relationship with the hotel's dashing concierge, Monsieur Gustave H. (Ralph Fiennes). But the specters of Zero's pain seem to lurk in the hotel's every corner. Zero mentions, though refuses to elaborate on, his departed sweetheart Agatha (Saoirse Ronan), a character who appears only a handful of times despite her central place in Zero's life. He also mentions yet doesn't expand on his fictitious Arabian homeland, the site of an apparent colonial genocide.

SWEETARTS

Aq Salim al-Jabat only comes up in Zero's story when it's mentioned by other characters—the well-meaning Gustave, who often jabs about Zero's heritage, or local militant police force the "ZZ," an allegory for the Nazi SS. History, in the world of

ARABIA

*Grand Budapest*, is disguised beneath layers of whimsy, so well hidden that it's hard not to be taken in by the film's rapid-fire humor, yet not so well hidden that one fails to recognize the fear on Zero's face when the ZZ arrests him for not having the correct paperwork as an immigrant. Those horrors are unambiguous.

The fantasy of Ennui-sur-Blasé serves a similar function in *The French Dispatch*, evoking horrors both distinctly American and distinctly modern, despite the film's mid-twentieth-century European setting. French cinema has long been a central influence for Anderson—the first critic to review his work (Matt Zoller Seitz, this book's custodian) said of his 1994 French New Wave–inspired short *Bottle Rocket* that the director shot Dallas, Texas, as if it were Paris, France— while even his first foray into Asia, *The Darjeeling Limited*, is preceded by the Parisian short film *Hotel Chevalier*. France has made its way into Anderson's creative DNA the same way Asia and America have: in the form of stylistic flourishes recalled from cinematic muscle memory but often divorced from real-world history. Until *The Grand Budapest Hotel*, no characters of color made their way to the forefront of his creative focus as protagonists (though Indian actors like Waris Ahluwalia and Kumar Pallana have frequently featured in his ensembles).

DALLAS

DNA

But the more Anderson has couched his work in fantasy, the more he appears to have done so with the express purpose of letting reality seep in to a greater degree. As much as Ennui-sur-Blasé might speak to an imaginary France, whose streets and buildings feel like an enormous playset, it also speaks to the realities of American life that have often gone ignored throughout Anderson's work. The first of the film's three short stories, "The Concrete Masterpiece," is recalled by art critic J. K. L. Berensen (Tilda Swinton) and is based on S. N. Behrman's six-part *New Yorker* feature about Joseph Duveen, a British art dealer. Duveen is fictionalized in the film as Julian Cadazio, a Frenchman played by Adrien Brody, albeit with an American accent. The story centers, however, on Mexican-Jewish painter Moses Rosenthaler (Benicio Del Toro and Tony Revolori), a man working under the harsh conditions of incarceration, and the object of Cadazio's predatory pursuit.

BEHRMAN

DUVEEN

Curiously, when Rosenthaler first meets his muse (the prison guard Simone, played by Léa Seydoux), he straps

ELECTRIC CHAIR    ELECTRIC CHAIR

himself to an electric chair in the hope of being executed as a form of relief. A macabre precursor to the segment's livelier scenes, but a distinctly American one as well—the electric chair has never been a fixture of French capital punishment the way it has in America, but in Anderson's film, French and American history appear to have been smashed together. Rosenthaler's story may be one of romance and creative endeavor, but it's also about his shackles, and the brutality of the four walls on which he chooses to paint. The conditions under which he creates his art loom large over the story, even when that story is presented cartoonishly (Anderson, as if taking the next step on his aesthetic journey, now presents several scenes as living snapshots, or dioramas in a pop-up book, as the camera dollies from one set of motionless actors to the next).

SNAPSHOT CAMERA

Though where Anderson appears to most confront American realities often brushed under the rug is in the film's third and final section. It's based on the *Dispatch*'s "Tastes & Smells" article "The Private Dining Room of the Police Commissioner" by African American writer Roebuck Wright (Jeffrey Wright), based in part on civil rights activist James Baldwin and the time he spent in France. This segment uses the framing device of a televised interview years later (à la *The Grand Budapest Hotel*) and tells of Wright's bizarre adventures while chronicling the culinary works of an Asian chef/policeman

BALDWIN

in Ennui-sur-Blasé, Lieutenant Nescaffier (Stephen Park). Rather than a straightforward review of Nescaffier's kitchen, Wright wistfully tells the story of Nescaffier solving the high-profile kidnapping of the commissioner's son, using poisoned delicacies, which he, himself, ingests as a means to fool the kidnappers.

This adventurous tale unfolds at a mile a minute, occasionally in the form of illustrated cartoons in the

POISON

style of *The New Yorker*, but it culminates in a devastating conversation between Wright and Nescaffier, the latter of whom ends up a sacrificial lamb in the commissioner's tale and now lies on a recovery bed. The chef and the writer exchange withheld but meaningful words about being outsiders in this largely white tapestry of stories—they're perpetual foreigners, forever in search of that which eludes them

LAMB

even in their homelands. Anderson's whimsical, it's-a-small-world-after-all settings have housed many kinds of people over the years, but they've only ever felt like home to a few, and he seems to recognize this.

Wright's narrative often stops dead in its tracks, in a way that feels uncharacteristic of Anderson's bubbly momentum, so that Wright may solemnly reflect on horrors only he and

IASWAA

Nescaffier seem to recognize. When visiting a police station, Wright comes across a mob accountant (Willem Dafoe) locked in a chicken coop. Their eyes meet in a surreal, silent moment as if Wright recognizes—deep in his bones—the inhumanity and indignity foisted upon the accountant, in what appears to be a case of mistaken identity. By the end of the film, it's revealed that were it not for Nescaffier remembering to feed the accountant, he would've starved to death.

The largely black-and-white *The French Dispatch* bursts to life in color when it presents art, food, and other hallmarks of aesthetic beauty. It's during these fleeting moments, however, in Wright's story—moments of solidarity and unspoken persecution—that the film feels most vivid, and most human. Reality now permeates even Anderson's most caricatured settings, each created to mirror childhood comforts; their idiosyncrasies can no longer mask the harshness of the real world outside their margins. On paper,

*The Grand Budapest Hotel* is the story of Gustave H., but there's a cunning reason it's told through the eyes of Zero, a man frequently brushed aside, but a man ultimately given the power to decide how his story

LIVING COLOR

should be told: whimsically, but through sighs and pauses, never forgetting the real pain and uncertainty that comes with recalling the rare comforts of his youth.

To someone like myself, who discovered Anderson's work as a stranger in a strange land, these quiet exchanges—between Zero and the author, between Wright and Nescaffier—speak volumes. As if Anderson's fictitious settings have now begun to gaze inward, at the real meaning behind the places and cultures he turns into fairy tales. The first word that comes to mind when describing his work is "whimsy," but the reasons behind that whimsy are what define him as a filmmaker, one whose imaginative

ASIASL

signature involves smoothing over the rough edges of history—not so that those edges can be forgotten, but so that they may be better understood, and accepted more readily.

**SIDDHANT ADLAKHA** IS A FILMMAKER, ACTOR, AUTHOR, TV WRITER, AND FILM CRITIC FOR VARIOUS OUTLETS INCLUDING THE *Village Voice*, THE *New York Times*, AND *New York* MAGAZINE. HE WAS THE RECIPIENT OF LA PRESS CLUB'S AWARD FOR BEST TV CRITICISM AT THE 62ND SOUTHERN CALIFORNIA JOURNALISM AWARDS IN 2020, AND HE WON THE 2ND PLACE AWARD FOR BEST FILM CRITIC AT THE 14TH NATIONAL ARTS & ENTERTAINMENT JOURNALISM AWARDS IN 2022. HE WAS ALSO INVITED TO SERVE ON THE NARRATIVE FEATURE JURY AT THE 2022 EDITION OF THE SOUTH BY SOUTHWEST FILM FESTIVAL (SXSW). ORIGINALLY FROM MUMBAI, HE NOW LIVES IN NEW YORK CITY.

# the CONCRETE MASTER- PIECE

### PADDY JOHNSON

A PERFECT CALLING CARD

A PERFECT SPARROW

NEW YORK WATER TAXI

The great fallacy of art is that it is accessible to everyone. In reality, masterpieces often reside inside wealthy homes, only to be seen by a small handful of people. Other times, they are never discovered at all. Institutions build walls to exhibit art but also use them as barriers.

These themes emerge in Wes Anderson's *The French Dispatch*, which brings together three stories from a fictional magazine by the same name and takes place in the fake French city Ennui-sur-Blasé (much ado about nothing). The first story, "The Concrete Masterpiece," follows Moses Rosenthaler (Benicio Del Toro), an incarcerated murderer discovered for his virtuoso painterly skill while in prison. Its author, J. K. L. Berensen (Tilda Swinton), tells the story.

As the title suggests, every scene comes with a name, a label, emphasizing that the thing you're looking at is actually the thing. In fact, "The Concrete Masterpiece" might best be described as a thirty-minute-long visual joke and a rebuke of René Magritte's famed *The Treachery of Images*, a drawing that pictures a pipe with the words "Ceci n'est pas une pipe" inscribed below. If Magritte tells us what we see is a drawing, Anderson counters by telling us it's just a pipe.

Literalizing just about everything serves a larger purpose, making visible art mythologies and invisible truths. Perceived by the public as alienating and inscrutable, art provides Anderson with the theme of inaccessibility, a constant in art, no matter where the viewer lives or how fluent they become in its language.

Anderson gives no dates for the stories that unfold in *The French Dispatch*. As to the period in which "The Concrete Masterpiece" is set, my best guess places the narrative around 1950, a pertinent detail mostly because the world of art cares a great deal about periods, movements, and styles. Providing such information about an artwork imparts a level of seriousness. Its absence feels significant as the only detail Anderson leaves out in a short designed to poke fun at art through its own pretensions.

The vast majority of "The Concrete Masterpiece" takes place in a prison, possibly the most inhospitable viewing environment conceivable. That provides a few chuckles, but as someone who works in the fine-art industry, I also see it as a jab at the luxurious and inaccessible locations the art world seems to love. The vaunted art fair Frieze New York takes place on Randall's Island, which requires the fair to provide water taxis to art viewers. The famous quinquennial Documenta most recently hosted its citywide exhibition in not one but two countries—in Kassel, Germany, and Athens, Greece—requiring dedicated art viewers to travel even more than usual. That's to say nothing of the collector-led exhibitions in remote locations for the handful of friends who can afford to attend. A friend once told me auction house specialists often measured wealth by how many helicopter landing pads a collector had on their yacht.

In the movie, Berensen highlights a collector of similar means, Upshur "Maw" Clampette, whose wealth gives her the ability to make unusual purchases and transport them anywhere she pleases. Not unlike the real world, the reason a feature can be written at all has less to do with Rosenthaler's skill than it does the fact that a couple of wealthy people liked the work enough to find a way to move it.

The wealthy include not just Maw Clampette, an American collector, but the art dealer Julian Cadazio (Adrien Brody), who initially discovered Rosenthaler's work while serving a sentence for tax evasion at the same prison. Based on Joseph Duveen, a real British art dealer who almost single-handedly established an American market for European artwork,

CECI N'EST PAS UN MOINEAU

**ASHTRAY**

**POTS**

**MACRAMÉ**

Cadazio plots sales and charms buyers in and out of prison. "Europe had plenty of art, and America had plenty of money," Duveen famously once said. Anderson's near-obsessive labeling continues the jabs at accessibility. At the opening of "Ashtrays, Pots, and Macramé," an amateur artist exhibition in the lunatic section of the prison, the title of each work describes the art's form: "Utensils" is a collage of utensils, "Bust" is a clay bust, "Tower" is a paper tower. Rosenthaler's Abstract Expressionist painting, executed in a Francis Bacon meets Willem de Kooning style, acts as a final punctuation mark in this sequence. *Simone, Naked, Cell Block J. Hobby Room* is the longest and most specific title of the lot. It details what the painting depicts and where.

As visual-language wordplay, the joke works well, but it also speaks to the larger art-industry conventions. In this world, titling typically does little to give the viewer insight into the work, creating barriers rather than access to understanding. Idiosyncratic title choices that mean little to anyone but those doing the naming are common, as is the widespread usage of *Untitled*. (*Untitled* is so popular there's even an art fair that goes by the same

# CADAZIO
### UNCLES AND NEPHEW GALERIE

**VERNISSAGE**
dans deux semaines
3am
(Precise date to be confirmed.)

**NEW WORK BY MOSES**

# ROSENTHALER

**A PERFECT INVITATION**

name.) Arguably, the method of descriptive naming offers few insights, either, a truth Anderson reveals through layering levels in inaccessibility. When Cadazio shows his fellow dealers Rosenthaler's perfectly drawn sparrow as proof of his talent, the work later shows up at auction under the title "A Perfect Sparrow." It's a clever joke on the description and a title that only reveals meaning if the viewer knows the background.

In some cases, Anderson focuses exclusively on creating the concrete. Simone (Léa Seydoux), a corrections officer, serves as a mix of dominatrix and muse for Rosenthaler. She poses nude for him, rudely refuses his marriage proposals, and forces him out of a creative block by shocking him in the prison's electric chair. Simone tortures the tortured artist.

The best example of concrete, though, comes in the form of the segment's title. When Rosenthaler reveals his final masterpiece, a series of ten abstracted figures, it takes the form of a fresco embedded irrevocably in the prison's wall. The technique combines dry pigment powder with the lime plaster of a wall—it doesn't have much to do with concrete at all. But the title smartly refers to the contrasts within the film—the mystery surrounding ideas of artistic genius and the crude methods of evaluating it, and the desire to make abstract concepts more tangible through concreteness.

**MOSES**

# ROSENTHALER

"SIMONE, NAKED, CELL BLOCK J. HOBBY ROOM"

**A PERFECT POSTER**

Eventually, the audience and masterpiece make their way to Maw Clampette and her foundation's museum, located back in Kansas and buttressed by a large cornfield. The context for art may change, but its inaccessibility remains constant—America, land of opportunity for those wealthy enough to move walls.

**PADDY JOHNSON** IS THE EDITOR OF THE FORTHCOMING BOOK *Impractical Spaces* AND THE COFOUNDER OF THE COLLABORATIVE NATIONAL PUBLISHING PROJECT IMPRACTICAL SPACES (2017–PRESENT). SHE WAS THE FOUNDING EDITOR OF THE CONTEMPORARY ART BLOG *Art F City* (2005–2018) AND COFOUNDER OF THE QUEENS PUBLIC ART PROGRAM *Parade* (2018–2019). JOHNSON HAS CONTRIBUTED TO THE *New York Times*, *New York* MAGAZINE, THE *Economist*, CNN, VICE, GIZMODO, THE *Observer*, *frieze* MAGAZINE, THE *Christian Science Monitor*, THE *Art Newspaper*, AND *Hyperallergic*. SHE WAS A COLUMNIST FOR ARTNET, THE *L Magazine*, AND *Art in America*. JOHNSON WAS THE FIRST RECIPIENT OF THE ARTS WRITERS GRANT FOR BLOGGING IN 2008 AND A TWO-TIME NOMINEE FOR BEST CRITIC AT THE ROB PRUITT AWARDS IN 2009 AND 2010. SHE TEACHES NEW MEDIA ART AND WRITING AT PARSONS AND NJCU. SHE LIVES IN NEW YORK WITH HER PARTNER.

**FRESCO**

**FRESCA**

**FRISCO**   **FRITOS**

**FREDO**

**FRODO**

# The Purposeful Period FASHION of *The French Dispatch*

### ABBEY BENDER

If Wes Anderson weren't a filmmaker, he'd make an excellent fashion designer. All of the qualities we see as typically Andersonian—the symmetrical compositions, the pleasing colors, the dazzling level of attention to even the smallest details—dovetail with the hallmarks of couture. The pleasures of his on-screen tableaus are not unlike the pleasures of an expertly tailored suit or a dress made out of luxurious fabric: Everything fits, and everything looks impeccable. Anderson's characters run the fashion gamut. Sometimes they're seductive, sometimes they're athletic, sometimes they're professorial, sometimes they're a weird but unforgettable combination of the categories, but they're always dressed in a way that commands attention, even if viewers aren't clotheshorses themselves. Anderson's costumes are worlds away from the fast fashion we've become accustomed to. They are exceedingly thoughtful and idiosyncratic. It's no wonder his characters have served as hipster Halloween costume inspiration for years.

CANONERO

BARRY LYNDON

*The French Dispatch* marks Anderson's fourth collaboration with Milena Canonero, the veteran designer who got her start working with Stanley Kubrick and who won her first Oscar for *Barry Lyndon*'s sumptuous eighteenth-century costumes. Her most recent Oscar came for the irreverent take on thirties-era finery (smartly tailored purple suiting and all) of Anderson's *The Grand Budapest Hotel*. Both Kubrick and Anderson are creators of instantly recognizable tableaus, of which fashion is a key part, and Canonero is the bridge between two of cinema's most exacting auteurs.

*The French Dispatch* takes Anderson's worldbuilding to new heights. With its three-storyline structure and multiple time periods, the film is filled to the brim with great actors in stylish midcentury apparel. Creating multiple distinct aesthetics within one film while maintaining an overarching sense of purpose and style is no easy task, but Anderson and Canonero pull it off gracefully. The framing device of a New Yorker–esque publication sets the scene of the mythical times when writers not only worked in an office, but also dressed up to go there. The men (led, of course, by Anderson mainstay Bill Murray as editor Arthur Howitzer Jr.) wear collared shirts, ties, and vests, while the women wear demure, light-colored blouses tucked into knee-length skirts and sensible business-casual heels. It's all as tidy as the oversized "issue-in-progress" cork board that functions as the office's centerpiece. Staff writer Herbsaint Sazerac (Owen Wilson) bikes around the fictional town of Ennui-sur-Blasé, giving us a tour while wearing a beret. His costume suggests a storybook vision of the roving journalist. Like so many of Anderson's films, *The French Dispatch* is bathed in nostalgia. The classic silhouettes and carefully chosen accessories of the magazine's staff take us back to a fantasy of a simpler time—a time when a beret, at least to Americans, instantly signified French sophistication—but seen through Anderson's lens there's always a wink, an acknowledgment that Sazerac, with his borderline parody French name and hat, is, like so many of the director's characters, someone prone to affectation.

HOWITZER

SAZERAC

BERENSEN

*The French Dispatch*'s first main narrative arc concerns Moses Rosenthaler (Benicio Del Toro), an incarcerated, moody painter who takes on Simone (Léa Seydoux), an attractive prison guard, as his muse. The frame for the story is a lecture given by *Dispatch* writer J. K. L. Berensen, played by Tilda Swinton, an actress whose ability to pull off dramatic drapery is unparalleled. She stands at a podium in a swishy orange caftan dress that shouldn't work with her red hair but does. Throughout the film, Anderson toggles between black-and-white and color, and the orange dress makes for a vivid contrast with the monochromatic prison scene she presents. Rosenthaler wears a prison-issue smock, while Simone wears a tailored guard's uniform, complete with a hat (when she's not posing nude for the troubled artist, that is). The relationship between these two characters has kinky undertones, especially given the chicness that Seydoux brings to a traditionally masculine role. Her outfit is rigid (maybe even a little bit fascist), but balanced with just the right amount of feminine touches,

ROSENTHALER

SIMONE

**MARGOT**

**GRAND BUDAPEST**

like a skirt and a name tag reading "Gardienne" (the feminine version of the French noun) to add visual interest. It's one of many examples of amusingly fetishistic costuming from Anderson's filmography. Think of Margot (Gwyneth Paltrow) in *The Royal Tenenbaums*, balancing hard and soft, femme fatale and schoolgirl, with her striped polo dress topped off with a fur coat, or the uniforms in *The Grand Budapest Hotel*, with their tailored formality offset by bright colors. Sartorial icons of (often eroticized) power become less cliché and more playful in Anderson's world.

After leaving the prison, we're transported to a story of student revolutionaries in Paris, led by Zeffirelli (Timothée Chalamet). Chalamet's pretty petulance and poufy hair make him an ideal addition to Anderson's collection of rebellious yet precocious youths. This narrative thread bears

**ZEFFIRELLI**

**JULIETTE**

an obvious aesthetic and political debt to the French New Wave; Zeffirelli is the kind of young, charming, yet occasionally aggravating idealist who could've been played by Godard and Truffaut muse Jean-Pierre Léaud had the film actually come out in the sixties. A shot of the students crowded into a café presents a spectrum of sweaters, schoolgirl skirts, and berets. They are the arbiters of radical chic. Zeffirelli's girlfriend and fellow activist, Juliette (Lyna Khoudri), wears a leather jacket and a helmet topped with goggles. She seems tougher than Zeffirelli in his blazer, sweater, and collared shirt. The image of the offbeat, somewhat preppy suit is an Anderson signature that evokes Max Fischer (Jason Schwartzman) in *Rushmore* and the brothers in *The Darjeeling Limited*, to give just a couple prominent examples. Juliette, on the other hand, is dressed as though she could jump onto a motorcycle and take off at any moment. The story ends with Zeffirelli's image being immortalized on mass-produced T-shirts reminiscent of the iconic ones featuring Che Guevara, in a potent reminder that radical politics often have greater influence when there's a strong look attached. We know Zeffirelli becomes a fashion icon, but whether his political ideals likewise break through to the mainstream remains to be seen.

**GUEVARA**

**ROEBUCK**

In the third and final story, we can tell some time has passed by the seventies-era width and pointiness of journalist Roebuck Wright's (Jeffrey Wright) collar as he appears on a Dick Cavett–like talk show. Talking to the host (Liev Schreiber), Wright recalls an assignment given while he was behind bars; a mysterious chef; and an action-packed chase scene (shown in a fanciful animated sequence). The most dynamic fashion moment comes when a self-described "mixed-up showgirl" (Saoirse Ronan) suddenly appears, commanding her black-and-white scene in a long black negligee and stockings with garters. She has the worldly, sensual presence of a midcentury European arthouse star, and in one of the most stirring shots the scene briefly switches to color as we see a close-up of her face, her bright blue eyes and red lips setting the screen ablaze. She makes only the most fleeting of appearances, but her fashionable boldness (few can make lingerie look like an actual outfit and not just something flimsy for the bedroom) makes it count.

**MIXED-UP SHOWGIRL**

The film is filled with so many characters and stories within stories that at times it threatens to topple over, but costume design helps anchor it all. Because we spend relatively little time with any one character, each outfit really has to make an impact. Anderson is a master of the crowd shot, of lining people up with purpose and creativity, and fashion is a key tool for instantly conveying information about the group, whether they're in prison uniforms or the modish attire of hip teens. Throughout *The French Dispatch*, it's rare that we see characters in more than one outfit. Each costume helps situate us within an increasingly off-kilter narrative. Early on, Howitzer shares his mantra with his writers: "Try to make it sound like you wrote it that way on purpose." This line, delivered in Murray's inimitable deadpan tone, could just as easily apply to the costumes. Anderson and Canonero try to make every single outfit look that way on purpose, and it's a resounding success.

**ABBEY BENDER** WRITES ABOUT FILM, FASHION, AND NOSTALGIA. HER WORK HAS APPEARED IN THE *Washington Post*, *Time Out New York*, *Sight and Sound*, THE *Village Voice*, *Little White Lies*, *Filmmaker*, AND MANY OTHER PUBLICATIONS. SHE WRITES "COSTUME PARTY," A COLUMN ABOUT ON-SCREEN STYLE, FOR *Nylon*. SHE LIVES IN NEW YORK.

232   fondu enchaîné

# NO CRYING:
## How to Overcome Blasé Ennui

### DAVID BORDWELL

Russian impresario Sergei Diaghilev once commanded French poet Jean Cocteau: "Astonish me!" Every artwork, he suggested, should be a tour de force. Something like this seems to me Wes Anderson's mission statement. At least since *The Royal Tenenbaums* he has sought to make each of his films extraordinary—every scene a uniquely memorable moment, every shot an arresting pictorial event. There are no mundane scenes, no filler material of people getting out of cars or drifting along a street. The films are bell jars.

They're also cabinets of curiosities, Wunderkammers. They juxtapose solemnity and silliness, simplicity and recondite reference, satire and sentiment. Their aesthetic is at once flamboyant (riotous color, stuffed settings) and austere (strict principles of staging and shooting). They are the most maximalist minimalist films anybody has made. Every instant is designed to astonish us.

Even overdesigned. The Anderson aesthetic digests all that it touches. No material is left in its raw state. Every inch of the image has been processed to the fullest. The worlds that result, a few degrees off center from the more or less realistic realms we see in other movies, have the gravity and density of our own. They achieve that rarefied state through strategies of narrative form and cinematic style.

*The French Dispatch* of the Liberty, Kansas *Evening Sun* shows us the risks and rewards of this refined aesthetic. They are on crisp display in one, apparently digressive, sequence we can take as a model of the Anderson method.

### REMEMBERING THE SUICIDE

Lucinda Krementz (Frances McDormand) interrupts her account of the Chessboard Revolution by noting Mitch-Mitch Simca's (Mohamed Belhadjine) epiphany during his stint of national service. Another young soldier, Morisot (Alex Lawther), refusing to live in his parents' world, commits suicide by plunging out a high window. This impels Mitch-Mitch to desert the service and return to his pals at the Sans Blague Café. But instead of presenting his account of the incident, or giving us a flashback as his memory, the film presents the suicide at several removes.

Nudged by Krementz's voice-over, we see a British production of Mitch-Mitch's autobiographical play, *Goodbye, Zeffirelli* (**1**), in which actors re-create the suicide. That play was translated by Krementz. We have a character's memory chronicled in his play text, which passes through a translation and then a specific production for a foreign audience. Weirdly, the stage sequence we see is at once a flashback (in the chronology of Mitch-Mitch's play, but also in his café explanation) and a flash forward (because Krementz's translation is made five years after the revolution we're seeing). And of course the entire Mitch-Mitch episode is swallowed up in Krementz's overall narration, which is a cinematic representation of her story, "Revisions to a Manifesto." That, it turns out, is a 1975 reprint of an article published years earlier.

The suicide, then, passes from memory to play text to translation to performance to journalistic article to a reprint, the whole reconstituted as a stream of images and sounds. As a kind of palimpsest, the suicide scene is an extreme case, but typical. Anderson has always framed his stories not just cinematically but bookishly, through letters, journals, and other texts. The sense of a story filtered through many tellings in many media comes to the fore in *The French Dispatch*, not least because it frames itself as a tribute to a magazine. The greatest-hits format of its final issue allows Anderson to create his own version of a portmanteau film reminiscent of those European "omnibus" films *Les plus belles escroqueries du monde* (1964) or *Paris vu par...* (1965). Unlike those, however, Anderson's tales are presented not simply as episodes but as enacted texts, each with its own array of narrative filters and veils.

1

Herbsaint Sazerac (Owen Wilson), the city reporter, gives us a tour of Ennui-sur-Blasé in straightforward, to-camera address, the simplest way to enact his written text. As a curtain-raiser, the episode surveys motifs in the stories to come: the prison/asylum, the Sans Blague Café with its motor scooters, and the hookers and nighttime gunplay of the final police siege. With J. K. L. Berensen's (Tilda Swinton) account of "The Concrete Masterpiece" we get something more oblique. Her lecture in the Clampette gallery is channeled through video cameras, her photographic slides, and, ultimately, her written text.

Krementz's account of the Chessboard Revolution is a visualization of her journal, with her speaking voice kept distinct from her action in the events she recounts. Yet at times her voice is interrupted by Zeffirelli's (Timothée Chalamet) commentary and imagery, notably the fantasy motorbike escapade with Juliette (Lyna Khoudri). In the cinematic version we get, her journal becomes a collaborative collage with his input. (Tit for tat: She rewrites Zeffirelli's manifesto.) Yet another sort of narrating at a distance is

2

given in Roebuck Wright's (Jeffrey Wright) talk-show interview. He provides an oral performance of his memorized article from earlier years, while also reflecting on his past in Ennui-sur-Blasé—a luxury afforded to no other narrator.

As Wright's confessions remind us, the three main stories not only refract the events they present. They twist time. Berensen's lecture must take place at least twenty years after the triumph of Moses Rosenthaler (Benicio Del Toro), but when? The lecture corresponds, as best we can tell, to her *French Dispatch* essay. Did she publish the text she read at the gallery, or did she simply deliver her write-up as her lecture? We've already seen the curious time-bending in Krementz's inclusion of Mitch-Mitch's play, a glimpse of a distant future event. Is it an interpolation she added to the 1975 publication of the older piece? Or is it an aside to us, cut free of her *French Dispatch* text? Wright's poignant reflection on the source of his story indulges in time-jumping as well. It flashes back to his first encounter with the magazine's editor, Arthur Howitzer Jr. (Bill Murray), and draws some incidents from a comic strip "published the following week."

Given that all these narrative refractions play with the order of story events, we might take Wright's reference to "three overlapping timelines" as a hint about how these tales benefit from their layering. Despite the strict siloing of stories, each one bookended by a page and a final reckoning with Howitzer, they quickly slip into benign disorder, spilling out beyond strict timelines and into digressions and detours. Perhaps Alumna's (Elisabeth Moss) prodigious sentence diagram is a tip-off to the way scenes will proliferate on the slightest pretext (**2**). *The French Dispatch* gives us a floating, teeming array of substories that evoke the many ways experiences get transformed in the telling.

## GEOMETRIES OF VISION

As a display, the Mitch-Mitch suicide scene is a flamboyant scale model of Anderson's visual style. Fourteen shots over nearly three minutes are framed with a meticulous geometry. Apart from the first shot, a view over the shoulder of the Drill-Sergeant (Rupert Friend) looking out at the darkened audience, all the other shots are presented as straight-on views of the stage space. Cutting enlarges portions of them, but the oblique angles of orthodox shot/reverse shot are abandoned in favor of lateral cuts and sidelong camera movement, rigorously parallel to the boys and the bunks. The layout of the bunks creates a pictorial grid that frames faces with maniacal precision (**3–4, next page**). Every bit of the frame can be activated for our attention. (Anderson is one of the few directors today who tries to explore the vertical dimension of the image.) And the sheer panache of Anderson's style overrides the theatrical premise, turning the play into pure cinema. When Morisot jumps from his bunk and vanishes, he disappears in the cut.

Anderson has long explored the resources of what we might call planimetric staging (shooting frontal or profiled

performers at right angles to the rear plane) and compass-point editing (cutting "on the line" between camera and subjects). *The Grand Budapest Hotel* revised that approach by adjusting to the demands placed on him by differing aspect ratios. In *The French Dispatch*, he confines himself to just two ratios, the classic 1:1.37 and the contemporary "scope" proportion 1:2.40. Within these he pushes to new limits his tendencies toward rectilinear imagery, dense compositions, and movie citations.

The precise positioning of the draftees in Mitch-Mitch's play reminds us how Anderson integrates characters and milieu. The sequence makes a veritable fetish of what we might call aperture framing, the enclosing of characters or objects within windows, doorways, and other openings. A virtuoso instance of this strategy opens the film, as we see an Advent calendar framing of the waiter carrying his tray up to the *French Dispatch* office (**5–6**). Thereafter, any inch of screen space might harbor a point of interest.

Anderson announces his commitment to all-over compositions when Cadazio (Adrien Brody) praises Rosenthaler's masterpiece: "Perhaps the most interesting contemplation of peripheral vision I've ever seen." At this moment a waiter (Felix Moati), on the left edge of the shot, is massaging Uncle Joe's (Henry Winkler) shoulder (**7**). We get peripheral detail not only in the heads dotting the boys' bunks but also in a waiter's sidelong delivery of a drink (**8**), in Howitzer's tactful entrance to Krementz's apartment (**9**), and in that sinister hand creeping into the edge of Gigi's (Winsen Ait Hellal) ceiling (**10**).

These gestures stand out in fairly clean frames, but Anderson's cabinet of curiosities is often stuffed with pictorial splendors. *The French Dispatch* has an astonishing density of visual detail—not only the somewhat fussy recruiting of period props and furnishings, but also the cramming of faces and bodies into the frame. The tactic is most obvious in the Sans Blague Café, with kids piled into almost baroque depth (**11**), but every episode has its crowd scenes and jammed interiors (**12–13**), all disconcertingly deep.

Nearly every image is choreographed, of course, within planimetric coordinates. Characters address us frontally or in

3

4

5

6

7

8

9

10

238  fondu enchaîné

11

profile. (Orthodox shot/reverse shot is reserved for the TV interview and moments of quasi-reportage on the barricades.) If characters move, they move parallel or perpendicular to the camera axis, seldom diagonally or in a serpentine or wayward path. One of Anderson's great accomplishments is to show just how much visual variety he can get with a few simple principles of construction.

His tendency toward pictorial tableaux likewise emerges flagrantly here.

Now he indulges in homemade freeze frames: dense, rich moments of halted action during the salon controversies over Rosenthaler's genius (**14–15**). The fact that they're executed by trembling actors holding their postures gives them a charming blend of amateurishness and virtuosity. But then that blend is present throughout the movie, from the low-budget special effects of Sazarec's bike ride to the jittery drawings on the *French Dispatch* covers (which in turn evoke the childish pleasures of bande dessinée album design; [**16–17**]).

12

13

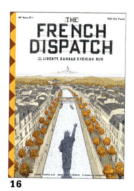

16

14

15

17

The French Dispatch 239

As you'd expect, the style of *The French Dispatch* cites French cinema and pictorial culture. The waiter's zigzag ascent to the magazine offices recalls Jacques Tati's *Mon Oncle* (**18**), as does the "awakening" of the street, which activates different zones of the frame one by one (**19–20**). Shots in the "Manifesto" episode pay homage to Godard's "blackboard" compositions of the 1960s (**21–22**). The cartoon chase at the climax draws on the "clear line" heritage of Hergé and other comic-book artists (**23–24**). It seems to me as well that the salon-brawl tableaux evoke early cinema. So does the cutaway set during the gang's imprisonment of Gigi. True, Anderson has always used dollhouse sets, while gracefully tracking laterally from room to room, but here I'm reminded of how Louis Feuillade and other French directors employed cutaway sets in tales of anarchic intrigue (**25–26**).

Refracted storytelling, self-conscious artifice in the imagery: The rewards of this refined aesthetic are clear. We're gripped, from moment to moment, by the sheer audacity of form. But there are risks as well. By putting narrative situations at such a remove, by sculpting them so fastidiously, aren't we stifling emotion? Howitzer's office motto, "No Crying," might seem to be the slogan of a filmmaking practice that tamps down feeling in favor of cleverness.

Well, there are feelings and feelings. Speaking for myself, I find emotion—specifically, aesthetic rapture—in the moment-by-moment dazzle of Anderson's storytelling and style. Form can thrill us, too. But I'd also add that the films of his I value most, above all *Moonrise Kingdom*, show how an ambitious, eccentric formal design can transform its subject and still retain strong emotion. To see how that happens in *The French Dispatch*, we need to consider one more aspect of the Mitch-Mitch suicide scene: its banality.

18

19

20

21

22

23

24

25

26

27

28

## ALL TOO FAMILIAR

In Jacques Tati's *Playtime*, vistas of guidebook Paris are subjected to a calculating style that makes us see them afresh. A flower seller ("That's really Paris!" exclaims a visitor) stands out in a valley of gleaming skyscrapers. The Eiffel Tower and the Arc de Triomphe are glimpsed in the reflections of swinging doors, as is Sacré Coeur (**27**). By the end, however, a kitschy souvenir scarf and a sprig of plastic flowers evince spontaneous feeling (**28**). We come out of this pageant of stereotypes appreciating the human contact that people can still find in the modern world.

Something similar is going on in *The French Dispatch*. Sazerac's bike tour of Ennui-sur-Blasé introduces not France but Frenchness, a cozy landscape of postcard clichés. Police ride bikes, people take the Métro, prostitutes lounge on the street, and cats roam rooftops. The tour announces that this film will defamiliarize these clichés, trying to tap them for fresh stories and true feeling. And those stories and that feeling are invigorated by interruptions, digressions, stylistic flourishes, and references that, as I've tried to show, keep catching us off guard.

Clichés make you blasé, and they breed ennui. But they wouldn't endure if they didn't have a little bit of emotional appeal. Our Mitch-Mitch scene, for instance, is pretty conventional. The scene of recruits sharing their dreams of what they'll do when they're back home is a staple of war movies. Yet such scenes remain irrevocably touching no matter how many times we see them. And here, even when hedged by artifice, Morisot's death and Mitch-Mitch's sorrowful response become both startling and moving. In this scene and from story to story, Anderson preserves the lingering appeal of his clichés, distances them through formal play, and then reinfuses them with emotion—mostly, a dose of muted sadness.

What does everybody know about France? The French love fine art, the more outrageous the better. The first story, a tale of a criminal, suicidal painter, plunges us into the art world. Dealers, schools, rich American collectors, muses, and Bohemian carnality are the stuff of the tragic artist biopic.

The French Dispatch **241**

Rosenthaler's story recycles other clichés as gags. He's dilatory and undisciplined until he meets Simone (Léa Seydoux). Like all geniuses, he has a fatal need to fail; his dealer, Cadazio, has to coax and bully him into making art. Ever since *The Rite of Spring*, a work of genius arouses violent controversy, so we see, frozen in tableaux, salon visitors and auction-goers in cataleptic battle. Cadazio, a middling impresario, embraces the Philistine notion that Rosenthaler must be good because he can draw realistic pictures and just doesn't want to. Just as *The French Dispatch* brings the world to the Midwest, Upshur "Maw" Clampette gives the avant-garde a home in fields of Kansas corn. French clichés aren't the only ones on display.

What does everybody know about France? The French are hyperintellectual, especially when it comes to politics. (There's the old line about French philosophers studying a bridge: "Yes, it works in practice, but does it work in theory?") The second story presents spring 1968 refracted through a Lewis Carroll lens, treating student rebellion as a chess tournament. So we get glossy-magazine images of student culture; yé-yé music, hanging out in cafés, weird hairdos, weirder dances, petty cliques, adolescent idealism, factional squabbles over manifestos, and a Sartrean hijacking of politics by literature in Mitch-Mitch's autobiographical play.

Again, the gags and citations multiply. Zeffirelli becomes Marat, with turban and manifesto, braced in his bath by Mrs. Krementz as Charlotte Corday. French poetry is satirized (Baudelaire's "Spleen" becomes "Postscript to a Burst Appendix"), and academic debate is mocked as a matter of hand signals. Radical chic takes over when after Zeffirelli's death his defiant image becomes a publicity icon for a brand of cigarillos. The French love politics, but they also love the beau geste.

What does everybody know about France? The French love gourmet cuisine and urban crime stories. "The Private Dining Room of the Police Commissioner" combines both elements in an account of the "gastromanic gendarmerie." The episode brings in imagery from silent-film feuilletons, film noirs, slapstick chases, and comics. A pan-European gang of crooks and molls can call time-out at the prospect of fine dining. For the cops, the siege becomes an occasion to sample unsavory dishes fit for a Continental palate ("Blasé Oyster Soup . . . City Park Pigeon Hash"). What must the citizenry of Liberty, Kansas, make of this menu?

Each absurd tale harbors pockets of wistful failure. An artist's model inspires him but will not love him. A young man discovering love and political action dies and leaves grieving parents behind; a middle-aged reporter confronts her isolation and the failings of her youth. ("I am convinced they are better than we were.") A chef in search of a new flavor finds it in poison; two foreigners share their sense of loneliness in an alien culture.

One bright spot is the reunion of father and son, the Commissioner (Mathieu Amalric) and Gigi (Winsen Ait Hellal), in the last story we see. A similar muted ripple of affection reappears at the very end of the film. The stories we have seen/heard/read will endure as reprints in the magazine's obituary issue, as a tribute to Howitzer's love of France and his devotion to his writers. His corpse, stretched out on his desk, presides over the last staff meeting, where the tone swerves from restrained mourning ("No Crying") to enthusiastic chatter.

As *Playtime*'s final stretch yields a burst of exuberance, the end of *The French Dispatch* spares a moment for heartfelt grief followed by exhilaration. Admittedly, Anderson is more recondite and self-consciously intellectual than Tati. But I think his film yields the sort of sprightly delight that Tati would have enjoyed. Cocteau, too. He fulfilled Diaghilev's command with the ballet *Parade* (1917), which sent a jolt of avant-garde bad manners through stereotypes drawn from circus and cinema. Later, Cocteau's absurdist ballet *The Wedding Party on the Eiffel Tower* (1921) mocked the worship of that touristic landmark. When our best-loved clichés are framed by rigorous form and then made to yield flashes of authentic feeling, we can be—well, astonished.

**DAVID BORDWELL** IS A MADISON, WISCONSIN–BASED FILM THEORIST AND SCHOLAR. HIS BOOKS INCLUDE *Narration in the Fiction Film, Ozu and the Poetics of Cinema, Making Meaning,* AND *On the History of Film Style.* HE AND HIS CREATIVE PARTNER AND SPOUSE, KRISTIN THOMPSON, WROTE THE TEXTBOOKS *Film Art* AND *Film History.*

# THE First Cut Is the DEEPEST

### AARON ARADILLAS

Wes Anderson's use of pop music is one of his most distinctive features as a director. His choices come out of a particular school of thought on how music should be used to score on-screen action: not just to amplify its feelings as a megaphone does the human voice, or repeat what the images and sounds and dialogue are already telling the viewer (the "play a happy song when a character is happy" approach), but also to add something; to ironically subvert what should be a moment of triumph; to undercut despair with a premonition of hope; to widen the context of a moment so that it's not just about the characters, but something larger. A smart filmmaker (or, just as often, the filmmaker's music director, who is in charge of researching and licensing existing music and suggesting tracks) can do all these things and more.

Oddly, however, there are not as many practitioners of this approach as there ought to be. Too many cuts add nothing to a scene but an element of redundancy: a character is walking in the rain following a traumatic event, and the soundtrack is "Runaway," which begins, "I'm a-walkin' in the rain/tears are fallin' and I feel the pain," etc. There is a more complex and subtle approach to

"RUNAWAY"

THE JAZZ SINGER

"ROCK AROUND THE CLOCK"

needle-drop scoring, but it doesn't have as long a history as you might think. From Al Jolson's synchronized sound performance in the first "talkie," *The Jazz Singer*, through the first cinematic use of rock-and-roll in *Rock Around the Clock* (so electrifying that some teenage viewers cut up theater seats with switchblades), popular music has always had a home in movies. And of course there were always musicals, original and adapted. But the cinematic vocabulary of the needle-drop didn't reach its full expressive potential until the 1960s, when a new crop of art-minded filmmakers figured out how to use the music in bold and clever new ways. An early landmark was Stanley Kubrick's *Dr. Strangelove or: How I Learned to Stop Worrying and Love the Bomb* (1964), a psychosexually fraught satire on the war-making impulse that opened with shots of jets refueling in midair scored to an instrumental version of "Try a Little Tenderness" and closed with a montage of atom bombs wiping out humanity as Vera Lynn sang, "We'll Meet Again."

KUBRICK

"WE'LL MEET AGAIN"

The following year brought Kenneth Anger's *Scorpio Rising* (1965), a dialogue-free experimental film that backed homoerotic biker imagery with songs by Ricky Nelson, the Angels, the Crystals, Bobby Vinton, Elvis Presley, and Ray Charles. The film's many disciples included George Lucas and Martin Scorsese. Lucas's 1973 breakthrough feature, *American Graffiti*,

ANGER

AMERICAN GRAFFITI

would later be described as one of the first "jukebox movies." The soundtrack of wall-to-wall, late 1950s/early 1960s needle-drops evoked nostalgia for an already vanished era, but it also created a feeling of time-space suspension, mirroring the developmental stasis affecting the characters and giving each scene an ebb-and-flow rhythm. Scorsese's *Mean Streets* (also 1973) used pop music to accentuate action, enhance character, and comment on aspects of the story in the manner of an omniscient narrator or a Greek chorus. When Robert De Niro's self-destructive hellraiser Johnny Boy makes a slo-mo entrance into a bar while the Rolling Stones' "Jumpin' Jack Flash" booms on the soundtrack, it foretells a running theme in Scorsese's filmography: the aura of attraction-repulsion that radiates from people who flout rules others must abide by.

SCORSESE

"JUMPIN' JACK FLASH"

After that: the flood. Almost every contemporary filmmaker of any significance developed a strong musical voice to complement their visual sense. Scorsese used an eclectic classic rock collection to enhance his street-level stories of masculine prowess and eruptions of violence (*GoodFellas, Casino, The Wolf of Wall Street, The Irishman*). David Lynch turned love ballads into siren songs for the Apocalypse (*Blue Velvet, Wild at Heart*). Quentin Tarantino recontextualized sixties Pop artifacts and seventies R & B deep cuts into postmodern reveries (*Pulp Fiction, Jackie Brown, Death Proof*). John

"BLUE VELVET"

"PRETTY IN PINK"

Hughes used New Wave and eighties Brit pop to complement the fashion and restless energy of his tales of modern American teen life (*Sixteen Candles, Pretty in Pink*). The cosmopolitan sophistication and unabashed yearning of Kar-Wai Wong's films (Chinese in locale, international in spirit) is communicated by the soundtrack, a blend of Chinese, English, and American pop hits. Cameron Crowe uses his rock-crit knowledge of music history to provide the emotional melody to his tales of romantic entanglement (*Jerry Maguire, Almost Famous, Vanilla Sky*). Allison Anders mixes Brill Building pop with SoCal grooves into a continuous feminist anthem (*Grace of My Heart, Sugar Town*). Spike Lee's movies are a catalog of the many contributions that African Americans have given to music, from hip-hop to jazz to funk and soul (*Do the Right Thing, Mo' Better Blues, Jungle Fever, Crooklyn*). The beat goes on.

WONG

ANDERS

"SUGAR TOWN"

And then there's Wes Anderson. The director specializes in stories about makeshift families banding together and attempting to achieve a specific goal while forces, impossible to control, try to thwart their efforts. Most often the music in Anderson's movies is used to provide an emotional

LEE

The French Dispatch **243**

layer to a scene or to enhance or act as ironic counterpoint to the action. Unlike, say, in a Scorsese movie, where the volume of a musical selection goes up and down depending on the emotional intensity of a scene, the music in Anderson's movies is rarely "live." It's not used as another "color" on his palette. Instead, the music is used to set tempo and control the energy of a scene. This is true on the rare occasions when a song is heard live within a scene (like in *The Life Aquatic* or *Moonrise Kingdom*).

"YPGTTO"

In the opening of *Moonrise Kingdom*, twelve-year-old Sam (Jared Gilman) is preparing to run away from home. As he prepares, he puts on Benjamin Britten's "The Young Person's Guide to the Orchestra" as conducted by Leonard Bernstein. Composed in the 1940s, and a staple among Gen-X kids throughout the sixties and seventies, the piece is an introduction to how an orchestra works. It informs us that an orchestra plays a "theme," and then proceeds to demonstrate how the four sections of the orchestra (woodwinds, brass, strings, percussion) perform "variations" on the theme. This is also an illustration of how Anderson approaches music in his movies. By this point we all know what a "Wes Anderson soundtrack" sounds like. But what does that mean? It's not a one-size-fits-all descriptor. And unlike a lot of filmmakers who have gone out of their way to cultivate a known musical preference—three decades into his career, Tarantino, for instance, is still mainly associated with retro sixties and seventies pop and funk, and sampled music from existing film and TV soundtracks (also a Scorsese tendency)—Anderson uses each project as an opportunity to create new soundscapes to surround his frames. Yes, there are certain wellsprings that he returns to (the Rolling Stones, the Kinks). But he's not attached to one specific sound to the exclusion of others. Each movie is given its own distinctive sonic "voice." And as the story progresses, Anderson will do variations on that "voice." His approach to music mirrors his approach to filmmaking in that he uses various storytelling devices (books within movies, plays within movies, documentaries within movies, flashbacks within memories) in order to tell a story that is larger than the sum total of its characters and subplots.

There are really only two other filmmakers who operate like this. The first is an obvious one, and that would be Stanley Kubrick. Like Anderson, Kubrick's attention to detail was legendary (or, for detractors, notorious). His musical selections and precision in the blocking and

*2001: A SPACE ODYSSEY*

"2001"

CLOCKWORK ORANGE

editing to a certain piece of music turned each movie into a kind of musical, one where the images rather than the characters danced. Think of the clean, graceful ballet of the docking of the space station in *2001*. Or Alex the droog prowling a mall in *A Clockwork Orange* accompanied by a synthesizer cover of "Ode to Joy" from Beethoven's Ninth Symphony. (Kubrick even does a bit of self-referential promotion by putting the *2001* soundtrack on display in a record store.) Even in late works like *Full Metal Jacket* and *Eyes Wide Shut*, Kubrick showed a deftness in choosing the right 45 single as a story-setter. The use of Nancy Sinatra's "These Boots Are Made for Walkin'" in Kubrick's Vietnam War epic is at once an obvious sight gag, heralding the entrance of a native-born sex worker in go-go boots who propositions US Marines; an acknowledgment that at that point in the historical narrative, American boots are walking all over Vietnam; and a confirmation of an inevitability that the Americans either don't know

"TBAMFW"

"BABY DID A BAD BAD THING"

or cannot admit, seven years prior to the fall of Saigon: that ultimately Vietnamese boots are gonna walk all over them. (Additionally: The song is placed right after Vincent D'Onofrio's Private Gomer Pyle blows his brains out, heralding the second and third acts' expansive mix of satire, action, and exhaustion.) Chris Isaak's "Baby Did a Bad Bad Thing" in *Eyes Wide Shut*, playing when stars Nicole Kidman and Tom Cruise make out in front of a mirror, preminisces the entire course of a story in which a wife confesses not infidelity, but a fantasy of infidelity, sending her insecure husband on an all-night wandering that at first seems like it's going to become *1999: A Sex Odyssey* but that ends up affirming the comforts of domestic partnership and the necessity of trust. That the Isaak song is not just a prophecy but a joke on the characters only becomes obvious at the end: In the greater scheme, neither husband nor wife did anything all that bad. In fact, Cruise's rather hapless character, Bill Harford, did the best he could under surreal and often menacing circumstances, trying and failing to get to the bottom of what appeared to be a conspiracy to cover up a murder. The only "bad" thing either lead character did was be honest with each other and themselves at long last. That could be seen as *tactically* bad if your life involves a lot of risk avoidance. But morally, it's good. This is needle-drop filmmaking at a high level—conceptually so multilayered, and so revealing of untapped potential in a medium that had been around a hundred-plus years by then, that directors who are content to play a song about anger when a character is angry should turn in their cameras.

ASHBY

Another filmmaker who strongly influenced how Anderson uses music was New Hollywood legend Hal Ashby. Ashby began his career as an editor and was acutely attuned to a movie's tempo and

**HAROLD AND MAUDE**

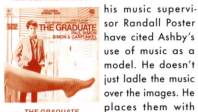
**THE GRADUATE**

**"MRS. ROBINSON"**

**SHAMPOO**

**"MANIC DEPRESSION"**

**SGT. PEPPER**

**"SYMPATHY FOR THE DEVIL"**

**"TIME HAS COME TODAY"**

**"WHIP IT"**

**MOTHERSBAUGH**

**ANIMAL HOUSE**

**"7 AND 7 IS"**

**TSMR**

how selecting just the right piece of music can make the audience get in sync with the characters' emotional arcs. In interviews, both Anderson and his music supervisor Randall Poster have cited Ashby's use of music as a model. He doesn't just ladle the music over the images. He places them with the fine precision of an obsessive worldbuilder. *Harold and Maude* (1970), a dark but wistful May-December love story between two outcasts, plays like a visualized Cat Stevens songbook. (The broad contours of its story, along with *The Graduate*'s, can be seen in *Rushmore*.) Ashby's sex-and-politics satire *Shampoo* (1975) plays like an all-night party slowly winding down, a pacing choice befitting a story set in the runup to reactionary Republican Richard Nixon's triumph in the 1968 presidential election, an event that marked the beginning of the end of the counterculture as a disruptive force for change in American life. An extended party sequence shifts from the gutbucket lament of Jimi Hendrix's "Manic Depression" to the Beatles' "Lucy in the Sky with Diamonds," a song about a beautiful trip that will eventually come to an end. In Ashby's *Coming Home* (1978), songs from the sixties are used as a nearly continuous "score." The movie allows cuts like the Rolling Stones' "Sympathy for the Devil," the Chambers Brothers' "Time Has Come Today," and the extraordinary Tim Buckley protest song "Once I Was" to play in their entirety, dictating the pace of the story, and making the movie feel in total like a cinematic concept album about the effect of the Vietnam War on the American psyche, each scene a song in pictures.

In *Bottle Rocket* (1996), Anderson's calling-card directorial debut about a band of naïve young criminals, budget constraints didn't allow him to fully express his musical inclinations. Yet there are definite hints of Anderson's future soundtrack aesthetic. The decision to collaborate with composer Mark Mothersbaugh, member of the great art-punk group Devo, instantly distinguished both Anderson and *Bottle Rocket* as something different in the world of hip nineties indie filmmaking. Much like Elmer Bernstein's early comedy scores for movies like *Animal House* (1978) and *Stripes* (1981), Mothersbaugh's scores for early Anderson movies changed the way original music was used in low-budget indies. Mothersbaugh's Guaraldi-meets-Vivaldi cues provide a rock-solid foundation for Anderson to layer in musical variations in the form of pop songs.

In *Bottle Rocket*, the score keys us to the underlying mix of anxiety, depression, and mental illness that keeps three would-be career robbers bonded to one another. The movie's two standout uses of pop music nicely bookend the story of Dignan (Owen Wilson) attempting to reconnect with his crew, including recently released mental patient Anthony (Luke Wilson) and lovable hothead Bob (Robert Musgrave). Their first attempt at a shock-and-awe-type robbery is scored to Love's "7 and 7 Is," a blistering piece of sixties surf-style garage rock that sounds so much more threatening than the robbers actually are that it becomes a comment on their laughable delusions of badness. (At times, the soundtrack is more aware of the characters' limitations than they are.) The other important song selection is the Rolling Stones' "2000 Man," a folk-tinged psychedelic rocker from their wildly overproduced *Their Satanic Majesty's Request* (1967). The song is used during a key getaway sequence as Dignan sacrifices himself for the good of the crew and tries to elude capture after attempting their biggest caper. The clashing of acoustic and electric guitars, along with the song's midtempo-then-quick-tempo rhythms, give the sequence a wistful feel. The sequence gets across the idea that crime may not pay, but there are other (often ironic) ways to be rewarded: Dignan makes like a movie hero and goes back into the building, getting captured and beaten by police, but his defeat as a robber is a personal victory. He got busted and will do prison time, which means he's finally a real criminal.

*Rushmore* is where Anderson's mastery of mise-en-scène was put on full display. Released during the winter of 1998–99, a period that also produced *Election* and *The Matrix*, it was a cinematic touchstone for the Y2K generation. Max Fischer (Jason Schwartzman), known as "the worst student at Rushmore Academy," was the latest youthful anti-authority nonconformist in a long tradition of confused rebels that includes Jim Stark (*Rebel Without a Cause*), Benjamin Braddock (*The Graduate*), and Lloyd Dobler (*Say Anything*). But Max's nonconformity was tinged with control-freak madness that originated in the loss of his mother, plus working-class resentment of private-school kids who had everything handed to them.

**REBEL WITHOUT A CAUSE**

**THE FOUR SEASONS**

**THE FOUR SEASONS**

We get our first hint that *Rushmore* is going to add something new to the high-school comedy when we hear the opening bit of original score by Mothersbaugh over the Touchstone Pictures logo. Titled "Hardest Geometry Problem in the World," the Vivaldi-inflected piece recalls *The Four Seasons*, which suggests that we're about to enter a buttoned-up and orderly world like the one in *Dead Poets Society*. This assumption is shattered by a subsequent montage of the many clubs and societies that Max founded and/or led during his years at Rushmore, scored to the British Invasion deep cut "Making Time" by the Creation. The snarling guitar riff screams "youthful rebellion," but the song's placement (over images of prep-school extracurricular activities that are meaningless in the real world) is a winking acknowledgment that this is not actually rebellion but assimilation through sheer force of will: Max conquered a series of clubs that wouldn't normally have someone like him as a member. The song also momentarily punctures the

**"MAKING TIME"**

invisible wall of Anderson's diorama-like framing, confirming that somewhere inside of the director's everything-is-just-right compositions lurks the heart of an anarchist, like a kid who spends all day building elaborate Lego cities and then crushes them while roaring like Godzilla. (The use of "Making Time" made such an impression that it showed up in multiple TV ads and inspired the release of two CDs worth of Creation singles and B-sides.)

**"CONCRETE AND CLAY"**

Initially, Anderson had wanted to score all of *Rushmore* with songs by the Kinks but expanded his musical selections to include forgotten nuggets from the British Invasion. Songs like Unit 4 + 2's "Concrete and Clay" (used during a montage of Max successfully saving Latin), and Chad & Jeremy's "A Summer Song" (used during a montage of Max getting to know the widowed teacher Miss Cross), strike the right balance of playfulness and melancholy. Anderson even gets to use a song by the Kinks, the ominous acoustic heartbreaker "Nothin' in the World Can Stop Me Worryin' 'Bout that Girl," which is used to score the moment when steel tycoon Mr. Blume (Bill Murray) realizes his marriage is a sham. And the Rolling Stones pop up again, this time with "I Am Waiting," a haunting ballad from the great *Aftermath* (1966). Over the years, Anderson and Poster would refer to the Stones as their unofficial house band. Unlike Scorsese, who uses Stones songs from their late sixties/early seventies catalog, Anderson opts for album cuts from their early ABKCO years. Does Anderson

**"A SUMMER SONG"**

**KINDA KINKS**

**AFTERMATH**

relate to those songs' searching, restless quality? It sure looks and sounds like it.

*Rushmore* makes it clear that the songs are meant as score. This is most evident in an extended sequence where Max and Mr. Blume declare war over the affections of Miss Cross. A series of retaliatory actions is scored to the Who's "A Quick One, While He's Away," a mini-opera about infidelity and forgiveness that seems to dictate the editing and camera movements of the sequence. (The raucous version used in the movie is not the version heard on the motion-picture soundtrack.) But this is not the music of Max's choosing. Unlike, say, the four-to-the-floor beats that Tony Manero strutted across Brooklyn to in *Saturday Night Fever* (1977), Max, with his school blazer and capital-R patch that he wears like a medal of honor, is defined by songs that indicate the richness of his imagination, the naïveté that he fails to hide, and the strains of anger and madness that can cause his creativity and organizational skills to tip over into hostility and abuse.

**"AQOWHA"**

**SATURDAY NIGHT FEVER**

**"NIGHT FEVER"**

There are few *Rushmore* moments when we hear music "live"—not literally, as a performance by somebody in a room, but what filmmakers call "diegetically," from "diegesis," meaning that the song issues from a radio or record player or other on-screen source. *Rushmore* uses pop diegetically in the scene where Max pretends to be wounded in a final attempt to seduce Miss Cross. He pops in a cassette he's conveniently brought along of Yves Montand's "Rue St. Vincent" to set

**"RUE ST. VINCENT"**

246  fondu enchaîné

the mood. When Miss Cross finally puts an end to Max's charade, he abruptly stops the music. The sound of the cassette being ejected from the tape player is like a final note of humiliation.

*Rushmore* collapses diegetic and non-diegetic music in its final scene. After all of Max's failed attempts to exert his power over everyone who cares for him, he finally is humbled and seems to be entering a healthier headspace. At an after-party for his latest theater production, a big success, every significant character in the film joins together on the dance floor. Max signals to the DJ to put on another record. We hear the sound of a needle being picked up and a new record starting. The Faces' "Ooh La La" starts to play. And in a brilliant bit of visualization, Anderson uses a brief moment of slow motion as Max and Miss Cross start to dance and Ron Wood (in a rare vocal performance) sings "I wish that I knew what I know now." It's the perfect curtain call for Anderson's triumphant production. And it cements the association between Max Fischer and Wes Anderson, by making it seem as if Max successfully directed his own life, but in a healthy and giving rather than an angry and suffocating way—which means that he, or somebody like him, is capable of directing a movie like the one you just watched.

"OOH LA LA"

*The Royal Tenenbaums* (2001), Anderson's admixture of J. D. Salinger, Charles Schulz, and Orson Welles's *The Magnificent Ambersons*, swings for the fences by invoking the Beatles in its opening moments. Framed as a film version of a popular novel, the movie opens with a prologue showing the three Tenenbaum prodigies achieving early stardom. We see financial wizard Chas playing the stock market in his bedroom; twelve-year-old "adopted" daughter Margot writing and directing a play; and tennis prodigy Richie developing his skills. The sequence is scored to an instrumental version of "Hey Jude" arranged by Mark Mothersbaugh that excises the lyrics but still climaxes with a choir singing a snippet of the "Nah na na nah na nah nah" refrain. Despite the children's early successes, *The Royal Tenenbaums* is a movie about making peace with failure. Paul McCartney wrote "Hey Jude" to comfort John Lennon's first son, Julian, after his parents divorced.

"HEY JUDE"

It's about picking yourself up after defeat. Juxtaposing the scenes of prodigious success with "Hey Jude" keys us to the film's melancholy mood. The lyric "Take a sad song and make it better" sums up the story you're about to see.

*The Royal Tenenbaums* is where Anderson and Poster integrate pieces of existing classical music with the pop tracks, as if to affirm the idea that pop and classical cuts differ more in scale and duration than in basic compositional principles. Following the prologue, we get a quick introductory montage of all the important characters in the movie accompanied to the second movement of "String Quartet in F Major" by Maurice Ravel as performed by the Ysaÿe Quartet. A reintroductory sequence of the adult versions of Chas (Ben Stiller), Margot (Gwyneth Paltrow), and Richie (Luke Wilson) is accompanied by a snippet of "Sonata for Cello and Piano in F Minor" by George Enescu.

YSAŸE QUARTET

ENESCU

Mothersbaugh's score takes its inspiration from such pieces when placing original classical compositions in the score, often for scenes involving the entire Tenenbaum family. It's only when the characters break off into pairs or by themselves that they are given their own musical voices, and these tend to be mid- to late-twentieth-century popular music. For example, whenever patriarch Royal Tenenbaum (Gene Hackman) goes to an ice-cream shop with Margot, Vince Guaraldi's "Christmas Time Is Here" can be heard faintly on the soundtrack.

"CHRISTMAS TIME IS HERE"

"THESE DAYS"

There is a feeling of impending tragedy that runs throughout the movie, for acoustic folk songs of longing and death follow Richie wherever he goes. When he sees Margot, whom he has been in love with for his entire life, for the first time after many years, the moment is scored to Nico's version of Jackson Browne's "These Days." Many have often mistaken the song as belonging to Margot, but the movie makes it clear that the song plays from Richie's point of view. Richie's attempt at suicide is scored to Elliott Smith's "Needle in the Hay," a haunting ballad about heroin addiction. Nick Drake's "Fly" plays over the film's plaintive wrap-up montage. As for Margot, she is associated with the romantic ballads of the Rolling Stones, especially those found on the US version of *Between the Buttons* (1967). In a sequence where Richie returns from the hospital after his suicide attempt, he finds Margot listening to music in the tent he has set up in the Tenenbaum house. As they admit to being in love with each other, the Stones' "She Smiles Sweetly" and "Ruby Tuesday" play. It's a rare moment where

ELLIOTT SMITH

DRAKE'S *BRYTER LAYTER*

BETWEEN THE BUTTONS

"RUBY TUESDAY"

the film's music is heard diegetically.

Yet there are moments when Anderson has some knowing fun without breaking the musical spell the film has woven. The moment when Etheline Tenenbaum falls in love with accountant Henry Sherman (Danny Glover) is scored to Bob Dylan's "Wigwam," a borderline joke song that is considered one of Dylan's worst. The character of popular pulp Western writer Eli Cash (Owen Wilson), the working-class kid who grew up across the street from the family home on Archer Avenue, is shown to be as special as the Tenenbaum kids but lacking their resources and pedigree. He loses himself in drugs and is given to listening to the unsettling sounds of the Clash, particularly songs like "Rock the Casbah" and "Police and Thieves." And then there's Royal, a liar, cheat, thief, and casual racist but still capable of expressing positive emotions and appreciating life. A sequence of Royal and his grandsons partaking in some lighthearted criminality is scored to Paul Simon's jaunty "Me and Julio Down by the Schoolyard," an ode to the feeling of invincibility that fuels childhood adventures. The movie ends with Royal's funeral being scored to the strings-heavy, up-tempo "Everyone" by Van Morrison. The song is the inverse of "Hey Jude," as it speaks to the Tenenbaum family's ability to overcome tragedy and remain a united (albeit dysfunctional) group.

*The Life Aquatic with Steve Zissou* (2004) finds Anderson hitting his stride with his approach to the music. In *The Life Aquatic*, the overriding musical voice belongs to David Bowie, except the variations on Bowie's music are bolder, innovative. Framed as a seafaring quest for revenge, the movie is really about parental insecurity. Legendary underwater explorer and documentarian Steve Zissou (Bill Murray) sets out to avenge his friend's death while being confronted with the existence of his long-lost son Ned (Owen Wilson). Anderson prefers the lo-fi sounds of early Bowie tracks like "Space Oddity," "Rebel Rebel," and "Life on Mars," while Mothersbaugh's score creates an ethereal underwater vibe. Pieces like "Let Me Tell You about My Boat" and especially the low-tech electronic cut "Ping Island" complement otherworldly sounds of Bowie.

The masterstroke is the use of stripped-down "live" covers of Bowie songs by Brazilian singer Seu Jorge. As in the use of curtain calls in *Rushmore* or the chapter headings in *The Royal Tenenbaums*, Anderson uses Jorge's covers of songs like "Rebel Rebel" to provide a pause for reflection in the middle of the action. "Life on Mars" appears in the devastating early scene where Ned meets the man he believes is his father. Jorge kicks things off, and Bowie's version suddenly takes over when Zissou turns away from his maybe-son, walks the entire length of the boat, stands on the bow, and sparks up a joint, processing Ned's revelation. At first, the Seu Jorge versions of Bowie songs might seem like a stunt, but they are quickly woven into the movie's free-floating feeling of exploration.

The few times the musical selections deviate from the Bowie aesthetic, the songs have a surprising consistency. A brief chase scene is set to the extended intro to Devo's "Gut Feeling." A song titled "Here's to You" is by Ennio Morricone, but startles us with its lovely vocal performance by Joan Baez. A couple of songs explicitly fill in Zissou's emotional state. The most striking is Zissou's rampage against the pirates, scored to Iggy and the Stooges' "Search and Destroy," a hard-charging punk anthem. This is easily the funniest example of Anderson's use of an aggressive pop sound to amplify transgressive behavior, but it's a well he returns to as necessary: see also Love's "7 and 7 Is" in *Bottle Rocket* and the Ramones' "Judy Is a Punk" in *The Royal Tenenbaums*. Later, when tragedy befalls Steve and his crew, the Zombies' nearly a cappella "The Way I Feel Inside" plays over a burial at sea. As an actor, Murray is best at expressing insolence and making narcissism seem almost charming (see: *Stripes* and *Mad Dog and Glory*). He has a more difficult time showing empathy (see the last ten minutes of *Scrooged*, where it's initially hard to tell if the Murray character's reawakened idealism is a put-on). The songs penetrate Murray's deadpan facade and give us access to Zissou's

"WIGWAM"

"ROCK THE CASBAH"

"MAJDBTS"

MOONDANCE

"REBEL REBEL"

"SPACE ODDITY"

"LIFE ON MARS"

"GUT FEELING"

"HERE'S TO YOU"

"SEARCH AND DESTROY"

"JUDY IS A PUNK"

"QUEEN BITCH"

"THE WAY I FEEL INSIDE"

emotional interior; the Zombies song in particular fills up what might otherwise read as an emotional void. In the end, Zissou has changed, but not completely, and Bowie's snarky "Queen Bitch" plays as he exits stage right.

*The Darjeeling Limited* (2007) finds Anderson playing around with form and expanding his musical palette. Instead of a prologue, *Darjeeling* opens with a short titled *Hotel Chevalier*. Featuring Jason Schwartzman as Jack and Natalie Portman as Jack's ex-girlfriend, the film takes place in a hotel room over a twenty-four-hour period as the couple spend one more despairing night together. With sparse dialogue, it establishes a sense of missed opportunities that is sustained throughout the movie proper. For *Hotel Chevalier*, the soundtrack digs up an obscure skiffle-folk ballad by Peter Sarstedt entitled "Where Do You Go To (My Lovely)." In part, the song and the short (and by extension, the feature) are about futile attempts to recapture a feeling. In the end, all you have are memories.

"WDYGT(ML)"

*The Darjeeling Limited* is presented as a travelogue through India. Francis (Owen Wilson), recovering from a near-fatal wreck, reunites with his brothers Peter (Adrien Brody) and Jack (Jason Schwartzman) sometime after their father's funeral. The trip is meant as a bonding experience. The travelog format provides Anderson with a very loose structure for the movie and justifies a dive into Indian music, particularly the scores composed for the films of world cinema giant Satyajit Ray. The opening of the movie shows a train leaving a station. The moment is set to a track entitled "Title Music," from Ray's *Jalsaghar* (1958) and composed by Vilayat Khan, which seamlessly transitions into the Kinks' "This Time Tomorrow" from *Lola Versus Powerman* (1970), a hyperacoustic tune with the line, "This time tomorrow, what will we know? / Will we still be here

LOLA VERSUS POWERMAN

watching an in-flight movie show?" "This Time Tomorrow" resonates throughout a film permeated by that slightly numb feeling that washes over you in the aftermath of sudden tragedy. The funeral that follows is scored to the Kinks' "Strangers," a mournful unplugged number that has the line, "Strangers on this road we are on / We are not two, we are one." Like the Zombies' "The Way I Feel Inside" in *The Life Aquatic*, the song becomes a requiem for unspoken emotions.

As it turns out, Francis has had a plan the entire trip. He means to "rescue" their mother Patricia (Anjelica Huston), who left America following her husband's funeral to join a convent in the Himalayas. The reunion is less than joyous. Patricia matter-of-factly tells her sons she's not interested in looking back. She says, "Yes, the past happened, but it's over now, isn't it?" Francis replies, "Not for us." Then, she says, "Maybe we can express ourselves more fully if we think what we want to say." At that moment the Rolling Stones' "Play with Fire" starts to play. A haunting ballad with a chiming guitar riff, the song plays over a trademark Andersonian all-in-one tracking shot that *The Wes Anderson Collection* described "as a dream train" shot that "violates the laws of time and space." The closing-credit song is Joe Dassin's "Les Champs-Élysées," a jaunty number with a refrain that gets lodged in your ear. Dassin, son of blacklisted filmmaker Jules Dassin (*Rififi*, *Topkapi*), has a lilting, singsong voice that recalls Ron Wood's vocal on "Ooh La La." In fact, "Les Champs-Élysées" is the best closing-credit song in an Anderson movie after *Rushmore*. Like "Where Do You Go To (My Lovely)" from *Hotel Chevalier*, the song is a list of highlights from the past. This time, it's about France, not Britain. But the tone is decidedly different. Instead of regret, Dassin takes comfort in the memories. This time tomorrow what will we know, indeed.

"PLAY WITH FIRE"

*Isle of Dogs* (2018), Anderson's animated Japanarama, mirrors *The Darjeeling Limited* in its approach to music. An original mash-up of George Orwell, fifties disaster movies, and Japanese folklore, the movie is Anderson's take on the classic boy-and-his-dog story. Attacked in some circles for being culturally insensitive, the movie is acutely aware of its surroundings as it depicts the misadventures of a pack of dogs trying to fend for themselves on the bombed-out ruins of Trash Island, which looks a lot like a cross between Hiroshima and Tokyo after Godzilla has run rampant.

As in *Darjeeling*, the movie is aware it is inhabiting and appropriating a foreign culture while the characters attend to their immediate needs. As the story progresses, the pack of dogs (led by the attack-prone stray dog Chief, voiced by Bryan Cranston) gradually assimilate into their new world. "Taiko Drumming" by Kaoru Watanabe is an inspired piece of score that is used at key moments throughout the movie. The acceleration and intensity of the piece is so commanding that we start to laugh whenever it begins to play. It's funny, but not just funny. Alexandre Desplat's score takes its cue from that piece and other bits of source music. Desplat's score is a constant, as *Isle of Dogs* is Anderson's most music-driven film. (It's the least dialogue-driven Anderson picture.) When Desplat isn't keeping the movie's beat, Anderson seamlessly integrates pieces of score from classics of Japanese cinema, like "Kanbei & Katsushiro" from Akira Kurosawa's *Seven Samurai*. As in *Darjeeling*, Anderson is aware of whose backyard he is in.

WCPAEB

The movie's most inspired selection is the out-of-nowhere use of the psychedelic-folk-rock nugget "I Won't Hurt You" by an obscure sixties outfit called the West Coast Pop Art Experimental Band. Sounding like a cross between the Del-Vikings and Nick Drake, the song is a haunting number that plays as the dogs wander the wreckage of Trash Island. The song deliberately breaks from the rest of the soundtrack, yet there's an internal logic to its inclusion. The movie's purposeful lack of subtitles tunes us in to the barriers of communications between the canine world and everyone else. At certain points in the story, every character is placed in the position of the "other." "I Won't Hurt You" is the one piece of music where the emotions are universal.

*Fantastic Mr. Fox* (2009) is both Anderson's first animated feature and his first collaboration with composer Alexandre Desplat.  FINCHER

Desplat, who is one of the leading lights in film music over the last twenty years, has garnered worldwide recognition for his work, like his haunting score for David Fincher's *The Curious Case of Benjamin Button* (2008) and his majestic work on Terrence Malick's *The Tree of Life* (2011). His work for Anderson (*Fox, The Grand Budapest Hotel, Isle of Dogs,* and *The French Dispatch*) shows a more playful, lighthearted side that allows room for Anderson's increasingly more experimental song choices.

For instance, the banjo-inflected opening fanfare titled "American Empirical Pictures" effortlessly blends into the Wellingtons' "The Ballad of Davy Crockett," a piece of Boomer nostalgia that also sets up a folkloric tone for the rest of the movie. (It's also Anderson's tip of the cowboy hat to his Texas roots.) Based on a Roald Dahl story, *Fantastic Mr. Fox* is Anderson's version of a domestic family comedy. Mr. Fox (voiced by George Clooney), his  "TBODC"

long-suffering but patient and loving wife, Felicity (Meryl Streep), and their moody twelve-year-old son, Ash (Jason Schwartzman), attempt to hold their clan of friends and family together while fighting off a trio of vicious farmers. Banjo- and/or ukulele-influenced music dominates both the score and the song selections. There's a child's sense of improvisation as Desplat uses everything from finger snaps to rollicking banjos to spaghetti-Western–style whistling. When Mr. Fox decides to return to his more animal instinct and starts stealing chickens again, the score becomes devious in its freewheeling style. (At times,  "BONNIE AND CLYDE"

 "BONNIE AND CLYDE"

 "BONNIE AND CLYDE"

 BURL    IVES

the score during the sequences of outlaw behavior recalls the galloping banjo themes from *Bonnie and Clyde* [1967], a movie about charismatic thieves.)

The songs seem to fuse with a score. The multiple tracks by Burl Ives, with his deep, courtly cadences, invoke the paternal authority and comfort of a bygone era. (They also make you think of the Rankin-Bass animated specials that Anderson grew up watching.) The songs are heard at a low volume during scenes of domestic life. "Fooba Wooba John," "Buckeye Jim," and especially "The Grey Goose" (about the hunting and shooting of a goose) provide a soothing foundation for the movie's more rambunctious events to occur. A lot of the songs have the feel of early 45s that children would play over and over again on their first record player. There's an original nursery-like rhyme that warns of the evil farmers and an inspired campfire song by Pulp frontman Jarvis Cocker—a banjo-and-kazoo ditty titled "Fantastic Mr. Fox" that could have been a Burl Ives B-side. Anderson uses several

 "HEROES AND VILLAINS"

 SMILEY SMILE

 "I GET AROUND"

songs by the Beach Boys. The opening scene of Mr. and Mrs. Fox walking together is scored to "Heroes and Villains" from *Smiley Smile* (1967). The classic "I Get Around" is used to kick off the final showdown between the evil Farmer Bean and Mr. Fox and his friends. And, in the end, after peace and order have been restored, the Beach Boys' lovely cover of "Ol' Man River" is like a balm. Oh, yeah, Anderson's house band, the Rolling Stones, makes an appearance with the anarchic "Street Fighting Man" from 1968's *Beggars Banquet*. The riotous song is used to comic effect during a sequence of utter destruction as the farmers use tractors to destroy the Fox family tree.  "OL' MAN RIVER"

The musical highlight comes at the end, after Mr. Fox, Felicity, Ash, and all their animal friends have relocated to the sewers. They've broken into the grocery store of their archnemesis Farmer Boggis. As they plan to raid the store  "STREET FIGHTING MAN"

BEGGARS BANQUET

before it opens, the Bobby Fuller Four's "Let Her Dance" starts to play as everyone dances in the aisles. The song, with its bouncy guitar riff and vocals, is a departure from the rest of the movie's music. The sequence plays like an actors' improvisation, a stop-animation first.  "LET HER DANCE"

*Moonrise Kingdom* (2012) uses Britten's "Young Person's Guide" as the catalyst for the entire story, which is Anderson's skewered take on the classic

*fondu enchaîné*

children's story *From the Mixed-Up Files of Mrs. Basil E. Frankweiler*. As Britten created "Young Person's Guide" as an introduction to understanding the orchestra, *Kingdom* is Anderson's guide to the early days of young adulthood and all the disappointments and contradictions that come with it. Sam and Susie (Jared Gilman and Kara Hayward) are twelve-year-olds who have decided to run away together because they can see the hypocrisy and shortcomings of the adult world and don't want anything to do with it. The Britten piece tells us that they are just postponing the inevitable: In its droll, genial way, the record is preparing children to understand and accept a system of expression that was invented centuries earlier and that isn't going away.

One character who is just as world-weary as the heroes: Deputy Sharp (Bruce Willis). In the midst of a midlife crisis (he's having an affair), Sharp is sharper than any of the other grown-ups on the small island that he oversees. He feels an unspoken connection with Sam. Sharp is long past the point where a "Young Person's Guide" can comfort him. Hank Williams speaks to his life experience. Unlike most of Anderson's movies, a lot of the music in *Moonrise Kingdom* is heard diegetically, which gives the songs an emotional immediacy. There's real poignancy when Williams's "Ramblin' Man" comes on following Sharp's midday liaison.

"RAMBLIN' MAN"

Desplat's version of "Young Person's Guide" plays over the closing credits. The composer creates his own theme and then has every single instrument play a variation of the theme as the credits roll. It's like an updated version of "Young Person's Guide," except more complex and detailed, as if to concede that, since the 1960s, adult life has gotten even more complicated.

*The French Dispatch* is Anderson's version of an anthology movie like the literary-bent art-house curio *New York Stories* (1989), featuring three *New Yorker*–style short stories directed by Martin Scorsese, Francis Ford Coppola, and Woody Allen. (The movie is also Anderson's speculation on his legacy and how he will be remembered by his collaborators.) The three short stories and scene-setting travelogue that comprise the bulk of the movie are taken from the final issue of *The French Dispatch*, an arts-and-culture publication whose editor in chief, Arthur Howitzer Jr. (Bill Murray), has died of a heart attack. The three main "articles" deal with the different ways in which the artistic impulse manifests itself.

Like *The Grand Budapest Hotel* (2014), the music in *Dispatch* is heard almost constantly. Yet it rarely, if ever, overwhelms a given scene. In *Grand Budapest*, Desplat's Oscar-winning score relied on inspiration from European composers. It was the first time Anderson didn't use any notable source music. (No pop songs.) In *Dispatch*, Anderson uses a mix of symphonic pieces and underused pop songs to complement Desplat's Baroque-inspired score, which features pianist Jean-Yves Thibaudet.

THIBAUDET

For instance: Anderson uses very specifically chosen jazz music in "The Private Dining Room of the Police Commissioner," a convoluted tale involving kidnapping and French cuisine that's recounted by Roebuck Wright (Jeffrey Wright), a James Baldwin–style bon vivant. (The story appears in the magazine's "Tastes & Smells" section.) There's a late-fifties jazz-nightlife-in-Paris vibe reflected in songs like "'Round Midnight" (although you'd be hard-pressed to hear it on the soundtrack). (The appearance of "'Round Midnight" conjures Bertrand Tavernier's 1986 masterpiece *Round Midnight* starring Dexter Gordon. That movie was implicitly about Frenchman Tavernier's infatuation with American culture. *The French Dispatch* is about Anderson's love of French culture as seen through the prism of his lifelong subscription to *The New Yorker*.) The story climaxes with three timelines converging and a getaway chase ensuing. This moment is further dramatized by having the elegant black-and-white photography switch to comic-strip-inspired color animation. The accompanying piano score mixes beautifully with jazz selections like Sonny Rollins's "Swingin' for Bumsy."

ROUND MIDNIGHT

SONNY ROLLINS

In the first story, "The Concrete Masterpiece," convicted multiple murderer Moses Rosenthaler (Benicio Del Toro) is inspired by love to express himself through painting, and becomes a once-in-a-generation artist. It's a fun-house answer to Scorsese's "Life Lessons" segment from *New York Stories*, starring Nick Nolte as Lionel Dobie, a bare-chested, womanizing "action" painter who likes to indulge his appetites and paint to loud rock music like Procol Harum's "A Whiter Shade of Pale." Here, Moses takes to grunting and snarling like an animal whenever he is made unhappy when discussing his art. Civilized pieces of music by such composers as Chopin are used as

"A WHITER SHADE OF PALE"

MANDOLIN   CONCERTO IN C MAJOR

ironic counterpoint. In a crucial moment, Moses unveils a "masterpiece" three years in the making. The moment is dramatized by having the black-and-white photography switch to full color, and a trio begins to perform Vivaldi's Mandolin Concerto in C Major. That the music originates in that very room makes the moment more effective. It isn't just the filmmaker who is contrasting the lethal rage and lyrical primitivism of Moses with the softness, shallowness, and effete materialism of his wannabe patrons. They did it to themselves. They're the ones who hired the musicians.

In "Revisions to a Manifesto" (for the "Politics/Poetry" section), Anderson finally allows for some "contemporary" music, albeit of the French pop variety. Echoing Bernardo Bertolucci's *The Dreamers* (2004), the story follows a yearlong uprising within the student body over access to the girls' dormitory at a Parisian university. The story is chronicled by Lucinda Krementz (Frances McDormand), a single woman who prides herself on her "journalistic neutrality" while secretly aligning with the student resistance. The political and personal become entangled when Lucinda starts sleeping with the young Zeffirelli (Timothée Chalamet) and assists him by "copyediting" his manifesto. Inspired by the Paris student uprising in May '68, the story dives into the sexual politics of the moment as an older journalist tries to be objective while becoming increasingly infatuated with the young. Early on, Lucinda meets Zeffirelli at a dinner party on the night authorities decide to unleash tear gas on the streets. Zeffirelli's big entrance is accompanied to Ennio Morricone's "L'Ultima volta," a track from the 1964 Italian documentary *I Malamondo*. He's wearing a gas mask. The kicker to the scene is when Lucinda emerges wearing one, too.

I MALAMONDO

"TU M'AS TROP MENTI"

"J'EDQJT'A"

Like all student bodies, this one comes most alive when coffee and music fuel the exchange of ideas. The jukebox provides a steady stream of pop songs that serenade the youth as they fantasize remaking the world in their image. The first song we hear "live" is Chantal Goya's bumptious "Tu M'as Trop Menti." Goya's appearance on the soundtrack has a boomerang effect. Known as a singer, her one major movie credit is the leading female role in Jean-Luc Godard's *Masculin Féminin* (1966), a movie that 1968 Paris revolutionaries would have seen more than once. We also hear "J'en Déduis Que Je T'aime" by Charles Aznavour, often referred to as "the Frank Sinatra of France." The most indelible use of music is "Aline," performed by Jarvis Cocker. The song was originally performed by Christophe and was the number-one single in France in 1965. Here, Cocker performs the song in the guise of the fictitious pop star Tip-Top. The song goes from "live" to playing over a montage of escalating protests, culminating in the Chessboard Revolution. The decision to use a cover version instead of the original is a peculiar one: Anderson didn't want the wildly popular original to overwhelm the sequence. Unlike Joe Dassin's "Les Champs-Élysées" at the end of *The Darjeeling Limited*, "Aline" is a more reflective piece of French pop. Cocker's cover is moodier, a little sadder than the original. His deep tones create a nice distancing effect that allows us to be one step removed from the story. There are other snatches of Europop, but "Aline" is the song that echoes throughout the segment. A song about heartbreak, it has a youth-oriented fatalism that reflects the "touching narcissism of the young."

"ALINE"

There is no one set style for Wes Anderson when it comes to music. At this point we can predict some of the artists and eras he is likely to return to, just as we might guess what playlist an old friend is about to put on when a party has reached the dancing phase. But his relationship to music as a filmmaker continues to surprise.

**AARON ARADILLAS** IS A FILM CRITIC AND JOURNALIST. HIS WRITING HAS BEEN PUBLISHED AT ROCKCRITICS.COM, *Slant*, VULTURE, AND INDIEWIRE. ARADILLAS HAS ALSO WRITTEN AND COPRODUCED VIDEO ESSAYS FOR THE MUSEUM OF THE MOVING IMAGE, *The L Magazine*, AND INDIEWIRE'S NEWEST SITE, PRESS PLAY. HE WAS THE PRODUCER-HOST OF THE INTERNET TALK RADIO SHOW *Back By Midnight*.

## ACKNOWLEDGMENTS

Every volume in *The Wes Anderson Collection* is a bespoke effort that took a circuitous route to bookstore shelves, but this one's path was more complex than most. Thanks are due to the author's family, who had plenty of onerous challenges to contend with during the research and writing period (2019–21), yet graciously endured the additional disruption of phone and Skype and Zoom conversations taking place at odd hours, many of them in French with an interpreter, in kitchens, living rooms, bedrooms, airport lounges, train stations, movie theater lobbies, and, in one case, from the front seat of a rented truck.

The writer would have been bereft without the assistance of production consultants Ben Adler, Octavia Peissel, and Jeremy Dawson, and of course Wes Anderson, who encouraged and validated a different approach from previous volumes and gave notes that made the end product better. Thanks are also due to editor Eric Klopfer; designers Martin Venezky and Shawn Dahl; design manager Danielle Youngsmith; managing editor Annalea Manalili; production manager Larry Pekarek; and publisher Michael Sand. We also appreciate the individuals associated with the production who shared personal photos and art, including Robert Yeoman, Sandro Kopp, Tony Revolori, and Steve Park.

And then there's our regular *Wes Anderson Collection* series illustrator Max Dalton, who always has an unerring sense of what will make a section pop: I adore you, my friend. Also filmmaker Nicolas Saada, whose playful, conversational introduction set the tone for the book, and who became a trusted adviser; and essayists Paddy Johnson, Aaron Aradillas, Abbey Bender, Siddhant Adlakha, Marc Cerisuelo, and the one and only David Bordwell, to whom this book is co-dedicated (along with his wife and frequent collaborator, Kristin Thompson). Olivia Collette, who contributed an essay to the *Grand Budapest Hotel* volume of the *Collection*, served as an interpreter for interviews where the subject only spoke French; she also helped clarify idioms, spellings, and grammatical principles during the writing and revision process, as did Ben Adler. Their fluency and keen judgment were blessings.

At Searchlight, thanks to Diana Loomis, Sarah Peters, Melissa Holloway, Jacquelyn Silverman, Rachael Lyon, Andy Bandit, Emma Ofria, Dylan Holfus, and Kelsey Rivkin, as well as Carol Roeder and Angela Ontiveros at Disney Publishing Worldwide who helped make this book possible.

Most of all, the author wishes to thank Judith Carter, executive director of our publishing company, mzs.press, and his partner in life, for lifting his spirits when they were at their lowest and urging him to move forward with this book rather than give up, repeatedly assuring him throughout the process that the tragedies and challenges that made the task seem unachievable were an energy source that would make it stand apart. *Tu avais raison, ma chère.*

*Dedicated to David Bordwell and Kristin Thompson*

**EDITOR**
Eric Klopfer

**DESIGNERS**
Martin Venezky
Shawn Dahl, dahlimama inc

**DESIGN MANAGER**
Danielle Youngsmith

**MANAGING EDITOR**
Annalea Manalili

**PRODUCTION MANAGER**
Larry Pekarek

**COVER AND ORIGINAL ILLUSTRATIONS**
Max Dalton

**UNIT PHOTOGRAPHY**
Roger Do Minh

Library of Congress Control Number: 2020944147
ISBN: 978-1-4197-5064-9
eISBN: 978-1-64700-117-9

Copyright © 2023 Matt Zoller Seitz

THE FRENCH DISPATCH © 2021 20th Century Studios and TFD Productions LLC.
All rights reserved.

Unit photography and still-frames from THE FRENCH DISPATCH © 2021 Searchlight Pictures.
All rights reserved.

For additional credits, see www.abramsbooks.com/resources/.

Published in 2023 by Abrams, an imprint of ABRAMS. All rights reserved.
No portion of this book may be reproduced, stored in a retrieval system, or
transmitted in any form or by any means, mechanical, electronic, photocopying,
recording, or otherwise, without written permission from the publisher.

Printed and bound in the United States
10 9 8 7 6 5 4 3 2

Abrams books are available at special discounts when purchased in quantity for premiums
and promotions as well as fundraising or educational use. Special editions can also be created
to specification. For details, contact specialsales@abramsbooks.com or the address below.

Abrams® is a registered trademark of Harry N. Abrams, Inc.

**ABRAMS** The Art of Books
195 Broadway, New York, NY 10007
abramsbooks.com